ECONOMICS

Guiding you through the A to Z of contemporary economics in all its forms, *Economics: The Key Concepts* is an essential, affordable and accessible reference for students, lecturers and economists at every level.

Key concepts covered include:

- Competition and monopoly
- Development economics
- Equality
- Ethics and economics
- Game theory
- Happiness
- Property rights

Entries include extensive guides to further reading and are fully cross-referenced throughout to give readers a comprehensive pocket reference to the ideas, issues and practice of economics in the twenty-first century.

Donald Rutherford is Lecturer in Economics at the University of Edinburgh and the author of *The Routledge Dictionary of Economics* (2002).

YOU MAY ALSO BE INTERESTED IN THE FOLLOWING ROUTLEDGE STUDENT REFERENCE TITLES

Fifty Major Economists (Second Edition)
Steven Pressman

Economics: The Basics
Tony Cleaver

Business: The Key Concepts
Mark Vernon

Fifty Key Figures in Management
Morgen Witzel

The Routledge Companion to Global Economics
Edited by Robert Benyon

Management: The Basics
Morgen Witzel

Internet: The Basics
Jason Whittaker

ECONOMICS

The Key Concepts

Donald Rutherford

Routledge
Taylor & Francis Group

LONDON AND NEW YORK

First published 2007
by Routledge
2 Park Square, Milton Park, Abingdon, Oxon OX14 4RN

Simultaneously published in the USA and Canada
by Routledge
270 Madison Ave, New York, NY 10016

Routledge is an imprint of the Taylor & Francis Group, an informa business

© 2007 Donald Rutherford

Typeset in Bembo by
Taylor & Francis Books
Printed and bound in Great Britain by
TJ International Ltd, Padstow, Cornwall

British Library Cataloguing in Publication Data
A catalogue record for this book is available from the British Library

Library of Congress Cataloging in Publication Data
A catalog record for this book has been requested

ISBN 978–0–415–40056–5 (hbk)
ISBN 978–0–415–40057–2 (pbk)
ISBN 978–0–415–94661–9 (ebk)

Mixed Sources
Product group from well-managed
forests and other controlled sources
www.fsc.org Cert no. SGS-COC-2482
© 1996 Forest Stewardship Council
FSC

CONTENTS

LIST OF KEY CONCEPTS

Accelerator
Aid
Altruism
Arbitrage
Auction
Austrian economics
Balance of payments
Banking
Bubble
Capitalism
Capital theory
Classical economics
Clubs, theory of
Coase theorem
Cobweb
Collective bargaining
Comparative economic systems
Competition and monopoly
Consumer's surplus
Consumption
Contract theory
Cooperation
Core
Corruption
Cost
Cost-benefit analysis
Credit
Cultural economics
Currency
Customs union
Cycles
Debt

Demand curve
Development economics
Discrimination
Disequilibrium economics
Division of labour
Dual economy
Economic anthropology
Economic concentration
Economic demography
Economic growth
Economic integration
Economic methodology
Economic modelling
Economics as rhetoric
Economic system
Economic welfare
Economies of scale and scope
Efficiency
Elasticity
Energy economics
Entrepreneur
Environmental economics
Equality
Equilibrium
Ethics and economics
Evolutionary economics
Ex-ante, ex-post
Exchange rate
Exhaustible resources
Expectations
Experimental economics
Externality

Say's law
Scarcity
Search theory
Segmented labour market
Self-managed enterprise
Social capital
Social choice theory
Socialism
Spatial economics
Stabilisation policy
Stockholm School
Structural adjustment
Structure of an economy
Supply-side economics
Surplus value

Taxation
Technical progress
Terms of trade
Time in economics
Trade theory
Trade (labor) union
Tragedy of the commons
Transfer income
Transfer pricing
Unemployment
Utility
Value
Wealth
Welfare economics

INTRODUCTION

Economics has been studied for centuries as there has always been great curiosity about the nature and determinants of wealth and well-being, and how scarce resources should be employed. Economics operates at different levels: the theoretical, the technical and the advisory. Sometimes all are combined in one concept, for example, an examination of prices requires a consideration of theory, methods of pricing and prices policies. Some economic ideas are basic to much of economics discourse, such as cost; others are related to the analysis of particular problems, as is the case with environmental economics. Economics has long been sectarian so attention has to be paid to the many schools of thought. Political and social problems often have an economic dimension so different types of economic policy abound.

Central to the study and understanding of any academic discipline is an awareness of the nature and limits of the concepts used. The central themes of this work were chosen by consulting a range of economics books and economists. In this book over 170 concepts justify separate articles but subordinate concepts are mentioned within each discussion. Each entry takes a central concept and relates it to the variants which form a cluster of related ideas. A short definition introduces the concept and, where relevant and known, the origins of it are mentioned. At the end there are cross-references and further reading. The reading amplifies what has been written in the text.

There is a list of concepts, and an index of the names of economics writers cited in the text. Birth and death dates are stated to locate these writers intellectually in the successive ages of economics, whether mercantilist, classical or neoclassical either propounding the dominant theme of what economics was then or dissenting from it. Further information can be obtained on these writers by using reference books such as M Blaug (ed.) (1983) *Who's Who in Economics* (1983); D Rutherford (ed.) (2004) *Biographical Dictionary of British*

Economists; and RB Emmett and J Madison (eds) (2006) *Biographical Dictionary of American Economists*.

A guide to concepts takes its place in the working library of an economist alongside textbooks on the basics and specialisms of economics as well as manuals on mathematical methods and econometrics. Knowing concepts allows the economics researcher to build the foundations of an investigation theoretical or applied. Conceptual awareness ensures greater rigour.

New economics terms are coined every year but they are not important concepts until they inspire a body of economics literature. Economic concepts are surprisingly durable. Even an abandoned type of economic policy is a permanently useful idea as it exists as an option for the future.

ECONOMICS

The Key Concepts

ACCELERATOR

The relationship between an increase in net investment and changes in real income or output. This early twentieth-century theory is especially associated with Aftalion and JM Clark.

Although regarded chiefly as a theory based on a macroeconomic relationship between a change in aggregate income and aggregate net investment, it has microeconomic roots. When incomes increase, there is an increased demand for goods which will increase in price when the capital to make those goods is fully utilised. Manufacturers will increase the capital stock to meet the expected increase in demand. The accelerator can apply to a particular industry or to the economy as a whole. In the simplest expression for the accelerator it is the amount by which an increase in income is multiplied to predict the amount of net investment. It is also regarded as the desired capital–output ratio and will be more than one as the value of output from capital is much less than the value of the capital itself. The basic accelerator equation has been modified to deal with the problems of the time it takes to respond to an increase in income and the existence of excess capacity. Making net investment a function of previous income deals with slow responses; subtracting the value of the capital stock multiplied by the degree of excess capacity produces a better estimate of net investment.

An important application of the accelerator principle is in trade cycle theory. Hicks combined the accelerator with the multiplier, ceilings and floors to generate cycles. Increased income leads to increased investment through the accelerator, that extra investment creates more income through the **multiplier**, then the accelerator operates again. Only the full employment ceiling prevents infinite expansion of the economy; net investment independent of income will enable an economy to recover from the floor. In the first phase there is disinvestment as the extra demand is met from stocks, in the next there is induced investment and in the third oscillations as depreciated reserves are increased or run down as replacement takes place.

See also: **cycles**; **investment**

Further reading: Clark 1917; Hicks 1950

AID

Grants of money or of goods and services by national governments or private organisations and individuals to poor countries or regions.

There are different degrees of aid. Emergency help at a time of crisis such as an earthquake, medium-term assistance until a country establishes its own services, such as the loan of teachers and doctors, and long-term investment in infrastructure and business enterprises are the major categories. Multilateral aid consists of the distribution of donations from many sources through an international agency such as the World Bank to the recipient country. Bilateral aid flows directly between donor and recipient. Aid to foreign countries still amounts to a tiny fraction of the national income of developed countries.

There are many motives for aid. For strategic military reasons, superpowers help countries in return for military bases and to maintain internal political stability within them. From the nineteenth century large countries have tried to extend their power by creating spheres of influence: to be successful, such a policy needs continuous flows of help. This aid will be largely bilateral. For **balance of payments** reasons it is cheaper to offer goods and services in one's own currency, but the value of that aid can be devalued by inferior and more expensive goods than available in world markets. But aid offered by supposedly impartial international agencies has its own problems. Lobbies in such organisations will achieve more for some countries than others. Also the potential amount of aid can be devalued by the large administrative costs of allocating it. Idealists genuinely hope that through aid there can be a movement to a greater equality of per capita incomes throughout the world, but the small volume of aid makes that unlikely.

Generous individuals through charities and religious organisations send monetary and other help to poorer countries. A sense of moral duty motivates such aid. Often it is untainted by the political motivation of official aid. But it can be only enough to launch new initiatives or supplement inter-governmental assistance.

Aid is an example of a **transfer income**. Boulding conceptualised aid through distinguishing a grants economy from an exchange economy. Grants are non-coercive, an expression of benevolence and a method of creating an international community: aid has these characteristics at its best.

Aid can be part of a plan, or the encouragement of the spontaneous mechanisms of an indigenous economy. Aid is either a means to making a country more dependent or a stimulus to sustainable development. Experience of managing aid programmes has modified them. Increasingly there are safeguards to avoid destroying local cultures and environment. The choice of technology is important as the recognition that large reserves of labour have to be considered, as has the expense of choosing capital intensive methods. The contribution of aid to encouraging trade is essential, otherwise one tranche of aid has to be succeeded by another. The method of distribution of aid is vital if those most in need are to be helped, and it is important that **corruption** is minimised by careful monitoring which keeps gifts out of the hands of the ruling elite and military. The greatest danger of aid is the creation of aid dependency, which means that a country loses its economic independence and is unable to plot its destiny. But it can be argued that few countries have any autonomy because of the growth of international corporations and the process of globalisation.

See also: **development economics**; **equality**; **globalisation**; **poverty**; **trade theory**

Further reading: Boulding 1973; Singer 1984

ALTRUISM

A philosophy of preferring the welfare of others to one's own; unselfishness; the opposite of egoism.

Altruism can be practised within a family; perhaps the commonest examples are gifts, extended **credit** and the sharing of risk, within the wider population through private charity or government transfers, or even in the world as a whole through economic aid. This ideal has formed the basis of utopian communities.

It is agreed that it is the opposite of selfishness, which has often been confused with self-interest. This term was invented by the positivist Auguste Comte in 1851 and derived from the Italian word *altro*, other. The altruist forsakes personal gain and advancement in order to help the weak. Generally this attitude is derived from a moral stance, rather than the practicalities of economic life. The pursuit of **profit** under **capitalism** and the insistence on workers receiving the product of their labour under **socialism** are both hard to reconcile with altruism. It is possible to have short-term altruism in order to establish good industrial and international relations, and then to revert to usual market principles. Others would argue that the awareness of social cost in an environmentally conscious age necessitates the curbing of private interests for the others who constitute the wider community. Economic analysis of charities and religion has to consider altruism as a central motive for institutional behaviour. However, **globalisation** has had both the consequence of new opportunities for exploitation and also an awareness of greater and more distant needs, which inevitably will move the altruistic to action.

Altruism can take many forms. It can be intergenerational, where economic and social activities are restricted now for the sake of future generations' enjoyment of the environment. It can be private or public. A wise government might select the amount of help requisite to others more capably than less informed individuals and charities, or not. **Taxation** can be used both to discourage bad action against others and to make individuals pay the social costs of their actions.

Embedding altruism as a principle in economic institutions and economic policy is always controversial. It is difficult to sum individual preferences to form any scheme of improvement. Also qualities of self-reliance, ambition and risk taking can be discouraged by recreating an economy according to a social model. The problem of altruism having destructive effects is recognised in the Samaritan's Dilemma, in which helping others can lead to one's own destruction. Buchanan recognised that there are predators within one's own species in his account of the dilemma. It has many applications to welfare states.

Altruism is not always as genuine as it appears, as Collard pointed out. It can be enlightened self-interest, when what is ostensibly for others also benefits oneself. Gifts are prompted by many motives. They may be implicit exchange because we expect something back. They might be a form of personal security to appease potential enemies. The benevolent person in society has enhanced reputation and status so can benefit commercially.

There is a loose relationship between the stage of economic development and the incidence of altruism. In richer societies there might be few on low incomes and the government can afford through its fiscal policy to eliminate the needy.

Altruism requires imagination, empathy and a benevolent disposition. This can be practised directly, or by proxy, when voters require other people who are richer to help the poor. Altruism can be practised for the benefit of the present or future generations. What is crucial is the proportion of income consumed. By restraining consumption there can be more saving and investment for the future. Also the environment is improved by restraining the consumption of non-renewable resources.

See also: **homo economicus; social choice theory**

Further reading: Andreoni 1989; Buchanan 1975, 1977; Collard 1975; Fontaine 2000; Simon 1993

ARBITRAGE

Parallel simultaneous purchases and sales in different markets in order to gain from **price** differentials. Arbitrage is extensively practised in stock, bond, commodity and currency markets.

By this process efficient and consistent prices emerge despite places and times of sales and purchase being different. In pure arbitrage a riskless **profit** emerges as it costs nothing to hold contracts for different dates. The amount gained through arbitrage can be small but it has to be large to cover transaction costs, otherwise it is pointless. This form of arbitrage does not require the commitment of capital.

Under arbitrage pricing theory in a stock market selling a homogeneous stock, or share, the expensive will be sold and the cheap purchased in order to reach an equilibrium. A few risk factors will affect the price of an asset, including the rate of interest and the price of the asset relative to the price of a portfolio of assets. As financial markets have become more innovative, introducing a host of financial derivatives, so have the techniques for conducting arbitrage, including the use of stochastic differential equations.

Arbitrage can also be part of a merger and takeover strategy when an equity holding is acquired with a view to a company being taken over at a higher price. There can also be arbitrage over the current price of a company and its liquidation value.

See also: **risk and uncertainty**

Further reading: Ross 1976

AUCTION

A method of selling through a process of bidding which ultimately reaches an accepted price.

The simplest of these is the English auction, in which the auctioneer proposes a starting bid then conducts subsequent bidding until no one is willing to bid any higher. The successful bid must reach the seller's reserve price. As 'auction' is derived from the Latin word *augere* meaning to augment or increase, there is the possibility that the English form of bidding has its origins in the Roman empire.

Other types of auction abound. The Dutch auction is conducted in reverse order to the English. The auctioneer deliberately starts with a price far higher than buyers are likely to accept then reduces the price until a buyer accepts by shouting 'mine'. An automated version of this auction uses a 'clock face' with a hand moving from the highest to lower prices. Auctions are open, in the English or Dutch cases. The first-price auction uses the method of sealed bids being submitted and, when opened, the highest being accepted. This is used by the US Treasury for selling short-term securities. Similarly in second-price auctions there are sealed bids but the second highest is chosen. In hybrid auctions the bidders bid for quantities and the prices are negotiated subsequently. All these auctions have different outcomes. Auctions are assessed according to the revenue raised and passing the efficiency test of whether the person with the highest valuation succeeds.

The auction is important in understanding the working of **markets**, as it is the device for reaching equilibrium through the process of tatonnement, or groping, in general equilibrium theory. Under that Walrasian system the auctioneer announces a price and the buyers and sellers write down on pieces of paper whether the price is acceptable or not. The auctioneer can then collect the papers and determine whether at the suggested price there is excess demand or excess supply. The process will continue until demand and supply are balanced.

An auction is only one mode of selling. That they occur at all is to be questioned. They are public so can attract into a market more potential buyers. They can have lower information costs. Where there is uncertainty about the worth of an article an auction is superior to pricing by using customary formulae. The revenue equivalence theorem shows how risk-neutral traders will achieve the outcome of the sellers and buyers, achieving an equivalent exchange in terms of expected revenue to the seller and expected profits to the bidder. Bidders are ignorant of the private valuations of their rivals but sometimes can guess because a common source of information is used by all the auction participants.

Vickrey analysed auctions as games of incomplete **information**. He examined markets in a state of imperfect competition by considering counter-speculation as a means of achieving efficient resource allocation, and devised second highest price as a solution.

See also: **price**

Further reading: Krishna 2002; Vickrey 1961

AUSTRIAN ECONOMICS

A school of economics which began with Carl Menger in 1871.

This branch of economics was a reaction to the German historical school which had despised timeless universal economic laws, preferring the view that economies develop through stages. Both macro- and microeconomic theories are propounded by the Austrians. The former has been concerned with the theory of economic **cycles** and the latter with **prices**, **interest rates** and **investment**.

The distinctive features of the school are its emphases on individualism, subjectivism, opportunity costs and the time preference in consumption and investment. Also they have made contributions to the study of entrepreneurship, **money** and **inflation**.

Carl Menger in his *Principles of Economics* (1871) demonstrated the usefulness of marginal concepts, but avoiding mathematics in the form of the differential calculus used by his contemporary WS Jevons. Implicitly using an idea of marginal utility, Menger showed how there would be a consumer equilibrium by equating marginal satisfactions from different goods consumed. He carefully considered a range of markets from an isolated exchange between two individuals to oligopoly and monopoly. Consumption and capital goods were shown to be in a continuum of lower to higher goods with the higher, capital goods producing the lower to satisfy consumer demand.

The next major figure in the school was Eugen von Boehm-Bawerk, who derived a theory of capital with only land and labour as original factors of production, asserting that capital initiated round-about methods of production, increasing the average period of production as first capital goods then consumer goods would be produced. His three-volume *Capital and Interest* of 1884, 1889 and 1921 surveyed theories of interest, rejecting ideas of exploitation and the labour theory of value. In his theory, interest is justified because of a time preference for present over future goods. He both explained how an individual producer allocates resources and also how allocation occurs in the economy as a whole to achieve full employment. Also in the first generation of the Austrians was his colleague Friedrich von Wieser. His significant contributions to the subject were the theory of imputation, deriving factor prices from product prices, and his theory of alternative, or opportunity, **cost**. Previously value theories had been sharply divided between value based on cost of production and value based on utility: Wieser saw there was a unity between the two approaches, for costs could be translated into utilities

because the cost of production determines the yield from the productive process.

The leading figures of the second generation were Ludwig von
Mises, Ludwig Lachmann and Joseph Schumpeter. Mises, in the
'socialist calculation debate', attacked **socialism** by arguing that as
the government owned the means of production there could be no
pricing for capital goods and hence no full system of pricing for the
economy as a whole. Lachmann did much to detach Austrian from
neoclassical economics and anticipated some of the capital controversies between the two Cambridges of Massachusetts and England
in the 1960s by tackling the problem of measuring the aggregate
capital stock through preferring to examine capital structures. He was a
subjectivist with a great interest in economic methodology. His views
on expectations were similar to Shackle's. Schumpeter expounded a
theory of entrepreneurship and **innovation** to explain economic
development, and was an early theorist of evolutionary economics.

The third generation included a galaxy of stars: Friedrich August
von Hayek, Oscar Morgenstern, Gottfried von Haberler, Fritz
Machlup, and Paul Rosenstein-Rodan. Hayek, with his wide intellectual range of economics, psychology, and political theory, opposed
Keynesianism by attributing the economic ills of the 1930s to over-
investment, and went on to write about the spontaneous order and
information generation inherent in markets. Morgenstern's early
interest in economic **cycles** led to a study of speculation and forecasting: with Neumann he was a founder of **game theory**. Haberler,
an authority on trade theory and cycles, shared with Hayek a dislike
of the Keynesian underinvestment approach to macroeconomics.
Machlup combined a training under Mises and Hayek with experience of manufacturing to write on the economics of **information**,
industrial organisation and international monetary economics; and
Rosenstein-Rodan, after early forays into the study of marginal utility
and the issue of time in economics, advanced the thesis that economic development depended on industrialisation as this brought
about increasing returns.

Through its opposition to central economic planning and government intervention, this school of economics is popular with libertarian economists. Austrian economics became popular in the USA,
particularly because of its robust pro-capitalist libertarianism. The
tradition lives on in neo-Austrian economics, led by James Buchanan,
with his **public choice** theory; Israel Kirzner and his theory of
entrepreneurship; and Murray Rothbard, a disciple of Mises and an
advocate of **libertarian economics**.

Austrian economics is not to be confused with neoclassical economics, as it is scarcely mathematical in its methodology and less interested in equilibrium economics, preferring disequilibrium notions of flux and evolution. To distinguish original Austrian from neoclassical economics, the 'marginal revolution' can be called 'the subjectivist revolution'. With its fervent belief in the efficacy of **markets** to provide information, it has favoured decentralised, unplanned national economies. Much of Austrian economics has always been microeconomic, but in the 1930s Hayek opposed the emerging Keynesian economics, arguing that increased savings would restore harmony to the economy.

See also: **freedom**; **libertarian economics**; **neoclassical economics**

Further reading: Caldwell 1990; Gloria-Palermo 1999; Hicks and Weber 1973

BALANCE OF PAYMENTS

The accounting record of monetary transactions between the residents of one country and another. This balance technically always has to balance under the rules of double entry accounting, but there can be structural imbalances when a balance is only achieved by continuous resort to external financing: this can occur through a chronic failure to export more than is imported.

Within the balance of payments there are several constituent balances. The visible balance consists of exports less imports of goods; the invisible shows the difference between exports and imports of services: these are as varied as payments for services such as shipping, travel and professional services, as well as personal and intergovernmental transfers, and incomes arising from financial investments. The current balance adds together the visible and invisible balances. Further there are balances for short- and long-term capital flows.

The accounting balance provides a record of all transactions between the residents of one country and those of another within the time period of a quarter or a year. For there to be a fundamental equilibrium in the balance of payments, the current and capital accounts have to be in balance and the economy internally balanced at full employment.

The balance of payments can be regarded in stock terms as the relation between stocks of commodities and stocks of cash, or in the flow sense of incomes being transferred across national boundaries.

See also: **trade theory**

Further reading: Stern 1973

BANKING

The activity of exchanging or lending money.

In many languages a similar word for a bank, derived from the bench on which the money exchangers sat, is used. In the Middle Ages the growth of banking into moneylending was impeded in Europe by the church's teaching on usury, the making of a charge for the use of money. Gradually a justification for the payment of interest was found. Today in strict Islamic countries there is also a condemnation of usury, so it is only possible to lend **money** by participating in a joint venture, rather than potentially exploiting the borrower by charging a fixed rate for the use of money.

London goldsmiths in the seventeenth century discovered it was possible to lend more than is deposited – hence goldsmith banking. A study of depositors' demand for cash can ensure that banks can both profit from lending and ensure they have enough on deposit to meet demands for the redemption of banknotes. A cautious risk-free banking system has 100 per cent reserves. Experience showed that it was possible to have a base of 10 per cent cash or a monetary base of about 30 per cent cash and liquid assets which could be changed into cash with little risk of capital loss. The money **multiplier** is the ratio of the increase in bank deposits to a change in reserve assets. In the twentieth century banks diversified into the provision of other financial products, often riskier because they were not repayable in such short time periods as bank loans or represented investments in other financial institutions.

Several tiers of banking exist – central, wholesale and retail. Central banking has the tasks of financing government borrowing, issuing currency, conducting monetary policy, maintaining the liquidity of the banking system, liaising with central banks of other countries and supervising component banks of the system. As the government's bank, a central bank will be engaged in debt management, ensuring that a shortfall in government revenue after expenditures have been incurred will be financed by the short-term issue of bills, often repayable in ninety days, and bonds with five years if short, five to fifteen if medium, over fifteen if long, to redemption, or even undated. As the ultimate source of **credit**, banks maintain liquidity by buying short-term bills held by banks or other recognised financial institutions to inject cash into the banking system to meet customers' demands, especially when mass panic causes a run on a bank. Liaising with other central banks will vary according to the currency regime but can involve inter-bank lending to support a faltering currency. To maintain the quality and solvency of commercial banks, central banks will be involved in audit and inspection, as well as setting capital standards. In a country with a federal constitution such as the USA, state chartered banks will be regulated by state commissions. Some central banks have a long history, such as the Riksbank of Sweden, founded in 1668, and the Bank of England, established in 1694, but others were created in the twentieth century, including the most important, the Federal Reserve System of the USA, which was established in 1913 as a group of twelve banks covering the geographical divisions of the country, with an open market committee, all under the control of a board of governors. Central banks have varying degrees of independence but have their duties defined by statute. The most important mark of independence of a central bank is the right to set interest rates: both the USA and the UK have central bank independence in this sense. There can be hybrid banks which combine the functions of central and private banks, servicing many clients: these were possible in the nineteenth century, when national economies were smaller and the role of government less ambitious in scope.

Wholesale banking has other financial institutions, not the general public, as its customers and is engaged in services which include borrowing and lending. They exist because some banks are secondary banks in that they lend to, but do not collect deposits directly from, the public. These banks can also provide liquidity for other banks, which can then avoid seeking the help of the central bank. Retail banking, meeting the financial needs of firms and private individuals, is usually conducted by a financial firm with many branches. In the past in the USA there was unit banking, which restricted each bank to operation within a narrow geographical area, even a single site. Branch banking has the advantages of reducing the risk associated with business recession in a particular area and of collecting savings more widely.

At the international level, the World Bank (the 'International Bank for Reconstruction and Development') and the International Monetary Fund provide banking services for member nations. The World Bank is heavily involved in making grants to less developed countries; the IMF lends money to member countries finding it difficult to pay external debt. In a sense the IMF is a bank and the World Bank a fund. Not only has the IMF collected **currencies** to lend to indebted nations, but it has also invented a reserve currency of its own, Special Drawing Rights.

The business of a bank has been described as the business of its balance sheet. Its liabilities are the deposits it has received or created for its customers: they are liabilities as they can be transferred elsewhere, electronically or by a check/cheque. The assets matching the liabilities will range from cash, deposits with the central bank, loans to money markets, bills, bonds, loans to customers and trade investments in other financial institutions. There is a spectrum of liquidity and a spectrum of profitability running through the assets. Cash is a zero interest asset and the most liquid; then there are short-term assets which are near liquid. Loans and trade investments are the most profitable and least liquid. Skilled bankers finely balance the composition of their assets.

The free banking movement in Scotland (1810–45) and the free banking state legislation in the USA, as early as 1837 in Michigan and more widely under the National Banking Act of 1863, took away control by a central bank or legislature, providing, in the American case, that banks were backed by bonds. Since the 1980s deregulation in the financial sector has blurred the distinctions between one financial institution and another so that retail banks will also offer advice on mergers and investments and sell insurance and real property. But this has made banking more risky through moving out of areas of traditional expertise and lending for longer periods.

The demand for banking services varies according to the state of economic development. A largely subsistence agricultural economy is not very monetised so needs little banking; then savings banks, chiefly interested in storing deposits, emerge. An extensive financial sector is a defining characteristic of a developed economy. But there can be 'disintermediation' when the banking system is used less as a financial intermediary because firms borrow and lend from each other, especially under **monetary policies** which reduce bank lending.

See also: **monetary policy**; **money**

Further reading: El-Garnal 2006; Heffernan 1996; Selgin 1988; White 1995, 1999

BUBBLE

An unsustainable increase in the price of an asset or commodity encouraged by speculation.

A bubble occurs when **prices** are different from their fundamental values because speculators expect prices to rise further. Bubbles occur in bullish markets and can be fuelled by fraudulent schemes, such as the Ponzi scheme in which prices rise because of high **profits** financed by the new investors themselves. For there to be a bubble, what is priced is in a sense unique as there cannot be bubbles if there is an elastic supply of substitutes. A bubble is measured by a volatility test, for example, the volatility of the returns from an asset. Bubbles occur in dynamically inefficient markets, especially markets full of information deficiencies where the determinants of fundamental prices, for example, of precious metals, foreign currencies and works of art, are obscure. As a bubble has to be financed it will grow at a rate equal to the rate of interest.

The most famous examples are the Dutch tulip mania of 1625–37, and the speculation in the shares of the English South Sea Company in 1720. Recent examples include stock markets in a bullish state, as with the dotcom boom around the year 2000, and the housing market where prices took off, especially in countries with rising housing demand and a low rate of new construction, as in the UK.

There can be a 'bubble economy', as Japan was alleged to be in the 1980s, in which security prices as measured by a stock market price index have reached heights unjustified by underlying values or expected earnings. In general, when prices are too high, there is 'irrational exuberance', to quote the previous chairman of the board of governors of the US Federal Reserve system, Alan Greenspan.

Determinants of bubbles include a deliberate cultivating of the mass psychology of investors by the media; financial fraud, often aided by a lax regulatory regime for financial markets; and repeated economic crises which lead to shortages in supply, as in wartime or siege conditions. Bank lending to support the purchase of financing by encouraging stock market inflation is known as 'bubble financing'. An examination of the psychology of investors can explain the herd-like behaviour which encourages the formation of bubbles. Poor investment techniques can cause many miscalculations and the encouragement of bubbles. In an economy accustomed to severe and regular cycles in output and profits there will be the repeated expectation of upswings in the rise in stock market prices which will encourage the formation of bubbles.

A bubble bursts through the announcement of bad news – for example, the cancellation of dividends, or the revelation of the low potential of a mine or other asset. Although in the early days of the formation of a bubble real **investment** can be encouraged, when the bubble bursts thousands of investors suffer wealth losses and even destitution, plunging the national economy into recession, or worse.

Further reading: Cohen 1997

CAPITALISM

Both a method of production and a type of **economic system**.

As a method of production it uses roundabout methods of production so that capital goods are produced first, then final consumer goods. A non-capitalist method of production would be a primitive activity such as picking berries or catching fish by hand. With a capitalist method some resources are devoted to immediate consumption and others for making capital goods in the form of tools and machines. By creating an extra factor of production, the productive process becomes longer and achieves a higher output. The early Austrian economists, especially Boehm-Bawerk, explained this at length. Another, broader and less technical notion of capitalism, was Marx's approach. He was keen to distinguish different modes of production, including merchant capitalism and industrial capitalism. The merchant capitalist obtains goods in one place and sells them in another. This requires the investment of capital in stocks of goods to be sold at a later date. Marx describes that circulation as money being exchanged for commodities which are sold for a greater amount of money. The industrial capitalist invests in machines and buildings to complement labour in the production process, and through such investment can extract surplus value through not paying workers the full value of their product.

In a capitalist economic system there is private **property**, and the economic independence of firms that can set prices, invest, recruit and dismiss labour, and decide what to produce in the absence of government interference. The values of the system are the pursuit of private gain, of **profit**, rather than the maximisation of any social **production function**. There is a clear distinction between capital owned often by absentees and the alienated labour it employs. Many types of capitalism have been identified, often according to the nature of ownership. Popular capitalism, for example, encourages widespread share ownership so millions of people each have a holding of capital. At the other extreme is state capitalism of the old Soviet-type economy, in which all land and industry were owned by the state.

Smith, influenced by the Physiocrats' **laissez-faire** ideas, made use of the idea of natural liberty, the **freedom** to use one's abilities without interference, in his discussion of economic systems in *The Wealth of Nations*. Self-interested individuals following their natures will produce the best outcome for society. Capitalism was, therefore, a natural development, not something created as happens with socialist schemes. Although Smith has been called the father of capitalism he had little need for the term 'capital', preferring to speak of 'stock'.

Except under state capitalism, which uses the apparatus of planning to allocate resources, capitalism is reliant on the price system to match production and desired consumption. Smith with his '**invisible hand**' concept, and Hayek's successor concept of the spontaneous order, expected economic activity to need no central direction. The working of **markets** was sufficient to supply the **information** economic agents need to operate the economy. Capitalism does not require a state of perfect competition. Private monopolies can flourish under capitalism in the absence of a strong competition policy.

Marx, as the title of his most famous work *Das Kapital* proclaims, chose capitalism as his principal research programme. The capitalist has command over the means of subsistence for workers so can control them and exploit them. Capitalism is a mode of production in which capital seizes the means of production. Whereas before industrial capitalism workers as small craftsmen owned their tools, when the factory age is born the capitalist owns all machinery so can decide who works and on what terms. With the advent of private ownership of the means of production, social relations have changed. The driving motive of the capitalist is accumulation of capital to acquire more surplus value in a competitive world. The population is dehumanised so that it can exist to serve the capitalist's ends.

Proponents of capitalism point to the strengths which have delivered economic growth and a widespread increase in per capita incomes. The mistakes of not too wise governments have been avoided by allowing markets to follow their natural course. Critics have been keen to point out that many forms of exploitation are inherent in capitalism. Large inequalities of **wealth** and income indicate that the rich are doing well at the expense of the poor. Workers endure long hours in factories and offices to provide a pampered life of leisure for the rich. In Marxist thought it is stated that the working day is longer than is needed to provide workers' subsistence so that surplus value can be created for the owners of capital. Workers are alienated because the system of production separates workers from the capital they use and the products they produce.

There is an intimate relationship between capitalism and political pluralism. Capitalist activity which is not heavily taxed or regulated is said to create economic freedom, the foundation of a free society. As capitalism makes possible the financing of political parties in opposition to a government, and the establishment of a free press, there is political freedom.

Capitalism has successfully fought off ideological competitors. Gradually 'Anglo-Saxon capitalism', the system which emerged in the 1980s in the USA and the UK, has become the dominant form of economic system in most countries. Its characteristics are private property, flexible **labour** practices, few **trade unions**, free trade, income inequalities, especially in the massive remuneration of senior executives, and a swift reaction to changing economic circumstances provoked by financial markets determining the industrial structure.

See also: **comparative economic systems**; **laissez-faire**; **socialism**

Further reading: Amable 2003; Broome 1983; Cowling 1982; Schumpeter 1954; Tawney 1926

CAPITAL THEORY

The debate about the nature of capital and its measurement.

A starting point is to regard capital as a fund, an accumulated stock of goods or financial assets. Financial capital consists of the funds to acquire real, mainly physical, capital. Also, as technical capital, it is a collection of productive resources, especially machines, used to achieve an output in conjunction with land and labour. It can be owned privately or by a community or the state itself. In classical economic theory a major element of capital was the wages fund, which made production possible through having a stock to maintain workers during the production period.

From the 1870s, Austrian economists, including Carl Menger and Boehm-Bawerk, made leading contributions to the theory of capital, particularly through emphasising the role of time through capital being a roundabout method of production. Menger thought there was a hierarchy of goods, with the higher-order capital goods producing the lower-order consumer goods. Boehm-Bawerk controversially would not accord capital the status of an original factor of production like labour and land.

The Cambridge capital controversies debates of the 1960s, between Cambridge, England and Cambridge, Massachusetts, centred on the measurement of capital in the aggregate production function. Paul Samuelson, Robert Solow, Frank Hahn and Christopher Bliss, in the

American group, used the largely neoclassical approach of an aggregate production function to attack Joan Robinson, Piero Sraffa, Luigi Pasinetti and Pierangelo Garegnani in the 'English' camp.

Measurement of capital is difficult when its heterogeneous character is recognised, abandoning a neoclassical assumption. Either its cost of production is computed or the present value of the stream of services it produces is calculated, but changes in the value of capital and its quality raise severe measurement problems. There are the problems of re-switching, where the same technique is chosen at more than one rate of interest, and capital reversing when a lower capital-labour ratio is chosen despite the **interest rate** being low. Static approaches were criticised for ignoring the relationship between capital and the passage of time. The neoclassical attempt to explain the rate of return using the concept of marginal **productivity** was shown to be limited to a world of homogeneous capital, and not the basis of allocating capital according to relative **scarcities**. A criticism of Joan Robinson and her Cambridge, England disciples is that they revealed difficulties but failed to construct an alternative.

Capital and growth theories overlap. Capital deepening occurs when the capital-labour ratio increases so that production becomes more capital intensive; capital widening means an increase in the amount of the capital stock in an economy with unchanged capital-labour ratios.

When the notion of capital was extended from physical to **human capital**, earlier in Petty and Smith, and more recently in the works of Schultz and his contemporaries, the distinction between separate factors of production became blurred.

See also: **investment**; **Neo-Ricardian economics**

Further reading: Cohen and Harcourt 2003; Dewey 1965; Felipe and Fisher 2003; Kregel 1976

CLASSICAL ECONOMICS

The theories of the group of economists headed by Adam Smith which were dominant in British economics from *c.*1750 to *c.*1870. Its leading figures included David Ricardo, Robert Malthus, Nassau Senior, John Stuart Mill and Karl Marx.

As the title of Smith's influential work *An Inquiry into the Nature and Causes of the Wealth of Nations* (1776) indicates, **economic growth** was central to their concerns. Smith, sharing in the Scottish Enlightenment's attempt to explain human nature, argued that the basic human desire for betterment will lead to **saving**, which is invested so that **division of labour** is possible, bringing about growth in productivity. Most classical economists feared an end to economic growth, with the exception of JS Mill, who welcomed the slower pace of a stationary economy, providing incomes were properly distributed.

Ricardo in his *Principles of Political Economy and Taxation* (1817) constructs an abstract model of the economy relating value to wages distribution. Malthus in his *Essay on the Principle of Population* (1798) and *Principles of Political Economy* (1820) forcefully asserts that an unchecked population would grow faster than its means of subsistence. He was also an important precursor of John Maynard Keynes in his study of an underemployed economy and his policy recommendation of public works. In his *Principles* he sets out some of the clearest demand and supply analysis of the period. NW Senior's achievements included a movement of value theory from labour to utility foundations, and a justification for profits as the reward for waiting.

Prominent in classical economics was the study of **value**. Three questions were asked. What is the nature of value? What is the measure of value? What are the determinants of value? Following Aristotle, value in use and value in exchange were distinguished. Smith also separated natural **prices** based on cost of production from market prices determined by demand and supply. Natural prices were the long-run 'central' **equilibrium** prices around which market prices fluctuated. Later Ricardo refined Smith's diffuse discussion of the relationship between labour and value into a theory of relative prices determined by relative labour quantities. Marx expanded Ricardo's value theory through introducing the notion of 'socially necessary labour time'.

The distribution of national income into **rent**, wages and **profits** was another central theme. The differential rent theory, which originated with the Scottish agricultural writer James Anderson, was a pillar of Ricardo's model of the economy. At the margin of cultivation no rent was paid, leaving the product to be divided between wages and profits, the latter declining as real wages rose. Wages were discussed at the macro and micro levels of the economy. Smith used the notion of the wages fund as the total amount which had to be accumulated to pay workers throughout the period of production. The justification for wage differentials, including the amount of human capital embodied in each worker, was also set out. Profits were subject to a minimum level reflecting risk. Factor mobility would tend to equalise wage rates, as well as profit rates.

Like the Physiocrats, the classical economists by recommending free trade reacted to the dominant mercantilist view that an economy to be strong had to be protectionist. To maximise the effects of division of labour a large, and international, market was needed. Smith argued that trade took place because of a country having an absolute advantage in production over another, Ricardo and Robert Torrens used a comparative advantage trade theory. Mill refined Ricardo by using the concept of reciprocal demand to determine the terms of trade.

These economists were writing at a time when Britain endured long wars with France, with severe consequences for the economy. A boom occurred during the war and a severe recession after 1815. Insufficient **taxation** was levied to finance the war with the consequence that there was a great increase in the national **debt** and discussion of using a sinking fund to reduce it. A shortage of bullion reserves compelled the Bank of England to go off the gold standard in 1797. A debate with many contributors on the nature of paper currency and the role of the Bank of England in central banking continued until the Bank Charter Act of 1844. Throughout this discussion reference was made to Smith's views on the nature of paper currency and Ricardo's doctrine that a **currency** had to fluctuate with the amount of precious metals in the economy.

The roles for national government proposed by Smith were few – defence, law and order, some public works partly financed by the users, and support for the sovereign. To achieve the public good intentional effort was not required. By the pursuit of self-interest economic agents would be guided by an **invisible hand** to help society at large. Smith saw **economic welfare** in material terms and fervently preached that it was in everyone's interest to be a specialist, following division of labour principles, so that the income of the society as a whole would grow. However, classical economists granted exceptions to extreme **laissez-faire** economics. Specific problems were solved through directed legislation. The Navigation Acts, which required Britain's trade to be carried in British shipping, were approved as a means of creating a reserve navy to boost Britain's defences. Banking regulations improved the liquidity of the banking system. JS Mill had some sympathy for socialism and public ownership; but some contemporary legislation was strongly opposed. Malthus wanted the Poor Laws to be phased out as they irresponsibly promoted population growth. Many, including Senior, criticised the Factory Acts, those regulations which were progressively reducing hours and the employment of women and children.

The commanding position of classical economic theories had been lost by 1870. The advent of **neoclassical economics**, with the more precise analytical tools provided by WS Jevons and especially Alfred Marshall, took over. But the individual themes of classical economics continue to be discussed.

See also: **Austrian economics**; **neoclassical economics**; **value**

Further reading: Eltis 1984; Hollander 1987; O'Brien 2004

CLUBS, THEORY OF

An explanation of the provision of goods which are part private and part public by a voluntary association of similar persons who share production costs.

Unlike pure **public goods** they are not consumed by all; unlike pure private goods, one person's consumption does not diminish another's. Cases of sharing are so common that theorising about them is sensible. There are costs and benefits of joining a club and differences in clubs with respect to their size and activities to be considered. Clubs exist because the costs to many individuals would be prohibitive, for example, owning an Olympic-size swimming pool, or because the activity can only be done by a group of people, as is the case with games and sports.

Without a club being formally constituted the provision of a good or service can follow the principles of a club, as with the supply of services to households by a local government or a commercial concern. Considerations of relative costs and benefits will determine the optimal size of sub- and quasi-governmental organisations. A complex club provides a mixture of benefits. Large clubs can afford to charge lower membership fees but will run the risk of reducing the advantages of membership through creating congestion and losing their exclusivity. Under the usual rules of optimisation, membership will expand until the marginal benefit of membership equals its marginal cost. Clubs can be homogeneous with members having the same relevant characteristic, or they can be mixed clubs with a diversity of members. Inevitably the measurement of costs and benefits is difficult. For members the opportunity cost of membership has to be considered: to finance the membership fee other consumption or saving has to be reduced.

The **cost** of preserving the existence of a club introduces the difficult interdependence of costs and benefits: present benefits might have to be reduced to guarantee a continued flow of them. Benefits are variable depending on how much other members consume of the output of the club, and might be disproportionately consumed by some members to the detriment of others, especially if the membership is heterogeneous. If there are spill-over benefits of a club, for example when the health of a community is improved by the provision of gardens, there is a case for non-members to subsidise the members. A club which has shared **consumption** and homogeneous membership is called 'discriminatory', as persons lacking the crucial characteristics such as race or gender are excluded. The costs of excluding non-members reduce the amount of resources which could be offered to members. Game theory recognises the usefulness of the theory of clubs in that it discusses the circumstances in which coalitions occasion a welfare benefit.

The analogy of the club has been used for the pricing of public utilities, road charging to reduce transport congestion, the provision of public services locally, migration, political alliances and international organisations.

See also: **public good**

Further reading: Buchanan 1965; Sandler and Tschirhart 1980

COASE THEOREM

An alternative approach to responding to **externalities** such as pollution, avoiding the charging of the polluter or imposing special taxes.

Coase argued that instead of analysing the problem of social cost in terms of A inflicting harm on B and restraining A, the reciprocal relationship between A and B has to be recognised. He uses the example of a factory which makes noise upsetting a medical practitioner. If the factory had to be silenced then it would harm the manufacturer so the parties have to negotiate. Another example is of a cattle farmer with straying animals damaging the crops of a neighbouring arable farmer. Rather than propose legislation to establish who is allowed to do what he proposes a private solution. Providing property rights have been defined, an agreement to allow cattle to stray can be attempted to compensate the arable farmer and allow the other farmer some freedom in animal management. How much is paid depends on the loss of net income. It is assumed that there are no transaction costs in reaching this agreement. Instead of examining the divergence between private and social **cost** he proposed that there be an opportunity cost approach, looking at the effects on the market value of production of different social arrangements. The starting point should be that the world as it is is not an ideal state of affairs. Further factors of production should be regarded as rights to do various things. He asserts that the cost to exercise a right can be measured by the loss elsewhere. Thus the total effects of one social arrangement rather than another are considered.

Originally the Coase approach assumed zero transaction costs, which is often regarded as virtually impossible. When there are positive transaction costs there is an even greater role for the law as it is concerned with duties and privileges. The whole nature of the negotiations between the parties will be not an exchange of things but of rights to act in particular ways, hence an exchange of property rights.

Challenges to the theorem include an attack on the assumptions that there is perfect competition, **property rights** are defined and the transaction costs of negotiating an agreement are low. The possibility of applying the theorem to real life situations is questioned, especially when several parties with different opinions are involved so the negotiations will be protracted. Environmental scientists have questioned the Coasian approach, especially the idea that there can be efficient levels of pollution.

Coase's original intention was to attack the Pigou approach of using taxes or other government action to deal with firms that are polluters. By using a new analysis of the problem of pollution he made a major contribution to environmental economics.

See also: **environmental economics**; **property rights**

Further reading: Coase 1960, 1988

COBWEB

The path of a change in a market as it moves towards, or away from, an **equilibrium** between demand and supply.

At the beginning of a cobweb demand will be less or more than supply. For the market to clear there has to be a movement in **price**. If there is excess demand, the price will rise to reduce demand and encourage suppliers to send more to the market. Under conditions of excess supply a lowering of price will encourage purchasers and discourage suppliers. The whole underlying principle is that there can be different responses to an imbalance between demand and supply. Assumptions have to be made about the price **expectations** of the producers, especially whether there is price rigidity. Crucial is the **elasticity** of demand and supply curves. If the demand elasticity is greater than the supply, there will be a movement to a stable equilibrium; if supply elasticity is greater, the cobweb will be unstable in that the path will be further and further away from equilibrium. This is a challenge to the optimistic classical view that **markets** tending towards equilibrium cobwebs can be divergent. If the cobweb mechanism results in a disequilibrium this will be manifest in unemployment or excess capacity.

Cobweb theory has been applied especially to pig (hog) markets where there is a long production period, but in principle any markets, including labour markets, can be analysed in this way.

See also: **disequilibrium economics**; **equilibrium**

Further reading: Kaldor 1934; Nerlove 1958

COLLECTIVE BARGAINING

Negotiations between a **trade (labor) union** and an employer or employers' federation to determine pay and other employment conditions.

As unionisation increased so did the replacement of individual bargaining between a worker and an employer by collective bargaining. This increased bargaining strength in turn made union membership more attractive through creating a union effect on wages. Rarely does collective bargaining cover the whole of a national labour force, unless union membership is compulsory. With the decline of traditional heavy industries such as coal mining and shipbuilding, and extensive de-industrialisation, private sector collective bargaining has fallen in some Western countries.

Most of collective bargaining is bilateral, but it can be multilateral when interest groups, for example parents' associations at teacher wage bargaining, are present. Its scope varies according to the aims of the negotiators. Pay and hours of work are the most basic of terms in agreements; more ambitiously a range of fringe benefits, including health insurance, can be included.

Collective bargaining can take place annually, when requested by one of the parties or under the terms of a previous agreement. Such systems have differing attitudes towards the law. In the USA the purpose of the bargaining has been to produce an enforceable contract, unlike in the UK. In a totalitarian state collective bargaining has no role. Also there has been a limit to the power of employers and unions in concert to determine the economic terms of their relationship in freer societies where **incomes policies** have been used.

See also: **industrial relations**; **labour**; **trade (labor) union**

Further reading: Beal 1976; Hutt 1975

COMPARATIVE ECONOMIC SYSTEMS

The study of the nature of national economies with a view to classifying them according to the type of ownership, the method of allocating output and the determination of incomes. Prior to the extensive repudiation of the Soviet-type economy in the late 1980s, it was common to contrast capitalist, socialist and mixed economies.

The differences in economic organisation used to be sufficiently stark to differentiate one economy from another. Whether businesses and houses could be privately owned was crucial: where they were not there was the possibility of total state economic and social control. The use of the **price** mechanism through free markets or central economic **planning** underlay the method of allocation in each type of economy and whether **income distribution** would follow on from market freedom or administrative diktat. Mixed economies attempted to soften the effects of capitalism, without adopting the strong central controls of many types of socialism. Where there is a fringe of experimental mini-economies such as producer cooperatives or privately owned small firms, the economy is also 'mixed'.

In the 1960s the 'convergence hypothesis' argued that different economic systems were converging to a kind of managerial capitalism with a measure of planning at the national level, but that there were still sharp contrasts in terms of ownership of businesses and the freedom of the price system. In the 1990s this branch of economics changed to the economics of transition, analysing the difficulties and costs of changing the basis of economic organisation in countries free to make more use of market mechanisms.

See also: **capitalism**; **economic system**; **socialism**

Further reading: Wiles 1977

COMPETITION AND MONOPOLY

Contrasting states of markets classified according to the number of firms participating in them.

Market structures are often arrayed on a spectrum of conditions between the extremes of perfect competition and its complete opposite, monopoly. Previously in the nineteenth century competition was contrasted with **cooperation**. Competition was regarded as an evil which pushed down wages and added to workers' misery; cooperation was supposed to guarantee a fair reward. In the more modern view of competition and other market states, the spectrum starts with the largest number of firms in perfect competition, then the number of firms declines through monopolistic competition, oligopoly, duopoly and finally to monopoly: these markets operate according to different principles in determining output and prices. Seen from a buyer's point of view, a market with a sole buyer would be a monopsony, or with a few dominant sellers, an oligopsony.

Perfect competition, a limiting case, is a popular market type for economic analysis. It is usually defined by the conditions necessary to establish it. There should be a large number of buyers and sellers, freedom of entry and exit to the market, a homogeneous product, an absence of government intervention and transport costs, and perfect information. The last condition, that potential buyers and sellers have full relevant information, is so demanding that sometimes it is called a state of pure competition. The large numbers assumption means that no market participant can influence the price: they are price takers. The homogeneous product assumption requires that all buyers regard the product as identical, even if there are some differences in, for example, its chemical composition. The **elasticity** of the **demand curve** for each firm will be horizontal, perfectly elastic as every firm's output is regarded as identical to the others'; the demand curve for the industry will be downward sloping with some inelasticity because by definition every industry has a distinct product. If there were product heterogeneity, individual sellers would have some monopoly power. Freedom of entry and exit, in the negative sense of an absence of barriers, ensures that firms in equilibrium earn only normal profit, the minimum return to an entrepreneur. Because governments stand back from the market, buyers and sellers are free, without interference, to arrive jointly at a market price; because there are no transport costs, local monopolies cannot develop. Some **information** assumption is necessary, otherwise economic agents could not behave in the market. As a result of these conditions holding, in equilibrium the price equals both average total and marginal costs.

Similar to perfect competition is monopolistic competition, a market state first recognised by Ed Chamberlin, and similar to the notion of imperfect competition devised by his contemporary Joan Robinson in the 1930s. Monopolistic competition is principally distinguished from its similar state, perfect competition, by allowing product differentiation. For this to occur, selling costs, especially through advertising, will be incurred with the consequence that there will be an upward shift in the average total cost, posing a barrier to entry of marginal firms and hence reducing the number of firms in the industry. Product differentiation will mean that the firm's demand curve will be elastic but not perfectly so. In equilibrium the firm will not be operating at a large enough output to minimise average costs, an effect called the excess capacity theorem.

Where a market consists of a small group of **firms** it is called an oligopoly. The temptation to collude is strong, and if it occurred then the firms would be jointly acting as a single monopoly setting a single price for its product. Competition law and its antitrust equivalent have outlawed collusion in many developed countries. Sometimes an industry consists of the output predominantly produced by a group of oligopolists with a competitive fringe of smaller firms: retailing in Britain exemplifies this well. If oligopolists have to fix prices separately they have nevertheless to anticipate their rivals' reactions. A famous model of a non-collusive oligopolist's behaviour is described by the kinked oligopoly demand curve. This shows that such a firm's demand curve consists of two demand curves joined together so that up to the price set the demand curve is elastic, for if the firm raised its prices no one would follow. The demand curve beyond the ruling price is inelastic, in fact the industry's demand curve, for if a firm cuts its prices its rivals follow. This description of oligopoly was used to attempt to explain price rigidity under oligopoly, although rigidity can occur for a variety of reasons, including the menu cost of changing product prices frequently. Empirical tests do not confirm that oligopolists behave in a herd-like manner only when they lower their prices.

Duopoly has been powerfully analysed by Cournot and Bertrand. The former posited the case of a market with two proprietors controlling a spring of water each. They are **profit** maximisers who will adjust their prices in reaction to the other until a market price emerges. In the Bertrand refinement the two producers pursue price strategies until an **equilibrium** is established.

Monopoly is the other limit to the spectrum of market structures. A monopoly is a sole producer so the firm and the industry are coterminous and the firm's demand curve, downward sloping, will be the industry curve. Monopolies are established in various ways. A government can by law exclude rival firms, perhaps on grounds of national security or public safety, and even own the monopoly. An early technological lead with patent protection for the invention used will keep out other firms. If the industry has largely fixed cost production and attendant economies of scale then it could be described as a 'natural monopoly'. Sometimes it is difficult for an industry to attract firms because the product is unsafe or unsavoury. Monopoly has its rewards – the quiet life of not having to meet competitive challenges and the supernormal profits through its average revenue being in excess of its average cost. It can be difficult for a domestic monopoly to retain its market dominance in its own country, unless there is protection to keep at bay international competitors. Infant industries, sometimes with monopoly status, have been encouraged as an exception to free trade.

Public objections to the exploitative behaviour of dominant firms have brought about laws to promote competition. In the USA at the federal level the Sherman Act of 1890 started the control of monopoly, mergers and anti-competitive practices. In the UK a competition policy started in 1948 with the mild Monopolies and Restrictive Practices (Inquiry and Control) Act and was succeeded by tougher legislation, especially on the control of agreements between firms.

See also: **game theory**; **industrial organisation**; **price**

Further reading: Fellner 1960; Stigler 1966

CONSUMER'S SURPLUS

The difference between the amount a consumer is prepared to pay and the amount actually paid.

This was devised by Dupuit and extended by the Cambridge economist Marshall, who illustrated the concept in a standard demand and supply diagram. In the case of a downward sloping **demand curve** at less than equilibrium output, consumers have a reservation price as they would be willing to pay more than the equilibrium price. Thus there is a notional surplus for each part of the demand curve between it and the equilibrium price. Marshall said that there could be 'thin parallelograms' under the demand curve: when these are summed into the area under the curve they are called the consumer's surplus. In **welfare economics** the consumer surplus idea has been repeatedly used in devising compensation tests to ensure that when there is an economic change there is a net welfare gain. In **cost-benefit analysis** the concept is crucial to estimating the benefits from **investment**. As the notion shows that richer consumers have a higher surplus, it is taken into account in devising price structures and schemes of indirect **taxation**.

Marshall also suggested there could be a producer's surplus because of it being possible to obtain supply of a good or service at less than **equilibrium** price.

See also: **welfare economics**

CONSUMPTION

The spending alternative to investment for a household, a firm or a government; the using of a service or the destruction of a good.

The whole point of production is to satisfy the wishes of the consumer. As Adam Smith put it, 'consumption is the end of all production'. Consumption is analysed at both the micro and macro levels in economics. At the micro level theories have been advanced to explain how a consumer makes choices between various goods and services in the face of an income constraint. From Jevons onwards a consumer has been seen as a utility maximising individual wanting to choose a combination of goods and services which will extract the most utility from a given income. Through equating the ratios of marginal utilities to prices a consumer **equilibrium** will be reached as the same amount of **utility** per unit of currency spent is obtained. In another micro-theory Lancaster attempted to break away from utility-based consumer theory with his characteristics theory of consumer demand, suggesting that consumers demand the attributes of goods rather than the goods themselves, for example, the location of a house rather than the building.

At the macro level, since Keynes the relationship between aggregate consumption and **national income** has been an essential part of macroeconomic modelling. Keynes stated that as income rises consumption also increases, but at a slower rate: this produces an absolute non-linear consumption function. Diverse theories of the consumption function arise from the use of different measures of income –

absolute, relative and permanent. Absolute income is current income without any qualification. Relative income is current income relative to a previous peak income, or the income of one group relative to another. Permanent and transitory consumption are contrasted with permanent and transitory income so that there are two consumption functions. It is possible to split aggregate income into these short- and long-run components by regarding permanent income as trend income and transitory as fluctuations around the trend, or by regarding some types of income as permanent, particularly contractual employment incomes, and others, such as windfall stock market gains, as transitory.

An Euler equation is used to estimate aggregate consumption growth over time. In this inter-temporal approach consumption can be deferred, encouraged by the prospect of high real interest rates.

Veblen in his analysis of the leisure class noted the phenomenon of 'conspicuous consumption', which is undertaken for the purpose of flaunting one's status in society. Hirsch devised the term 'positional good' to describe something rare and exclusive which cannot be reproduced in large amounts. Its appeal is its non-availability to more than a few. Various forms of education, artistic performances and properties have this character.

See also: **Keynesianism**

Further reading: Hirsch 1976; Lancaster 1971

CONTRACT THEORY

An extension of the analysis of exchange and production.

Aristotle in the *Nichomachean Ethics*, book V, stated that it is dis-similar things which are exchanged so that some rules are necessary to bring about fairness. Francis Hutcheson, who taught Adam Smith, in his *System of Moral Philosophy* (1755), book II, chapter 9, examined the obligations which arise from contracting. He argued that commerce would be obstructed if the contracting parties could repudiate imprudent contracts. The contract should be naturally possible and the parties should make every attempt to discover the factors which affect the value of the goods and restore any excess which has been given. In the 1880s Edgeworth used contract curves to describe bilateral exchanges in the absence of uncertainty and asymmetric **information**.

Contracting can be bilateral or multilateral. Employment contracts are often bilateral, even under collective bargaining as two bargaining bodies negotiate. Multilateral contracts are common in insurance, where risks are widely shared, and in industries such as construction, where many different contractors aim to produce a complex building; also multilateral contracts occur in sharecropping, partnerships and franchise operations. The presence of several contractors raises questions of collusion and competition, both of which can affect the optimality of the contract. In the formation of contracts the parties are faced with problems of hidden or misleading information and uncertainty. There can be repeated bilateral contracting when circumstances surrounding the contract are short-term, for example, demand is volatile or output is variable, so that a chain of contracts reduces uncertainty. Contracts can refer to a present sale or to a future transaction. Also the contract might be an option to buy rather than an actual purchase. An efficient contract will produce stable prices and output.

Through the voluntary creation of a contract the parties to an exchange attempt to produce a mutually acceptable exchange. Many complications arise. The contract might be obscure or even implicit. The parties could fail to foresee many events so that later renegotiation of the contract is necessary. Where there are high set-up **costs**, such as training costs for new employees, there is a strong motive for making a long-term contract but to do so raises problems of anticipating random events and also the fact that the less well-endowed party will be more risk averse. These difficulties have encouraged the use of game theory to devise a strategy for the design of the contract.

Much of the problem of contracting is that of informational deficiency. A way of diminishing this danger is by signalling, which provides a hint of a future state. The future performance and productivity of an employee cannot be guaranteed but the past education and employment record are pointers to performance. Also the behaviour of a contracting party at the time of forming the contract can be a clue, hence the use of interviewing to detect honesty and attitudes. Established habits and customs in a social group can indicate likely conduct under the contract.

The existence of long-term contracts has stimulated the development of incomplete contract theory. To encourage agricultural improvement, long leases are granted. Banks in financial markets and employers of highly skilled staff have to devise contracts for periods of time when much is unforeseen. The inability of the contracting parties to describe the subject of the contract can lead to disputes about the fulfilment of the contract which have to be resolved, perhaps by negotiation, perhaps by arbitration. The incompleteness of the contract's provisions can render the original ex-ante investment futile or disappointing.

The variety of contracts has given rise to the analysis of a range of commercial transactions, for example, 'mixed bundling' when there is a simultaneous separate and joint sale of two associated products. Throughout there is a search for an optimal contract which will maximise the benefits to the contracting parties.

Many of the difficulties of contracting can be reduced to the 'principal-agent problem'. The principal can be the owner of a business who delegates to managers and employees various tasks, or a principal can be a firm granting to other firms the power to act on its behalf. As with all contracts there is the difficulty of monitoring to ensure that an agreement has been effectively executed. An incentive scheme has to be devised to ensure compliance with the contract and thereby maximise the principal's expected utility. The contract has to determine how the risk is shared between principal and agent. The principal-agent problem can also be analysed by considering the costs and benefits to the principal of having one form of relationship rather than another.

Implicit contract theory raises different issues, especially in the labour market, which differs from many types of product market because the contracting parties do not spell out the terms of their relationship. The nature of the employment and expectations of promotion and job tenure are based on long-held practices. Subjective evaluations motivate the agreement rather than a stated component of a contract. Also, in commercial transactions where the parties have an established relationship, there is often sufficient trust to make explicit contractual terms unnecessary.

Contract theory is an important element of **labour** economics, **industrial organisation** and corporate finance. The modern analysis of the role of information in markets inevitably includes contract analysis. Insurers have long been aware of the dangers of deficient knowledge of the insured. A problem of 'adverse selection' can occur if through ignorance a bad risk is accepted. Also there is always the possibility of 'moral hazard' when the insured cares less when a risk is covered by insurance and can behave recklessly.

See also: **game theory**

Further reading: Azariadis 1975; Bolton and Dewatripont 2005; Hart 2001; Hart and Moore 1988

COOPERATION

Joint production or consumption by a group of people for their mutual benefit; the opposite of competition; a mild form of socialism.

In the literature of utopias there are many examples of producer cooperatives. Charles Fourier and Robert Owen both designed such communities. There was a fear of the deadening effect of **division of labour**, so producer cooperatives were devised which were both agricultural and manufacturing in their activities. Fourier attacked labour specialisation because of his belief that humans have a basic 'papillon', or butterfly, tendency so want to flit from one activity to another. Also, members of the cooperative would benefit by not having to distribute profits to outside owners. In low-technology industries such as shoemaking, producer cooperatives persisted in England well into the twentieth century. The self-managed enterprise is an extension of the cooperative idea.

Consumer cooperatives have enjoyed more success. The cooperative society founded in Rochdale, England in 1844 spread throughout the UK and has survived to this day. The advantage of such societies is the offering of goods at lower prices through reducing profit margins.

Cooperation is also a major theme of **game theory**. Instead of the aim of a game being to defeat and disadvantage an opponent, the joys of participation, fun and the exhilaration of the activity can be sought. Instead of individuals pitting themselves against each other there are coalitions of players.

See also: **competition and monopoly**; **game theory**; **socialism**

Further reading: Webb 1921

CORE

A set of **equilibrium** prices.

The Oxford economist Edgeworth in *Mathematical Psychics* (1881) examined a market with two commodities and two consumers and drew a contract curve linking all the possible equilibria. It is supposed that there is perfect competition and a barter economy. Instead of assuming that economic agents take **prices** as given, he introduces the idea of recontracting. In an exchange economy when there is a large number of players, it is more difficult to have collusive behaviour so the core, the number of equilibrium relative prices, is smaller. Later this idea was powerfully generalised in game theory, where the core is that set of allocations in which a sub-group cannot benefit by deserting the coalition (players bound together by the same strategy).

Also there is a Walras core. This is an allocation for a nation in which every trader has a budget balanced at the price schedule. It is an equilibrium position in that there is not a price schedule which would allow a coalition of traders to trade better.

A core economy is dominant in world economic relations, a core firm leads an industry and a core region determines the economic fate of the rest of a country.

CORRUPTION

The diversion of the revenues and assets owned by governments or corporate bodies for the benefit of officials and their associates; often narrowly defined as the misuse of public office for private gain.

In a sense much corruption is the consequence of an inefficient principal–agent relationship. Much of this is indistinguishable from ordinary theft, but some is more subtle and difficult to detect, taking the form of the splitting of benefits between legitimate and illegal recipients. The array of corruption techniques is great. There can be off balance sheet accounting to disguise the extent of a government's debt, and the continuance of a governmental body without acceptable auditing, such as the European Commission: such deception gives corruption a chance to flourish.

Corruption is a function of size. It is larger contracts, especially for construction projects, which give much scope for hiving off funds illegally. Smaller organisations have little scope for the corrupt to benefit, hence the attractions of employment in major banks. A large organisation can be hierarchical, with opportunities for rent seeking at all levels. Under a democracy there is less opportunity for corruption as a government is exposed to scrutiny. An independent civil service with a tradition of honesty helps to keep corruption at bay.

Levels of **taxation**, if high, can provoke the growth of a shadow economy where much activity is hidden, so potentially corrupt. Also, the structure of industry is important as monopolists lack the challenge of competitors and oligopolists can collude, despite severe competition and antitrust legislation.

The effects of corruption are severe. It can lead to the refusal of charities to help poor countries, a reduction in trade and investment, and the creation of societies with very unequal income distributions.

To eliminate corruption different strategies can be employed. The supervision by international agencies of governments reduces crookedness at that level. The creation of a framework of company/corporate law is a curb on the misappropriation of funds within firms. As corruption is the product of a political and social culture, it takes a long time to include transparency and honesty. Within a public body it is important to have enough remuneration and incentives so that corruption is less attractive, hence the importance of paying judges highly so that it is less necessary to accept bribes from litigants.

Corruption from country to country is often compared using measures such as the Corruption Perception Index (CPI) based for each country on surveys of businesses and residents who estimate corruption on a scale from 0 to 10. Since the corrupt always try to hide their activities the index produces questionable results.

Further reading: Jain 2001; Shleifer and Vishny 1993; Svensson 2005

COST

The sacrifice of time, effort or resources which makes production possible.

For every factor of production a cost is incurred through participation in the productive process. **Labour** needs sufficient means for its maintenance and subsistence according to the demands of that society. Capital incurs costs in its hire and depreciation. Rent must be paid for land for exclusive use on one occupation rather than another.

The accounting cost will be the sum of the expenses incurred to produce a given output and recorded in the books of a firm. It is a narrower concept than economic cost, which includes opportunity cost. Opportunity cost is a central idea in economics. Given that there is **scarcity**, the use of labour or another factor of production in one way means sacrificing other uses. The opportunity cost will therefore be what can be gained in the next best employment. Because of the choice between one use and another, in a diagram the production possibility lines showing the amounts of a product obtainable from combinations of two factors will be downward sloping. As both an individual and society at large are affected by a particular choice, there are both private and social opportunity costs:

there can be a loss of personal income as well as a fall in national income. Wieser expounded the idea of opportunity costs in his theory of alternative cost.

Buchanan, in the Austrian tradition, relates cost to choice in that it is what is sacrificed when one alternative is rejected. In this decision making process cost is subjective so cannot be measured by anyone else, but it can be dated, as a decision is made in time. It is an ex-ante concept because it is based on expectations.

Costs can be classified according to time, as in the distinction between fixed and variable cost. A long-term commitment such as a building will incur fixed costs, but the hire of casual labour, which is hardly a commitment at all, will be very variable. The nature of the contract buying the services of a factor of production will have a time element. The longer the time specified, the more fixed the cost is. With the growth of employment contracts labour has changed from mainly a variable to a fixed, or quasi-fixed, cost for many occupations. Marshall in his *Principles of Economics*, wanting to use terms known to contemporary businessmen, distinguished prime ('variable') from supplementary ('fixed') costs. Prime costs, also known as special or direct costs, will include the costs of raw materials and of labour employed by the hour or the piece. For it to be worthwhile to continue in business, at least prime costs have to be covered. Supplementary costs will include standing charges for capital and the wages of senior staff who are paid salaries rather than wages. Sunk costs are fixed costs incurred before production begins. They are so specific that they cannot be recovered on the closure of a business, so will constitute a barrier to exit: heavy industries such as shipbuilding provide good examples.

In the theory of the **firm**, marginal, average and total costs are separately calculated. Marginal cost is the cost of producing the last unit of output, or the average for the last range of output if it is impossible to vary output a unit at a time. Average cost is simply the total cost divided by output. Average cost can be calculated as average variable cost, average fixed cost and average total cost. These different notions give rise to cost curves. These are used to illustrate economies of scale which will produce falling average cost curves; diseconomies produce rising average cost curves. The optimum firm has been defined as the minimum point of an average cost curve if that curve is U-shaped.

Many types of cost are paid by an individual person or organisation and hence are called private. When the costs affect others in society they are called social costs. Much of **environmental economics** relies on this distinction. Despite the distinction, a single individual can incur both private and social costs, for example, by burning a fire which requires obtaining fuel and applying heat, and producing smoke which has a spillover effect on surrounding people. The bearer of costs will define the cost, whether private or social.

Specialist uses of the word cost include the 'cost of living', the total expenses of maintaining a person in a particular society at a particular time. The cost of living is usually measured with a view to showing different purchasing powers over time. Through employing a **price index** it can be seen whether the same group of goods and services costs more or less over time. Such calculations produce essential data for wage negotiations as the starting point is usually the preservation of real incomes.

Costs are also regarded as factor **prices** as they represent the amount which has to be paid for obtaining factors of production. This means that they emerge from the working of the market forces of various factor markets for labour, capital and land. Excess demand in both factor and product markets will usually lead to higher prices.

Cost is a foundation of product prices and central to any theory of **value**. In fixing prices, costs, marginal or average, can be used as a basis. Often firms find that a formula linking average cost and a profit margin can produce the final price. To allocate resources efficiently, prices are equated with marginal costs.

Theories of value have been divided into those based on cost, especially labour, as with Ricardo and Marx, and those founded on utility, as with Jevons. Cost of production theories of value explain basic prices and long-run equilibrium prices. Smith regarded natural prices based on the cost of production as the central prices around which market prices fluctuated. These basic prices related to cost are dominated by supply considerations. Wieser imaginatively showed that both costs and prices are related to utility.

Recent studies in industrial organisation have examined at length transaction costs, arguing that their existence justifies firms growing in size so that many transactions are within a firm and not between firms in the market. Transaction costs are the costs of running an economic system, or of effecting an exchange, so will amount to all the costs of negotiating and contracting.

So central a notion as cost has produced various forms of specialist analysis, including cost accounting, cost effectiveness analysis and **cost–benefit analysis**.

See also: **consumer's surplus**; **cost–benefit analysis**; **efficiency**; **firm**

COST-BENEFIT ANALYSIS

A method of **investment** appraisal for major projects such as transportation systems, energy installations such as dams, and public health and education projects.

Although first used for assessing projects under the US Flood Control Act of 1936, it has its intellectual roots in the writings of Dupuit in 1844 and Marshall in 1890 with his concepts of consumer's and producer's surplus.

The point of such exercises is to estimate if there will be a net benefit from undertaking investment. In order to make the comparison, both benefits and costs have to be measured in the same units, usually a particular currency at a particular date. As the flows of benefits and costs can be uneven and of a different duration, it is usual to discount them to their present value. To produce the fullest assessment, many costs and benefits without market prices have to be measured by shadow or proxy prices. By using a survey, the subjective valuations of a beautiful view, for example, can be determined. If an improved transport link saves time and reduces fatal injuries then the opportunity cost of the saving will be calculated and the value of a human life ascertained, beginning with the loss of earnings through dying before normal retirement age. A major project does enable increased **consumption**, which can be valued in terms of the extra units, for example of electricity, consumed times the marginal benefit to the consumer. To make the calculations manageable it is usual to consider the net benefit of a project to a region or city, rather than for a whole country. However, critics of this type of analysis always question the placing of a money value on so many intangibles and the accuracy of the expected income flows.

Further reading: Dupuit 1844; Marshall 1920; Mishan 1972

CREDIT

Finance available to firms and households which exists because of trust.

An early writer on this subject, Henry Thornton, in his *Paper Credit* (1802) analysed both the determinants of commercial confidence and the range of credit instruments within the context of a balance sheet for the economy as a whole. He regarded commercial credit as the confidence among the commercial classes which disposed them to lend money to each other and undertake other monetary engagements. There would be little confidence where there is a weak sense of moral duty and insecure property. Where there is confidence, paper credit, whether banknotes or commercial bills, can exist. If faith in the ability of a bank to honour its obligations collapses, then the credit it has issued is worthless.

There are many types of credit – loans from family and friends, loans from pawnbrokers on the security of deposited goods, bank loans, and bills of exchange. A traditional form of credit is trade credit, which consists of loans and permission to delay payment offered by manufacturers and wholesalers to retailers. One type can be a substitute for another but is often differentiated by the length of period the money is borrowed for.

The quality of debtors varies greatly. For individuals there is credit scoring, which consists of awarding points for each personal characteristic then seeing if the total meets an acceptance level. For corporations and governments there is credit rating to indicate the creditworthiness of the organisation. Crucial to these assessments is the probability of default in the servicing of the **debt**.

Increasingly in poor countries and neighbourhoods, informal credit networks have been established because of the reluctance of banks to lend to persons with little collateral. Credit unions of persons contributing small deposits and having the right to borrow from the association have been set up. This 'micro-credit' has permitted the borrowing of small sums to start up businesses. Increasingly micro-credit has been recommended as a route to economic development. The very poor, women and other groups suffering discrimination are given access to finance for the first time.

Credit rationing is used by monetary authorities to achieve an optimal distribution of credit. It can be used as an alternative to **interest rate** changes. Some borrowers have limited access to finance so for social reasons there can be special credit deals, for example to buy housing. A credit crunch occurs when a limitation on lending curtails the activities of businesses and other potential borrowers.

See also: **banking**; **money**

CULTURAL ECONOMICS

A study of the arts as an industry, investigating the nature of its output, productivity, employment, consumers and financing. The wide range of activities considered includes theatre, opera, radio, television, painting, sculpture and museums.

As with other industries the degree of monopoly is important, especially whether a state monopoly or a competitive structure is appropriate. The types of output range from the perishable live performances of the performing arts to robust sculptures which have survived millennia. Like other industries, quality issues and the efficiency of production of every type of 'artist' is examined to see if the same outcome could be realised with a smaller input. As so much of art is durable the relative claims of the present and future generations are considered, and used as an argument for current artistic activities being loss-making. As with other productive activities, it is necessary to decide the amount of production. Crucial will be the probable rates of return, not only in monetary but in aesthetic and educational terms, as culture is a very sophisticated type of output.

The resources required to achieve a great work of art can be immense, so questions of private and public financing arise. There is a long history of monarchs, state and regional governments sponsoring musical events and artists. Culture is regarded as a merit good, improving human character and creativity, so attracts subsidisation. As a consequence of democracy and the financing of the arts through **taxation**, questions are raised about the use of public finances in this way. Inevitably with the more refined productions appealing to a small proportion of society the fairness of subsidising, for example, opera is much debated. As some cultural products are entertainment (for example, the theatre) it is asked why the beneficiaries expect to consume them at less than full cost.

Culture has attracted many analytical approaches. Consumer theory can be used to analyse art lovers' preferences and the demand for a particular medium so that a more rational allocation of resources can be attempted. Ruskin's lectures of 1857 on the political economy of art are an early example of using economic concepts of the nature of **labour**, accumulation and distribution to analyse artistic activities. The labour market for the arts is complex. The nature of training, or lack of it, is unusual. The market is often characterised by excess supply of unpublished authors, resting actors and musicians and penurious painters. There is much self-employment and a variety of ways of selling artistic production, including present sales and second sales through auctions. The nature of incomes in this sector is complicated by the existence of copyright to generate long-term income streams. Baumol and Bowen argued that there is little scope for **productivity** increases in the labour intensive live arts, so that with increasing costs there would be a case for state subsidy – a view which was challenged by Peacock.

It is difficult to estimate all of the effects of the arts on a national economy: employment, the relaxing benefits of entertainment, the enrichment of education, the expansion of tourism and the long-term creation of a national heritage. Many estimation difficulties spring from problems of valuation. Performances are perishable, unless a recording is acceptable as a substitute, and it can be difficult to achieve a consensus about an object's value.

See also: **value**

Further reading: Baumol and Bowen 1966; Peacock 1969, 2000; Ruskin 1867; Scitovsky 1972, 1976; Throsby 1994

CURRENCY

The official money of a country or of an economic union.

A currency can be issued by a central bank, a national government or its agency. Under free **banking** individual banks have the power to issue notes without many restraints. It can also be produced by a federation of nations, as with the euro. It is the medium of exchange which is currently used for transactions within a currency area. It can take the form of coin, banknotes or other forms of liquidity such as the special drawing rights of the International Monetary Fund. A country can have its official currency but extensively use another because of its greater monetary stability or its popularity for trading purposes, hence the popularity of holding dollars in many small countries.

Currencies are classified according to their function. A reserve currency is held by central banks because of its stability of value and usefulness in trade. A dominant currency is widely held because of its stability and because it is issued by a major **national economy**. In the twentieth century the US dollar initially had this role, but later the rise of the Asian countries challenged the supremacy of the US economy and hence of its currency.

Currencies are regarded as hard or soft. A hard currency will maintain its value for many years because it is issued by country with strict monetary and **fiscal policies** which keep inflation at bay. The attractiveness of a currency as a store of value makes it popular as a reserve currency. So many foreigners might want to hold a hard currency that its issue is strictly controlled. The Swiss franc has a long-held reputation for its hardness. Soft currencies, associated with countries which have weak economies, poor control of government finances and trade deficits, are used primarily for internal trading purposes.

A currency can be flexible, with its **value** fluctuating continuously in foreign exchange markets, or it can be fixed to gold or reference currencies and allowed fluctuation only within a band, or it can be pegged to the value of another currency with no less of national independence in **monetary policy**. In the past fixed currencies existed under the gold standard and under Bretton Woods 1944–71. The growth of currency unions has revived fixed exchange rates. Under a currency union it is necessary for the area covered to be economically homogeneous, with a great mobility of labour and capital. A currency union is supposed to be an optimal currency area, one with factor mobility and exposure to similar shocks to the constituent economies, as set down by Mundell. Where there is a common currency transaction **costs** are lower and there is price transparency. The USA meets the conditions for being an optimal currency area better than the European Union, helped by the widespread use of the English language. The members of a currency union sacrifice much freedom in economic policy making. As a single currency can be too strong for the weaker parts of an economy, it is necessary to have fiscal transfers to deal with unemployment and low levels of economic activity.

The euro was the last major currency to be created. By the end of 2006 it was the currency of twelve European countries, member states of the European Union which has also become a currency union. The currency has circulated as banknotes and coins since the beginning of 2002. For three years the participating countries had irrevocably bound their currencies together with fixed conversion rates. The currency reduces transaction costs and facilitates the working of the single market but, as it is governed by a single interest rate, it has varying degrees of effectiveness in managing inflation and economic growth in the different member states. Just as it would be difficult to have a single currency for the whole world, it is difficult to have one for a wide area with varying degrees of economic attainment.

Governments want their currencies to be attractive so that it is easy to pay for imports and meet other international obligations. Maintaining its value is the most attractive attribute of a currency. In the nineteenth century the competing systems for anchoring the value of a currency were the gold standard and bimetallism. Under the gold bullion standard, which flourished from 1880 to 1914, national currencies were related to weights of gold. The central bank was required to inflate or deflate the national economy so that the currency could remain on the standard. The gold exchange standard linked the value of one currency to another on the gold standard, as happened in the 1920s in the UK and the USA. Bimetallism required the use of two metals, usually silver and gold, in a fixed ratio (Adam Smith approved of this basis for value). In the nineteenth century it was used in the USA and in the Latin Union (France, Belgium, Switzerland, Italy, Greece and Romania) until increased silver production made a dual standard unstable.

As a consequence of issuing a currency a monetary authority obtains seignorage, originally the charge for minting coin from precious metals, but now the income net of the cost of production for expanding the money supply. A government can induce inflation by the over-issue of currency then repay its debt more easily because its value has been reduced.

Some countries undertake currency reform by replacing their existing currency with a new one: this can happen because a period of inflation has made the number of currency units required to buy simple goods unwieldy. Schemes to improve the value and stability of a currency have often been ordered by the International Monetary Fund. These usually include reducing excessive government spending, and market reforms such as making labour markets more flexible.

See also: **exchange rate**

Further reading: Madrid Conference on Optimum Currency Areas 1973

CUSTOMS UNION

An economic association of independent countries that abandon customs duties between each other in favour of a common external tariff, or a system of import quotas.

It is a stronger union than a free trade association, which lacks the same customs duties and a common trade policy. It can be a stage towards a complete economic union with common monetary, fiscal, trade and other economic policies. Many examples abound, including the European Union and regional groupings in North and South America, Asia and Africa. Increasingly, the setting up of many regional trading blocs has led to economic losses among the excluded countries.

The consequences of a customs union can be divided into trade creation between the members of the union who have privileged access to each other's market and trade diversion through the abandonment of trade patterns which existed pre-union. Also there are expected to be efficiency gains, greater economic stability and a promotion of political and cultural ties. Static effects are largely associated with economies of scale; dynamic effects include behavioural changes and technological investment.

See also: **protection**; **trade theory**

Further reading: Janssen 1961

CYCLES

Regular movements in national economic activity, measured by output, **prices** or **unemployment**.

Each cycle moves between a trough and a peak then back to the trough again: its length is measured from peak to peak or trough to trough. There is an upswing to a ceiling, or upper turning point, then a downswing to a floor, or lower turning point. The types of cycle are classified according to their usual length and the type of investment which has generated the cycle. Cycles are transitory movements around a trend which shows potential output based on productivity growth. When studying cycles it is important to distinguish the impulse or shock which sets off the cycle from the propagation mechanism which sustains it.

Wesley Mitchell defined cycles as follows:

> Business cycles are a type of fluctuation found in the aggregate economic activity of nations that organise their work mainly in business enterprises: a cycle consists of expansion occurring at about the same time in many economic activities, followed by similarly general recessions, contractions, and revivals which merge into the expansion phase of the next cycle. This sequence of changes is recurrent but not periodic; in duration business cycles vary from more than one year to ten or twelve years; they are not divisible into shorter cycles of similar character with amplitudes approximating their own.
>
> (Burns and Mitchell 1946: 3)

Mitchell's views have been qualified in many ways. Different types of cycle have been suggested, distinguished by their length and associated type of investment. Kitchin suggested there were minor cycles, on average lasting 3.5 years or 40 months, evident in the data on bank clearings, prices and interest rates of the USA and Great Britain, 1890–1922. He particularly attributed these to mass psychology. The Juglar cycle was identified in 1862 as a cycle of seven to ten years, associated with changes in fixed investment in factories and machines. (The Juglar cycle is often called the 'business cycle' or 'major cycle'.) Kuznets identified cycles of twenty-two years on average in production and twenty-three years in prices for the American and British economies. A cycle in unemployment led to a cycle in the labour force and in net investment. He found that troughs and peaks in immigration coincided with highs and lows in output. In response to labour market shortages, immigration rose, leading to changes in residential building. Most controversial of all was the Kondratieff cycle, or long wave, of about 45 to 60 years. A long cycle of this kind would be launched by a cluster of innovations starting a new industry. The first of these started in the 1780s with cotton and the canal age, and the second in the 1840s with the railway age; the coming of the motor car in the 1890s and aircraft in the 1930s also stimulated long upswings. Thus as the cycle becomes longer the type of investment associated with it changes from inventories in the case of Kitchins, fixed investment for the Juglars, housing for the Kuznets cycles and major industries and infrastructure for the Kondratieffs.

Classical and later economists advanced theories of the trade cycle. Malthus wrote about oscillations in production. JS Mill had a psychological theory of alternating moods of optimism and pessimism. Marx argued that there were ten-year cycles reflecting the average age of fixed capital. JM Keynes argued that fluctuations in the marginal efficiency of capital were primarily responsible for cycles, although there are fluctuations also in the propensity to consume and in the state of liquidity preference. Doubts about future yields can cause a downturn. Hicks used an accelerator and multiplier mechanism, with an increase in income generating extra investment via the accelerator and the multiplier translating higher net investment into higher income. Expansion and decline will only be halted by ceilings of full employment, which will cause a downturn and a floor because there will have to be replacement investment which can generate an upturn.

The consequences of an economy being cyclical are severe. A downturn will lead to unemployment of labour and other factors of production; an upturn can produce the threat of inflation. Thus the search for stabilisation measures has long been sought. Wicksell, in his analysis of cumulative processes of expansion and contraction, hoped through setting out the conditions for monetary **equilibrium** to establish price stability and thence stability for a whole national economy. Price stability was regarded as a key to taming the cycle until the changes in macroeconomic theory from the 1930s put more emphasis on managing demand. In the 1950s and 1960s monetary, and even more, fiscal measures were used to 'fine-tune' the economy so that fluctuations would be slight. The public sector was seen, as the Stockholm School had earlier suggested, as crucial. Government financed investment projects could be advanced or halted to change the level of demand. More recently, with the popularity of central bank independence and the associated inflation targeting, price stabilisation has become a leading theme in managing economies prone to boom and slump.

Further reading: Abramovitz 1968; Burns and Mitchell 1946; Haberler 1968; Kitchin 1923; Kondratieff 1935

DEBT

A financial claim created by a borrower in order to obtain money; anything that is owed or due.

Governments and incorporated businesses issue debt in the long and medium term as bonds but in the short term as bills. Debt is fixed interest in nature, unlike equity, which entitles the holder to a share of net earnings. Banks can create deposits and issue them to customers.

Debt can be owed by individual persons, firms or governments. A sovereign debt is owed, or guaranteed, by a government (for example, the borrowing by a state-owned industry) and usually takes the form of bonds. The accumulated debt of a government is the national or public debt. It is either floating or funded with no immediate obligation to pay the sums borrowed. A more sophisticated financial sector will devise new forms of debt to meet the varied needs of borrowers. Some debts are for a long period, such as a mortgage to finance house purchase or a bank loan to buy consumer durable goods. Much of personal debt takes the form of unpaid balances on credit cards. Debt in the form of loans can be converted into marketable forms, especially bonds, through the process of securitisation.

There is a chronic tendency to over-borrow so that debts can be unsustainable, the worst case being a 'debt trap' when the cost of servicing a debt rises faster than the income of the borrower.

See also: **credit**; **fiscal policy**

Further reading: Jochnick and Preston 2006

DEMAND CURVE

The graphical representation of the relationship between **price**, or sometimes income, and quantity. The normal demand curve is negatively sloped downwards to the right as lower prices usually attract more demand. But some demand curves are horizontal or even upward sloping, depending on the elasticity of demand.

JS Mill in his *Some Unsettled Questions of Political Economy* hinted at demand curves without drawing them. The Edinburgh professor of engineering Fleeming Jenkin constructed some in an article of 1870. Demand curves were prominent in Marshall's *Principles of Economics* as part of his partial **equilibrium** analysis. His treatment of them raised two important questions. Do empirical demand curves exist? Is it possible to isolate the relationship between demand and supply under *ceteris paribus* conditions?

Marshall questioned whether more than a single point could exist on a demand curve. Friedman pointed out that movement along the demand curve for a good constituting a major part of a consumer's budget would change real income, a variable which has to be held constant if other things are to be equal. Later empirical work on demand curves used either time series or cross-section approaches. In the case of time series the quantity demanded at prices associated with particular dates is recorded; cross-section data can be obtained by setting prices in different markets, for example different regions, at the same date.

Further reading: Friedman 1953

DEVELOPMENT ECONOMICS

Theories and policies recommended for increasing **economic welfare** in low income countries.

These arise from theories of **economic growth** which investigate the relationship between saving and investment and the role of technical progress in the long run. As this branch of economics is a mixture of theoretical and applied economics, inevitably it has been split between a **laissez-faire** approach of allowing the natural processes of **markets** to produce growth, and the advocacy of planning and initiatives by national governments and international organisations such as the International Monetary Fund, the World Bank, and regional banks including the Inter-American Development Bank. Strategies such as balanced growth, growth poles and a big push were commonplace in the literature. Neoclassical economists argued that the capital needed for economic growth in poor countries would flow of its own accord, attracted by lower factor costs. A leading proponent of a non-interventionist approach was Peter Bauer, who looked at the traditional mechanisms of the West African and Asian economies to advocate a hands-off organic development strategy: he believed that many of the problems of poor countries were the consequence of bad bureaucratic government.

Mercantilists such as William Petty and classical economists led by Adam Smith, by making economic growth a central theme of their work, were precursors of later development economists. A major classical framework employed for studying growth was 'stages theory', describing the emergence of modern economies from early primitive states of hunting then nomadic shepherding to agriculture and finally commerce and manufacturing.

The target of development economics is developing countries. They are regarded as a special case in the world economy, often treated as having similar problems rather than being different. An initial measure of economic underdevelopment is low GDP per capita. However, in countries with subsistence agriculture much produce is for own consumption so measures of GDP will underestimate national income, requiring supplementary estimates of production. Many extreme cases of underdevelopment exist in Africa and Asia, especially in desert areas. Underdevelopment has other dimensions, including little infrastructure in the form of roads, schools and hospitals. There are also deficiencies in political and economic institutions, often with little democracy and a shortage of banking and corporate structures. **Human capital** stocks are small, with low proportions of the population even literate and capable of practising medicine and using modern management skills.

Later, development economics came to mean prescribing economic policies for the poorer countries of the world. The pioneers of this specialism include Arthur Lewis, Gunnar Myrdal, Raul Prebisch, Paul Rosenstein-Rodan, Hla Myint and later Hans Singer and Amartya Sen. Particular theories are associated with these economists. Lewis highlighted the **dual economy** nature of poor countries.

Myrdal combined economic and sociological approaches to analyse Asian development problems, being acutely aware of the problems of **corruption**. Prebisch considered **protection** and import substitution to industrialise underdeveloped countries and improve their **terms of trade**; also he recommended long-term loans to prevent secular decline. Rosenstein-Rodan wanted poorer countries to benefit from the increasing **returns** associated with industrialisation. Myint linked economic development to international trade theory. Singer was an advocate of balanced growth. Sen has applied social choice theory to inequality and poverty issues.

Partly inspired by Marx's theory of imperialism, 'dependency theory' was articulated. To explain relative development within the context of a world economy system the processes of capitalism were regarded as practising exploitation of Third World countries through controlling access to technology and markets. Development economics has long been an ideological battleground, especially between neoclassical and Marxian economists. As Resnick demonstrated, the neoclassical economists, many of them in international agencies, used a microeconomic approach of seeing barriers to development in the failings of particular markets. Inevitably, changes in tariffs, **exchange rates** and the monetary systems of less developed countries were recommended to improve these economies. The Marxian approach is more internationalist, taking into account the relations between centre and peripheral economies, and recognising the importance of different social classes historically when analysing exploitation.

Examples of wrong development strategies are plentiful, hence the reaction of 'sustainable development', which takes into account the need for long-term plans which prefer to use renewable rather than exhaustible resources, and invest in education and the infrastructure. The Brundtland Report, *Our Common Future*, of the United Nations World Commission on Environment and Development in 1987, linked meeting present needs to being able to respond to future needs when considering sustainability. Economic development is linked to social development and conservation of the environment. However, the urgency of present requirements can lead to forgetting the long term. The report recommended redistribution from rich to poorer countries as part of a growth strategy.

The problems of underdevelopment occur within the world economy, so international economic solutions are proposed. The New International Economic Order was proposed at the General Assembly of the United Nations in 1974, suggesting trading boards and the redistribution of monopoly profits to the poorer countries.

More recently campaigns to make **poverty** a thing of the past have started with schemes to write off the external **debt** of many poor countries. Many countries fell into the 'debt trap' of holding debt with servicing costs rising faster than national income. Poverty cannot be relieved permanently in this way until there are political changes in dictatorial regimes so that income can be redistributed more fairly within countries, and the governments of these countries adopt **fiscal policies** which can facilitate investment without incurring further foreign debt.

See also: **corruption**; **economic growth**; **globalisation**

Further reading: Gemmell 1987; Jomo 2005; Lal 1983; Meier 2005; Resnick 1975

DISCRIMINATION

Treating identifiable groups less favourably than others, because of their age, sex/gender or race; charging different **prices** for the same thing.

Discrimination can occur at different stages of life: when young through limited access to education; when older through restricted access to employment and housing. Discrimination is exercised in product **markets** by setting unfair prices, in the labour market through paying wages which are lower for the less favoured group, in the housing market by charging rents to exclude tenants. The less valued group will be offered something inferior, whether it be training, conditions and stability of employment or prospects of promotion. Discrimination can be vertical, between different layers of a hierarchical organisation, or horizontal, when persons in similar employment are rewarded and treated differently. Much of the legislation from the 1960s was concerned with horizontal treatment.

Various types of economic analysis have been applied to discrimination. The oldest is probably JS Mill's, in his discussion of women's wages in his *Principles of Political Economy* (1848); book II, chapter 14 analysed the segmented nature of the labour market such that women are only allowed into a group of occupations, hence increasing supply and reducing wages relatively. This approach can be applied to other forms of wage discrimination. Becker, with a different approach, asserted that employers could have a taste for discrimination. This is costly to the discriminator as she can deliberately reject a more productive worker because of sex or race.

Discrimination can be created and sustained by governments, reflecting their opinions of different sections in the population, especially different racial groups. This is usually carried out to maintain the relative position of successful elites. New migrants are often the target of indigenous populations afraid of competition. On the other hand, governments can practise positive discrimination, favouring the disadvantaged in housing, employment and education. Often this leads to a backlash from those not privileged in this way.

Discrimination is usually measured as a residual after data for two groups have been standardised for personal characteristics. Thus to discover if there is discrimination between men and women in wages the data will be standardised for levels of education, occupational title, length of service, working hours, etc. The problem with the residual approach is that it can always be argued that the data can be further refined to reduce the differential. The alternative approach is the legal approach of calculating the damage done by discriminatory acts, such as only allowing one sex to apply for a particular job.

Price discrimination consists of dividing up a market and charging different prices for the same good or service. Because the cost of production is the same for the different sub-markets, higher profits arise where greater prices can be imposed. Discrimination is according to personal characteristics such as age or location. It is essential to be able to keep the sub-groups separate. In formal terms, it is because the elasticity of demand is different for different sub-groups that this pricing practice is possible.

See also: **segmented labour market**

Further reading: Becker 1971; Benton 1994

DISEQUILIBRIUM ECONOMICS

The study of a **market** or a **national economy**, or part of it, which is in a state of persistent excess demand or excess supply.

Disequilibrium economics is a direct challenge to standard accepted **neoclassical economics**, as it outlines the forces in markets which impede movement to **equilibrium**. A lack of information can prevent economic agents responding to **price** signals. Monetary and psychic costs can make factors of production immobile. Forces of custom and statutory and contractual norms can create price stickiness, which prevents prices from having their equilibrating role. In the cobweb theorem, differences in the **elasticities** of demand and supply can make convergence to an equilibrium an impossibility.

According to **Say's law** a national economy would move to equilibrium as every producer is also a consumer so there could not be a 'general glut'. This was challenged by Malthus, who also presented another famous case of disequilibrium: population unless checked would tend to grow faster than its subsistence, thus hurtling along on a disequilibrium path. Wicksell outlined the conditions for a national economy being on a cumulative path of expansion or decline because of a divergence between natural and market rates of interest. JM Keynes in his *General Theory of Employment, Interest and Money* (1936) considered national economies with persistent **unemployment**. It is possible for disequilibria to persist for a long time because of government interference in markets, as happened in many consumer markets in the former Soviet-type economies because of deliberate restriction of supply. For shorter periods markets can be in disequilibrium because of the lagged responses to price changes.

Economists have made use of Open Systems Theory to examine processes which never reach equilibrium. This approach looks at the interdependence of the components of a system and how their relationships become more and more complex. Mechanical relationships become more fluid and biological, as Marshall recognised. Later, Boulding was interested in the importance of feedback loops in complex systems. This has been applied to **development economics** to show how spillover effects can keep an economy from equilibrium. Previously, equilibrium economics heavily used thermodynamics to explain states of rest.

Disequilibrium can deliberately be created by a government dissatisfied with the prices produced by a market; for example, **rents** can be regulated to obtain affordable accommodation. The inefficiency of markets themselves can sustain disequilibria for a long time, especially if the supply of information to buyers and sellers is sparse and market players are slow to react to prices.

A structural disequilibrium can exist in the **balance of payments** of a country for years. The continued sharp differences in income between countries suggest that the world economy itself is in a state of disequilibrium.

Disequilibrium has its costs in terms of unemployed resources and inflation, so many economic policies have been designed to encourage a movement towards equilibrium. In a labour market, once the type of unemployment is recognised remedies are suggested, for example, training to reduce structural unemployment, and labour exchanges to lower frictional unemployment. Disequilibria in population, **national income** and the balance of payments need more widespread measures both macro and micro.

See also: **equilibrium**; **Say's law**

Further reading: Vroe 1999

DIVISION OF LABOUR

The principle of economic specialisation between or within occupations.

There is both occupational division of labour, for example, the difference between a farmer and a physician, and sub-division of labour, when the performance of a job such as building a house is divided into its component tasks. If there is a fine division of occupations then the specialists arising from the sub-division of labour will have new job titles, thus making the sub-division of labour a type of occupational division.

Xenophon in his *Cyropedia* contrasts a small town, where all the manufacturing operations to make a pair of shoes are done by one person, with a larger settlement where different operations can be performed by different specialised workers. Adam Smith, using the example of pin-making from the French *Encyclopedie*, noted too that the division of labour is limited by the extent of the market. As division of labour was regarded by him as the principal cause of economic growth, he explained how productivity is increased by employing the principle. Through dividing up **labour**, time is saved in passing from one operation to another, workers would become more dextrous, and this subdivision of tasks would facilitate the introduction of machines. Later he noted that the performance of repetitive tasks could reduce mental capacity, but he never abandoned the principle. To have the greatest amount of division of labour requires free trade in a global economy.

Classical economists loosely regarded agriculture as subject to diminishing **returns** because of soil exhaustion and looked on manufacturing as being in a state of increasing returns through extensive practice of the division of labour.

See also: **returns**

DUAL ECONOMY

A national economy with two sectors, one traditional and the other modern.

Developing economies have been described as having a modern sector, with the capital city, industries, services and international trade, as well as a traditional sector with a low level of technology engaged in a low-productivity agricultural and primary sector. The different sectors represent different stages of economic development, with much of the older sector non-monetised and lacking labour and financial markets. In the modern sector capitalist production with profit-maximising **firms** employing workers is the norm; in the traditional sector employers tolerate low **productivity. Saving** can only occur in the modern sector, so the economic growth of the country as a whole is dependent on that sector's expansion.

Barriers to mobility sustain the dualism of such economies, but civil wars and climate change have forced populations out of rural areas into cities, where the attempt to enter modern economic life is often frustrated by a lack of capital and education. Economic policy can aim to bring about a convergence between the two sectors by transferring resources into backward areas, but caution is needed to prevent the creation of new imbalances and devastation resulting from the use of inappropriate technologies.

See also: **development economics**

Further reading: Lewis 1954, 1979

ECONOMIC ANTHROPOLOGY

An analysis of economic institutions based upon the observations and models of social behaviour devised by anthropologists.

Anthropologists have studied the relationships within many primitive and more advanced societies. Key issues discussed, with the insights of different schools of economics, are the nature of work, exchange and money.

In the Ancient Greek economics of Aristotle and Xenophon the study of the household linked social and economic analysis together. Later the stages theory of Adam Smith and his eighteenth-century contemporaries noted that countries develop from hunting to shepherding to agriculture, then commerce and manufacturing. In all of these stages, methods of production, resource allocation and distribution of national income are different. In other ways anthropology has the character of **classical economics** with a description of how simple physical barter evolves into modern money. Marxian analysis has been fruitful in applying concepts such as the labour process and commodity fetishism to explain the working of primitive labour markets. Also the Enlightenment interest in human nature linked economics to the other social sciences. In the substantivist meaning of economics suggested by Polanyi in the *Great Transformation*, economics is concerned with how individuals make a living in their circumstances.

Institutionalists, especially Veblen, linked economics and anthropology by importing the term *tropism*, the response of an organism to an external stimulus. **Neoclassical economics** has been used by anthropologists to provide conceptual frameworks, especially utilising terms such as competition, **rationality** and uncertainty.

See also: **altruism**; **homo economicus**; **public choice**; **social choice theory**

Further reading: Gudeman 2001; Polanyi 1944; Veblen 1900

ECONOMIC CONCENTRATION

The dominance of one industry, firm or activity within the industrial or regional structure of a country.

Concentration is inevitable in the industries of small countries where, if economies of scale exist, there have to be few **firms** if the market is small to keep **costs** low. In wartime industrial concentration is encouraged as governments intervene extensively in industry and use a measure of central planning. New science-based industries are concentrated as it is not possible for other firms to gain access to the technology.

Absolute, or aggregate, concentration is the dominance of a few large firms in the output, sales or employment of a particular industry, or in a national economy as a whole. This is distinguished from relative concentration, which is based on the size distribution of firms within an industry. Aggregate concentration is also known as the dominant firms ratios. Relative concentration is measured using the device of Lorenz curves and Gini coefficients. These curves plot the percentage of firms against the percentage of output, employment or income: if there is equal distribution the curve will lie along a 45 degree line; the further the Lorenz curve is away from that diagonal the less equality there is between firms. A Gini coefficient is the ratio of the area between the curve and the diagonal to the area between the 45 degree line and the horizontal access.

Calculations of concentration are used to identify monopolies and potential market abuse. Therefore concentration is a major concern of antitrust and competition laws in many developed countries.

See also: **competition and monopoly**

Further reading: Blair 1972

ECONOMIC DEMOGRAPHY

The study of the nature of human populations and their effect on economic conditions.

Population problems can be simply divided into the problems of under-population and of overpopulation. In the earliest stage of economic development a shortage of people can be a barrier to economic growth; later a declining population raises many concerns as it is invariably ageing. Over-population can lead to a shortage of resources to sustain a large number of people.

Early writers on population, especially the mercantilists, were concerned to have enough people to maintain the strength of a nation absolutely and relatively. With vast tracts of fertile land unpopulated, encouraging the creation and settlement of large families was imperative, even to the extent of using fiscal penalties and rewards to boost the birth rate. Whereas population growth could be encouraged in parts of the world, in the older countries such as England population growth was seen as a problem. In the eighteenth century an awareness of the dangers of rapid population growth led Thomas Robert Malthus to formulate his principle of population.

Many economics writers have highlighted the relationship between population and subsistence, including Steuart, Cantillon and Smith, but Wallace came closest to being Malthus' precursor in that he mentioned the checks to population growth. Malthus argued that food is necessary for a human population and that passion between the sexes is constant. His stark population principle was that the human population unchecked would grow in a geometric progression but subsistence only in an arithmetic progression. In the first edition of his *Essay on Population* of 1798, the checks mentioned were different forms of misery, including plague and war, and vice. In the second edition of 1803 he included the check of moral restraint through late marriages to reduce the birth rate. His critics were many. Christians argued that a benevolent God would not allow babies to be born with the certain prospect of fatal starvation. Others argued that technical progress would provide more subsistence, or a desire for improvement would entice potential parents to prefer luxury to more children. Although Malthus was not an advocate of birth control, some of his disciples, especially the 'Malthusians', were.

Students of population trends have noted that there is a 'demographic transition' between early societies with high fertility and mortality to advanced societies where the birth and death rates are lower. Mortality falls when there are public health measures to improve the quality of water and to eliminate major diseases. There is a further fall in the death rate when more people receive personal health care. The birth rate fell dramatically in many advanced countries through the widespread use of the contraceptive pill. Also the increased education and labour force participation of women is associated with a fall in the birth rate.

Populations grow through natural increase and net migration. Natural increase is the excess of births over deaths in a given population. Net migration is the number of immigrants less the number of emigrants of a given country. Fluctuations in the relative prosperity of countries will induce migratory population flows.

The composition of population is important, especially the ratio of births to deaths and of the young to the old. Through the ageing of a population, the 'dependency ratio', those outside the **labour** force as a percentage of the whole population, grows. The determination of Malthus to solve the problem of a disequilibrium between population growth and subsistence growth by having a balanced economy is still a modern concern.

Given the dialogue between advocates of population growth and opponents of rising numbers, it is inevitable that the notion of an 'optimum population' should arise. JS Mill and Edwin Cannan supported this idea. The population is optimal in the sense that a particular size maximises output per head. Such a measure can be attacked from different angles, especially that a nation might be a satisfier and not a maximiser keener to improve the quality of life than the quantity of output.

When a 'population problem' is perceived, population policy responses are often devised. Various ways of increasing a population have often been attempted. To stimulate natural increase, financial inducements can be offered to couples to have more children. Assistance with travel and housing can be used to attract international migrants. Reducing population size takes time, but family planning and immigration controls can be used.

See also: **migration and mobility**

Further reading: Caldwell 1972; Rosenzweig 1997

ECONOMIC GROWTH

An increase in **national income** caused by an increase in the quantity of the factors of production or of their **productivity**.

This concern, which has been prominent in economics from at least the seventeenth century, has continued vigorously, although dissenters have questioned the advocacy of materialism and the social costs resulting from higher production.

In the eighteenth century stages theory was popular, especially in writers such as Smith and Malthus. Economic development was traced from a primitive stage of hunting and gathering to the age of shepherds and thence to agriculture, finishing with manufacturing and commerce. Rostow revived stages theory in his account of economic growth. In his first stage of 'the traditional society' growth is curbed by the lack of technical progress; in the second stage of 'transition' there is an increase in the rate of investment to at least that of population growth. Then there is 'take-off' when growth is at a geometrical progression: this period lasts about twenty years. In the fourth stage, about a sixty-year period, is 'the drive to maturity' in which modern technology is applied throughout the economy. The growth process comes to the final stage of mass consumption of durable goods when a choice has to be made between such consumption and the pursuit of either national power or social welfare. Although initially applied to the development of the American and Russian economies, it has other national applications. The neatness of the division of history into separate stages is questionable, as the activity dominant in each stage can overlap with the process in the next.

Economic growth is usually studied by considering a series of theories and models. In the outburst of economic research into growth in the 1960s, a number of prominent approaches emerged. The Harrod-Domar model from 1948 onwards had a central place. It argued that there is both a natural and a warranted rate of growth. The natural rate is the maximum long-run growth rate equal to the sum of the growth of the population and **technical progress**. The warranted rate is equal to the ratio of the proportion of income saved to the capital-income ratio.

Lewis in 1954 outlined his influential model of economic growth based on the idea of a **dual economy** of modern and traditional sectors, the agricultural and the industrial. By transfers of labour from the underemployed agricultural labour force to industry, there would be an increase in overall productivity and food surpluses in rural areas after the agricultural population fell. Increased incomes would make possible higher amounts of investment. Food exports would be possible. Questions have been raised about the productivity assumptions and the trading regime of the world economy.

In the 1960s there was a quest for viable steady state growth models. The variants of these were produced by making different assumptions about **savings** and technical progress. The Solow growth model is based on a Cobb-Douglas production model with constant returns to scale. Then labour productivity is considered and a savings function and equilibrium condition of savings equal to the depreciated capital stock are introduced. Capital accumulation brings about economic growth.

Growth need not be deliberate. It can be an unintended consequence, for example, of learning by doing as in Arrow's model. In the process of production experience is gained which will increase productivity through economies of scale. Productivity will be subject to diminishing **returns**.

The economic growth theory industry continues to expand. Endogenous growth theory attributes economic growth to advances in innovation and extra human capital. Encouraging a knowledge-based economy will produce many spill-overs and a second stage of growth through increasing returns. Kaldor and Mirrlees in 1962 presented a Keynesian model of economic growth, using a technical progress function which related the rate of change of gross fixed investment per employee to the rate of increase of labour productivity on newly installed capital equipment. Technical progress was shown to be crucial to economic growth, giving rise to many endogenous growth studies.

The Ramsey-Cass-Koopmans model assumes that a constant number of households has income streams from its **labour** and from the income flowing from its capital assets. These households will attempt to maximise the present value of an infinite **utility** stream.

Growth accounting involves decomposing the growth in **national income** according to the amounts of inputs and adding a residual determined by total factor **productivity**. This production function, using as inputs physical capital and the size of the labour force, can be extended by including human capital as an input.

Policies to encourage regional and national economic growth abound. At the regional level, grants and fiscal incentives are used to increase the rate of net investment. At the national level, growth policies include the employment of existing monetary and fiscal policies to stimulate investment, and the introduction of policy innovations such as indicative economic planning.

Further reading: Arrow 1962; Deane 1967; Domar 1957; Hahn and Matthews 1964; Hamberg 1971; Harrod 1948; Kaldor and Mirrlees 1962; Kuznets 1966; Rostow 1960

ECONOMIC INTEGRATION

The harmonisation and combination of the economic activities of separate economies.

Integration, the bringing together of separate parts into a whole, can occur at the levels of the firm, industry or **national economy**. A firm integrates its activities by reducing the amount of diversification of its activities, often by selling off assets which are not relevant to the principal of the enterprise. An industry experiencing mergers will consolidate the number of firms into fewer and larger units: this can be under the encouragement of government when there is a severe shortage of resources. At the national level economic integration occurs when industries or regions have more linked activities. This can occur by providing incentives to specialise. Old industries are allowed to die gracefully and new industries are encouraged. Regions concentrate on their core activities.

There can also be integration between nations. This occurs as the consequence of the creation of a federation, as has happened under the European Union, or when by agreement joint activities are instituted. Firms can have cross-country activities: governments can implement joint monetary, fiscal, labour, industrial and regional policies.

Integration has many motivations. Reducing costs is a dominant aim. Also there are equity issues: for example, in order to have fair competition tax rates are harmonised. Economic integration can be used as a first step to political integration in the interests of avoiding international conflict. Integration naturally occurs when in response to differentials in wage or profit rates there is movement in factors of production, equalising rates in a unified market.

See also: **customs union**; **holism**

Further reading: Machlup 1977; Streeten 1961

ECONOMIC METHODOLOGY

The way in which economic analysis is conducted; the application of scientific method to economics.

Economics was slow to emerge as a distinct subject. Not until the second half of the eighteenth century were comprehensive surveys of economics, by Cantillon, Steuart and Smith, produced. In the early nineteenth century classical economists began to include a discussion of economic methodology and to ask what economics attempts to be. Nassau Senior, the first professor of **political economy** at Oxford University, thought that the focus of political economy was the study of wealth's production but that the subject was divided into two branches. The theoretical consists of deductions from obvious propositions. The practical depends on induction from phenomena.

JS Mill, attempting a definition of political economy in his fifth essay on *Some Unsettled Questions of Political Economy*, narrowed the subject to the 'moral or psychological laws of the production and distribution of wealth' and concluded that it was an abstract science with an a priori method. In his *Principles of Political Economy* he made a sharp distinction between the laws of production and those of distribution, which he asserted are only a matter of human institution.

Cairnes in his discussion of economics argued that it is concerned with the means to reach our ends. It explains phenomena without approving or disapproving them. Political economy is to be seen as a hypothetical science showing what tends to take place. Using as an illustration Malthus' population theory, he argues that the method to be adopted is to consider the nature and power of a principle of human nature, then consider how restrained it is by external conditions, see what happens if it were unrestrained and look at the strength of opposing economic agents.

Marshall in his *Principles of Economics* explains his partial **equilibrium** method of 'a bit at a time', isolating pairs of economic variables to see the relationship between them with the assumption of *ceteris paribus*, of other things being equal. He thought that economics is concerned with 'normal action' – what can be expected under certain conditions. He did not regard the laws of economics as precise as those of gravitation but more akin to the science of the tides which is based on probability. In the first stage of economic reasoning he advocated the use of mechanical analogies, including equilibrium, but in the later biological, dynamic ideas to show oscillations around a centre which is progressing.

JN Keynes distinguished positive science which determines economic laws from an ethical approach to economics. Physical laws are presupposed so that economics can study cases of voluntary human action. Also psychology is presupposed to examine social relations. Abstract economics can provide fundamental principles, such as on utility, which pervade all economic reasoning in the preliminary stages.

Friedman thoroughly approved of Keynes' positivist approach and explained how positive economics is conducted. Economic hypotheses are creative acts using assumptions which cannot be completely realistic but need enough reality to have predictive power.

Robbins' celebrated essay on the nature of economics used an a priori approach to attack Marshallian economics so that economics becomes a study of 'human behaviour as a relationship between ends and scarce means which have alternative uses'.

JM Keynes used a comparative statics approach, unlike his Cambridge contemporary Dennis Robertson, who made his economics dynamic by introducing time lags, and Swedish competitors such as Bertil Ohlin who employed a period analysis.

Later the methodological studies of Kuhn and Lakatos attracted much debate among economists. Kuhn in his explanation of scientific revolutions begins with a scientific community which practises *normal science* which is based on past scientific achievements. These *paradigms* are a mixture of theory and methodology to explain collected facts. They are solutions to what are regarded as the acute problems of a scientific discipline in a particular time period and will guide what a scientist does. Although the scientist works according to rules, there can be unexpected results from experiments. There is a scientific revolution, a paradigm change, through discovering a new fact or inventing a new theory. There can be repeated failures to solve problems with existing science as theories do not fit the facts and the social climate has changed. A crisis leads to a new scientific theory. The old paradigm is abandoned when a successful alternative has emerged constructed from new fundamentals. There is a discontinuity rather than a steady cumulative process. It can take some time for a new paradigm to be widely accepted; Kuhn did not regard paradigm changes as a march or evolution to 'the truth'.

Lakatos considered research programmes in science, beginning with Newton's gravitational theory and shifts in the definition of problems as a consequence of empirical discoveries. Initial conditions are gradually developed in a scientific programme. There is an increase in content through research programmes absorbing counter-evidence. He wanted competing research programmes rather than a particular model becoming a monopoly. Lakatos, studying the philosophy of mathematics, argued that science progresses by making conjectures and attempting to prove them; criticism produces counter-conjectures. Thus theorems are not ultimately true but awaiting possible refutation. He sought to reconcile Popper and Kuhn through introducing the idea of scientific programmes, or groups of similar theories. Programmes can be progressive or in decline.

See also: **economics as rhetoric**; **Keynesianism**; **neoclassical economics**; **new classical economics**

Further reading: Backhouse 1994; Cairnes 1875; Caldwell 1982; Friedman 1953; Keynes 1891; Kuhn 1996; Lakatos 1972; Latsis 1972; Machlup 1963; Mill 1844; Popper 1959; Robbins 1932; Robinson 1962; Senior 1827

ECONOMIC MODELLING

Constructing an abstract description of economic relationships, often the relationship between two or more variables.

Non-mathematical models were used by Cantillon and Ricardo, but as the nineteenth century progressed important borrowings were made from mathematics, especially calculus, to sharpen economic analysis, as in the works of Dupuit and Jevons. Richard Cantillon in his *Essay on the Nature of Commerce in General* (1755) used a macroeconomic model of the flows of **rents** between villages where the farmers lived, market towns with the larger farmers and artisans, and cities where the landowners resided. David Ricardo in his *Principles of Political Economy and Taxation* (1817) constructed a 'corn model' of the economy in which as the population expanded the **cost** of subsistence would rise, as would real wages, and the rate of profit would decline.

Models are everywhere in economics. In macroeconomics there are **national income**, growth and **planning** models; in micro-economics models of the behaviour of households and firms. By modelling, economics tries to be its scientific best, attempting to show that the discipline can approach the rigour of the natural sciences. Hypotheses are carefully chosen, the structure of the model designed and the data collected. As a popular test of the worth of a model is its predictive force, it is not surprising that modelling is crucial to economic forecasting. Modellers show their seriousness by engaging in computational modelling.

Models can be static or dynamic. Many **equilibrium** models are of the former category; period analysis with variables lagged to introduce time constitutes the latter. Inevitably the growing sophistication of statistics and econometrics has introduced further intricacies into models. Stochastic models test hypotheses concerning the values of economic variables at different times. Accounting models reflect the balance between debits and credits. Optimality and constrained optimisation models are used extensively in microeconomics in the analysis of profit and utility maximisation. Many models are criticised for the unrealistic nature of their assumptions and their limited ambition, for example, examining only the case of perfect competition. From their earliest steps in economics, students are familiar with Keynesian macroeconomic models, the **IS-LM model**, and consumer equilibrium models.

Models can be quantitative or, less commonly, qualitative, as with decision trees. Stochastic models usually employ time series and the techniques of econometrics. Non-stochastic models are less precise in their predictions.

See also: **game theory**; **macroeconomic forecasting**

Further reading: Kreps 1990

ECONOMICS AS RHETORIC

A postmodernist literary approach to economics texts proposed by Donald, now Deirdre, McCloskey.

This is the method of finding good reasons for assertions rather than using abstract methods, common to most scientific methodology, to prove something to be true. It is a reaction against the techniques and accumulated results of positive economics which are obtained through collecting observations to test hypotheses for their predictive force, using the falsification theory of scientific research associated with Karl Popper. Introspection is denied a role in justifying a theory, but shaky statistical procedures are credited with creating evidence. By argument and entering into conversation, meaning in economics is realised. Thus the rhetorical approach examines the metaphors which abound in economics, even when using mathematical analysis to show that there are not closed fixed interpretations.

By changing the practice of economics to recognise rhetoric, a broader and more rational approach to the subject occurs. Although mainstream positive economic methods can be free from a political bias, rhetoric is no less dangerous as it is humanistic and permits free inquiry in the broadest sense. The rhetorical method can build upon, rather than cut down, **neoclassical economics**, but has an openness which could make economics more like poetry than scientific prose.

See also: **economic methodology**

Further reading: McCloskey 1985

ECONOMIC SYSTEM

The institutions and methods of arranging production, exchange, distribution and consumption.

Economic systems have been classified according to the relative amount of private and public ownership, the mixture of **markets** and **planning** to effect allocation, and their openness to foreign trade.

In the simplest of systems, households engage in production and consumption, then exchange their surpluses through barter with no government intervening in economic activity. With the growth of markets and **firms**, economic life becomes more impersonal and complicated. Economic development brings a greater sophistication in consumer tastes and new goods made possible through technical change. With industrialisation and migration from the country to towns there was a call for governments to extend their functions and respond to social problems. The implementation of socialist doctrines, especially in the planned economies of Eastern Europe, and in the mixed economies with some partly private and partly state industries, reshaped economic systems. From the 1750s, when the Physiocrats succeeded mercantilist thinkers, there has been the basic distinction between economic systems which have organically grown to their present state and those deliberately designed to serve the ends of government. Government legislation and orders cut across the spontaneous economic order, to use the expression of Hayek, for economies adjusting through response to price changes.

The contrast between a production and an exchange economy distinguishes an economy viewed as a giant machine for producing goods and services from one where quantities of products are given but their allocation is affected by the nature of exchange. The latter is a monetised economy. Edgeworth in his *Mathematical Psychics* modelled an exchange economy with two commodities, and two consumers having identical preferences and initial resources.

See also: **capitalism**; **comparative economic systems**; **socialism**

ECONOMIC WELFARE

The benefits accruing to persons as a result of economic activity.

In **classical economics** the production of goods but not of services constitutes economic activity, so that welfare is measured in material terms. But increasingly economic activity was regarded as productive of **utilities** and **economic welfare** as the sum of human satisfactions or utilities. The welfare of an individual is contrasted with the social welfare of society as whole. Economics makes the distinction between 'goods' and 'bads' so that there has to be a preponderance of life-enhancing outputs over bads such as pollution and harder work for there to be a net gain in economic welfare.

Pareto devised a notion of optimality, that there is an increase in economic welfare if everyone is better off without anyone being worse off. The shorthand way of measuring economic welfare is of Gross Domestic Product per head, a concept pioneered by Smith in the introduction to his *Wealth of Nations*. From this starting point, basic national income data has to be refined to take account of the composition of output and the circumstances under which it is produced, for example the average number of hours of workers.

See also: **welfare economics**

Further reading: McKenzie 1983

ECONOMIES OF SCALE AND SCOPE

An economy of scale exists if an expansion in output causes the average cost of production to fall; an economy of scope arises from increasing the range of a firm's activities, including operating in more markets.

Marshall, in his explanation of scale economies, distinguished internal economies arising from the expansion of a firm from external economies caused by an industry having a higher output.

The causes of scale economies are shown by examining the exercise of the functions of a firm, especially its management, production, financing and marketing. A typical case of a scale economy is where production has fixed costs, for example, the preparation of a template, so that the unit cost will fall as the output increases. There can also be diseconomies, usually attributed to the inability of managements to control larger organisations. Economies are depicted graphically in a falling average cost curve; diseconomies in a rise. As a scale economy is the consequence of the relationship between two variables, output and **cost**, the *ceteris paribus* conditions that the same technology is used when output grows, that factor proportions are constant and the scope of the firm remains the same, are assumed.

To reduce its costs a firm can increase the scope of its activities in many ways. It can extend its product range and it can market its products in a larger number of markets. A major reason for scope economies is the existence of common costs which can be spread over a greater range of activities. Thus it is worthwhile to merge two firms requiring distribution of their products over the same places. Many cases of coordination illustrate the idea of an economy of scope. A sharing of inputs can be achieved within firms as they absorb other enterprises, and by contractual relationships between different firms.

See also: **cost**; **firm**

Further reading: Gold 1981; Panzar and Willig 1981; Robinson 1953

EFFICIENCY

Producing at minimum cost; achieving a goal with minimal effort.

Productive activities have to be analysed and excess activity eliminated to achieve maximum efficiency. In **neoclassical economics**, efficiency is a constant goal. Idealistic economies, especially those with a tendency towards utopianism, are more tolerant of waste and low productivity.

Different types of efficiency include technical efficiency and allocative efficiency. Technical efficiency can refer to a single factor of production, whereas economic efficiency is concerned with the output per cost unit whatever the factor is. It is dependent on the technology used; thus manufacturing efficiency will be related to the type of machine and the working methods of a factory. There are specific types of technical efficiency. In energy economics, for example, thermal efficiency is important: this is the ratio of the net output of a heat engine to the amount of heat supplied at high temperatures. Network efficiency is full utilisation of the network's resources. Productive efficiency necessitates cost minimisation.

Economic efficiency is regarded by users of a system as that level of performance meeting their requirements. Market efficiency is the extent to which prices reflect current information: this is an important notion in capital markets. Allocative efficiency occurs where the combination of goods produced maximises consumers' satisfaction and profits: the concept is often applied to monopoly and to international trade. From a welfare point of view, the benchmark for efficiency is Pareto optimality, of reaching a state of improvement which is not at the expense of anyone. Under it the marginal rates of transformation of production for different goods will be equal and the marginal rates of substitution between goods will be the same for consumers, and the marginal rates of technical substitution between pairs of factors of production will be the same.

Efficiency in economics is often regarded as achieving the maximum output for a unit of input, and is the consequence of the optimal use of resources. It can be the average efficiency for a whole range of output, or the marginal efficiency for the last unit produced. Also it is identified with the minimum point of a U-shaped average cost curve; if the average cost curve is L-shaped, then the notion of efficiency is the minimum efficient size, the output associated with the turning point of the curve.

Efficiency has many determinants, including choice of the appropriate technology and quality of factor inputs, especially labour. The relationship between a type of organisation and efficiency is often considered. In industries, monopolies are suspected of inefficiency because they do not have to be as cost-conscious as competitive firms. Large firms are potentially more efficient than smaller enterprises if economies of scale exist. Private firms could be superior in efficiency to public enterprises, as they have the extra financial support of government and lack the market discipline of possible takeover.

A leading concept in Keynesian economics is the marginal efficiency of capital, which Keynes stated was 'the relation between the prospective yield of one more unit of that type of capital and the cost of producing that unit'.

Leibenstein's concept of X-efficiency is broader than allocative efficiency, taking into account psychological factors. X-efficiency is the result of intra-plant motivation, external motivational efficiency and non-market input efficiency. He also argued that the return to inputs could be small because labour contracts are incomplete so do not maximise performance. Some factors of production are not marketed, production functions are unknown and the influence other firms can have is difficult to measure. He concluded through his research that neither was production maximised nor costs minimised, as many workers prefer to work more slowly and spend time in interpersonal relationships.

Many economic entities can be said to be efficient. An efficient contract concerns an exchange between a buyer and seller which encourages efficient effort and investment by not producing a loss for the contracting parties. A socially efficient contract will achieve a social optimum. An efficient market achieves an allocation which cannot be improved. It will produce, in the case of a financial market, the true value of an investment. Any deviations from the true value will be random. The price will be a reflection of all the information on which past prices are based and, possibly in the strongest form of efficiency, all public information also. In efficient markets no investment strategy can consistently beat the market. In the labour market efficiency wages are equal to the marginal products of workers. This will be achieved by trial and error. If firms pay less, workers are encouraged to reduce effort or move to other employers; if they pay more, they will attract better quality workers so marginal products will rise to the high level of wages.

Further reading: Leibenstein 1966

ELASTICITY

The response of one variable to another, especially the response of demand or supply to price or income. This is one of the most powerful tools in economics.

Mun, Mill and Marshall made important contributions to the development of the concept. Thomas Mun in *England's Treasure by Forraign Trade* (1664), writing of the vent (sale) of cloth in Turkey, made use of a primitive idea of elasticity: 'We find that twenty five in the hundred less in the price of these ... to the loss of private men's revenues may raise above fifty upon the hundred in the quantity vented to the benefit to the publique', thus introducing the idea of price elasticity of demand as the ratio of the percentage change in quantity demanded to a percentage change in price. JS Mill in his *Principles of Political Economy*, book 3, chapter 18, refers to the 'extensibility of demand'. Marshall in book 3, chapter 4 of his *Principles of Economics* presented the modern description of elasticity as responsiveness, taking the case of price elasticity of demand.

Elasticity has many applications. Price elasticities of demand are used to classify the usefulness of goods, with an inelastic demand indicating a necessity. Supply elasticities are connected with time: the shorter the period of production the less elastic (more inelastic) is the supply. Income elasticities separate normal goods from luxuries (elastic income elasticity). The cross-price elasticity of demand shows the responsiveness of quantity demanded of good X to a change in price of good Y: this measure indicates whether goods are complements (negative elasticity) or substitutes (positive elasticity) and is used in the analysis of **markets** to indicate monopoly power. The elasticity of substitution shows how substitutable one factor of production is for another: this version of the concept is used in the study of **production functions** and **economic growth**.

ENERGY ECONOMICS

The study of the production and distribution of coal, gas, oil and electricity, as well as wind and solar power.

A careful examination is made of the stocks of **exhaustible resources** and the means of production. Much of this branch of economics is interested in projecting supply and demand. There is a dynamic relationship between the price of energy and the supply of it. In the case of oil, a rise in price will make possible production from oilfields previously too costly to exploit. With the exhaustion of coal and oil reserves new sources of energy from the sun, the wind and the sea have been investigated.

With the rapid economic development of China and India, the demand for electricity has added to the continuing problem of energy deficiency. Given the scarcity of many forms of energy, there is a high level of interest in applying efficiency measures on the part of economics.

As countries have become less self-sufficient in energy, international trading has become necessary. This has created spot and future markets for energy. Some types of fuel, such as gas and coal, can be stored; others cannot. Each type of energy will have different supply conditions and often various demand circumstances as particular sorts of equipment will often have a peculiar demand for fuel, for example, vehicles usually use oil. However a variety of fuels can be employed for some purposes, for example heating a house. Demand for fuel will be uneven, with peaks in some seasons and at some times of day. This raises problems of peak-load pricing designed to finance extra capacity for peak times and to encourage a smoothing of demand over time.

Taxation has many roles in energy economics. The large profits made from oil have become a tempting source of extra tax revenue. The inelasticity of demand for basic heating and lighting also leads to a steady source of tax revenue. Taxes affect human behaviour, as most recipients of income want to maximise post-tax income, thus an indirect tax on dirty kinds of fuel will be likely to reduce their consumption.

Because energy is a basic necessity for production and consumption it is a sensitive political issue. Lower-income households will be deprived of minimal levels of energy unless there is price discrimination in their favour. Security of supply is essential if economic and social life is not to be disrupted. To meet their responsibilities, governments often interfere in energy matters. **Regulation** is common to ensure fair prices and wide distribution. Some countries have nationalised their major energy industries, as the UK did in the late 1940s, to attempt a direct furthering of the government's policy aims.

Energy use raises many environmental concerns. The growth in car and air travel creates pollution by producing carbon emissions. Industrialisation invariably leads to an increase in the amount of effluents.

Further reading: Griffin 1986

ENTREPRENEUR

The fourth factor of production after land, labour and capital; the bearer of risk; a creative person.

The functions of the entrepreneur are variously regarded as either the organisation of production or the bearing of risk. The reward to the entrepreneur is **profit**. According to Cantillon in his *Essai sur la Nature du Commerce en Général* (1755) the entrepreneur buys at a fixed price and sells at an uncertain price, thus bearing risk; the entrepreneurial function can be executed by any occupational group. Entrepreneurship in the pure sense of risk bearing can be undertaken by individuals, companies or corporations with distributed equity capital with a variable income. Governmental organisations can use their resources, including tax revenues, to undertake risky projects.

To be entrepreneurial is to be enterprising and innovative. There is the question of whether entrepreneurship can be innate or the product of training. Management schools have courses in entrepreneurship which include the mechanics of setting up a business. Certainly, many successful entrepreneurs in the past had little formal education, but the increasing use of science by modern industry rules out the inspired and ignorant. Entrepreneurship can be the product of necessity, as in a war economy engaged in military competition, or in a failing business with outdated products.

Kirzner regarded entrepreneurship as the quality of alertness, of knowing where to look for knowledge rather than having substantial information. What the entrepreneur achieves is to create a mutual adjustment of discordant elements arising from mistaken decisions and missed opportunities.

Further reading: Cantillon 2001; Casson 1982; Kirzner 1973

ENVIRONMENTAL ECONOMICS

The study of the **costs** and benefits of using land; an examination of the impact on the non-built environment of economic activity.

From the Ancient Greeks to the Physiocrats of the eighteenth century the environment was not 'a problem' but the prime source of wealth and income. Agriculture, the leading sector of early economies, was regarded as superior and to be encouraged. With industrialisation from the beginning of the nineteenth century, the problem of pollution of the air and water arose. Thomas Carlyle was an early observer of the environmental disasters brought about through industrialisation and associated urbanisation. In the twentieth century the measurement of these destructive consequences was attempted in the calculation of social cost. Most of the measures of pollution, however, are physical, not monetary, such as the quantity of particles of pollutants in a volume of air or water.

Apart from studying the effects of damaging the environment, this branch of economics also looks at the consequences of the **scarcity** of natural resources. Classical economists such as Ricardo emphasised that land was fixed in quantity: the same can be said of the earth's mineral deposits and many of its products. The curse of diminishing **returns** is that successive units of a variable composite factor of production, usually labour–capital, when applied to a fixed factor, land, will have a declining yield. Quite simply, the land will be exhausted with nothing more to offer to the user. Because the environment within which economic activity is conducted boldly displays its scarce nature, economists have devoted much attention to resource management. Agricultural economics has long employed advanced econometric techniques to estimate production functions. Forestry and fishery economics have analysed the effects of depleting a resource at different rates.

National governments have employed a variety of regulatory devices to improve the quality of the environment. Command and control **regulation** lays down acceptable standards and can lead to criminal sanctions against those in breach of them. Regulatory bodies have to pay attention to the optimal rate of pollution, which is that rate which equates the marginal social benefit of pollution control to the marginal cost of pollution control. Various taxes attempt to tackle pollution. A carbon tax can charge for the carbon content of coal, natural gas or oil related either to the quantity charged or the value of the fuel. The external cost of a discharge can be imposed on a private polluter in the form of an environmental tax. There can be effluent and emissions charges. A pollution tax is related to the marginal value of emissions. The range of environmental or 'green taxes' grows. Taxes on fuel can discourage the production of emissions. There can also be taxes on specific activities, such as shopping with plastic bags or filling land with rubbish.

No longer can environmental problems be regarded as a domestic problem of a particular country. Climate change, and air and sea quality, are not problems confined within national boundaries. By international treaty some activities can be proscribed, for example, hunting rare species to extinction. In other cases it is recognised that some pollution is inevitable if an industry is to continue in existence. The tradable discharge, or emission, permit allows a particular rate of pollutant discharge. If the permits are tradable then larger users can buy the permits of the smaller, and can cope with peaks in production.

Much of **environmental economics** is neoclassical, founded on the recognition that scarcity is the great economic problem, and with a heavy use of marginal concepts. Inevitably, several branches of economics have similar tools in their kitbags. The idea of market failure, **cost-benefit analysis** and **welfare economics** are imported into environmental economics. But there is also Marxian environmental economics. Some Marxists object to the agenda of environmental economics, as it blames environmental problems on the poor and ignores the role of social factors such as the class system by attempting to unite all classes to attack pollution and similar negative aspects of production. However, by promoting an increase in material production as a goal, Marxists have clashed with ecologists. Furthermore, the economies of Eastern Europe have had appalling records of pollution, which are no advertisement for Marxist ideas.

Pollution can be easily measured, but other aspects of the environment are more obscure as they rest on subjective opinion, as in the case of a pleasant view: techniques such as contingent valuation based on opinion surveys are tried to assess the worth of this. There is a strong normative element in much of environmental economics. It is assumed that in the midst of competing demands for land, conservation is vital. Also the promotion of biodiversity is asserted without question. As part of the environment is undeveloped wilderness beloved by environmentalists, it is assumed that perpetual preservation is intrinsically worthwhile. Growth of extractive and manufacturing industries will always be criticised for environmental reasons. However, a relative of environmental economics, ecological economics, which looks at the relationship between ecological systems and human activity, has a heavy scientific content, especially physics and biology.

Environmental economists have long been on a collision course with economic growth enthusiasts. Low sustainable growth is the hope of the former; increasing the supply of inputs and their productivities the desire of the latter.

See also: **exhaustible resources**

Further reading: Hay 2002; Mäler 1974; Tietenberg 1994

EQUALITY

Having the same size of income or **wealth**.

What is equalised varies from one advocate of egalitarianism to another. It can be equality of income, of wealth, of primary goods, of basic capabilities, of resources, or of access to the means of production. Inequality can take various forms. In the case of income inequality there is inequality between different groups in the **labour** market, between the recipients of income from labour and from other factors of production, and between those at work and those in receipt of various welfare benefits. To indicate the amount of inequality, Lorenz curves plotting the distribution of income against the standard of a 45 degree line of absolute equality and the associated Gini coefficient measure, the ratio of the area between the curve and the 45 degree line and of the area of the triangle under the 45 degree line, are used. Also it is usual to examine the median, quartile, deciles and percentiles of an income distribution to see how wide income differences are. One measure of inequality is the ratio of the levels of income at the upper and lower quartiles.

A popular distinction is between equality of opportunity (having the same access to education and employment) and equality of outcome (the same achievement of income). The distinction is spurious as opportunity is often the consequence of the endowments of parents. Those who believe that there is a separate concept of equality of opportunity will promote positive discrimination to help the worse off. The cost of such policies can be greater government interference and a lack of incentives. Formal equality means equal treatment, judging persons without taking into account characteristics such as gender and race. Substantive equality requires persons receiving similar amounts of income and wealth. To 'correct' an income distribution requires the arbitrary assignment of weights to members of a population so that their shares of total income increases.

The advocacy of equality has always been linked to that of justice. That human beings born with the same basic needs should be treated differently has long been challenged. Also at every stage of life the allocation of more resources and more income to one person or class rather than another has been questioned. The existence of blatant inequalities has stirred up political revolutions, including the French Revolution of 1789, to address perceived economic injustice. Issues of equity in distribution are raised because of persistent attitudes and prejudices. However, equality and equity have to be distinguished. Aristotle's distinction in the *Nicomachean Ethics* between commutative and distributive justice is a contrast between treating persons equally and recognising inequalities by rewarding in proportion, which is a more subjective exercise. Income from work is seen to be more justifiable than income from capital and property. It is feared that large disparities in income will occasion unrest and can lead to crime. If a society has some with very large incomes then pointless luxurious consumption is possible: there could even be crowding out of the production of necessities for the poor. A maldistribution in income can also be caused by discrimination against particular despised groups. Also there can be disproportionate incomes because of criminal or sharp practices.

Without sufficient income to support families a society will disintegrate. The labour market is not performing the useful function of providing a reasonable livelihood for all employed workers. The persistence of poor pay can affect productivity and slow down economic growth. Economics writers have argued that greater equality is a benefit to society and that inequality is a loss. Bentham and others argued that because of the diminishing **utility** of wealth, total happiness would be increased by redistributing a unit of income or wealth from the rich to the poor, conveniently ignoring the difficulties of making interpersonal comparisons of utility.

To advocate inequality of incomes is to say that a differentiation of incomes creates economic **incentives**. Rarely has a labour market functioned without wage differentials. Even in the USSR occupational wage differentials were necessary in order to encourage persons to train for the more difficult occupations and to accept greater responsibility. Inequality is a spur which encourages demand for training and hard work to get to the top. This prospect of social mobility becomes the key to economic growth, as Smith recognised in describing the desire for betterment. If one believes in life as a Darwinian struggle to eliminate the unfit, income differences are accepted. Also there are some high incomes, such as those of singers and footballers, which are widely accepted without criticism. Through inequality there can be some high incomes providing the opportunity to finance the arts and be philanthropic, rather than delegate such concerns to the state.

To reconcile equality and efficiency, which leads to a few becoming very rich, Okun proposed removing some social goods, such as income distribution, from the market. He uses the parable of a 'leaky bucket' to allow 1 per cent of redistributed income to leak away as waste.

Improved communications and the faster pictorial transmission of news have increased awareness of the huge differences in incomes and living standards between different parts of the world. Where there is rampant disease and high infant mortality rates, a call for greater equality between countries has been demanded; ending world **poverty** has become a marching cry. Inequality can be addressed by granting poor countries more access to developing countries' markets or by economic aid. The pursuit of equality is always easier when there is economic growth, because greater equality can be effected by letting lower income groups grow at a faster rate. In a static economy, to seek equality is painful as it means making some people worse off.

See also: **aid**; **discrimination**; **Rawlsian justice**

Further reading: Bronfenbrenner 1973; Charvet 1981; Green 1981; Okun 1974; Pen 1971; Tawney 1964

EQUILIBRIUM

A state of rest with no further movement in a market to change **prices** or the quantities demanded and supplied. In a traditional society using custom and the same technology for long periods, an equilibrium can persist for a long time. In modern societies an equilibrium will be more temporary.

The notion of equilibrium is longstanding in economics. In the mercantilist period, Steuart in his *Principles of Political Economy* discussed many balances in the economy, some of which would be 'in equilibrio'. Smith discussed the 'tendency towards equality' brought about in, for example, local labour markets, when workers responded to differences in wages and moved from low- to high-wage employment, driving wages down and making them more equal. In classical economics, heavily reliant on Newtonian mechanics and Le Chatelier's principle, a movement towards equilibrium was assumed but not always regarded as achievable.

In the last quarter of the nineteenth century an important distinction arose between general equilibrium and partial equilibrium. Walras presented the conditions for there being a general equilibrium, a state of a **national economy** wherein all markets have demand equal to supply. If there are n goods exchanged then there will be one price for an exchange of two goods, so $n-1$ for goods in general based on $n-1$ separate equations. At one level a general equilibrium appears an ideal of harmony. To explain the establishment of an equilibrium of this kind requires the study of a vast number of price and output changes in a large national economy. Marshall was the pioneer of much of partial equilibrium analysis. Using the established idea of *ceteris paribus* (other things being equal), he was able to examine the relationship between two variables, especially a price and a quantity demanded or supplied, assuming that anything which could influence that relationship would be unchanged and hence not influential. He regarded 'a bit at a time' method as a way of making economic analysis manageable. **Neoclassical economics**, which is dominated by the idea of an equilibrium, is concerned with whether there are unique or multiple equilibria, as well as whether an equilibrium exists. There can be a temporary equilibrium over, say, a week, or an equilibrium over time. An equilibrium can be stationary, persisting for a long period if the forces governing demand and supply are stable, as happens in traditional societies with no technical progress. No change is expected and none occurs. An equilibrium can be static or dynamic. If static, the notion of time is excluded; if dynamic, movement on an equilibrium path is considered.

With the rise of modern macroeconomics in the 1930s under Keynes and others, the equilibrium between aggregate demand and aggregate supply was investigated. As with microeconomic analysis, in macroeconomics 'scissors diagrams' showing an equilibrium at the intersection of the demand and supply curves expounded this idea.

If seeking an equilibrium is regarded as important then the route to that goal has to be explained. There is an initial choice between price adjustments and quantity adjustments. Prices can be moved up and down until the equilibrium price which will clear the market is achieved. Quantities can be altered by changes in the rate of production and in the use of accumulated stocks until there is neither excess demand nor excess supply. Reaching an equilibrium is not always achievable, as the cobweb theorem shows. Some markets remain in disequilibrium for a long time because of price rigidities. Much of the notion of equilibrium is associated with markets but there can be an equilibrium idea employed in central economic planning where the planners deliberately attempt a series of material balances. The stages of reaching or passing an equilibrium are akin to the phases of an economic cycle. A shock can set a market or economy on a disequilibrium path until forces, including income changes, bring it back to equilibrium.

An equilibrium is a desired state of affairs, so that without economic agents revealing their preferences and desires a judgement cannot be made. What might appear to be disequilibrium because of the presence of unsold stocks can reflect the desire of the supplier to have temporary or permanent excess capacity so that there is a higher chance of being able to satisfy customers at any time.

In **game theory**, a strategic equilibrium can take a multitude of forms. In the case of the Nash equilibrium, central to game theory, two or more players in a game cannot benefit by changing their strategies. A Bayesian equilibrium, recognising there is incomplete information, is the consequence of a game in which the players consider expected utilities based on private information concerning the characteristics of the players. A sunspot equilibrium is an allocation of resources dependent on an extrinsic random economic variable.

As an equilibrium is a balance between different forces or entities, the term can be applied broadly to cases of a general or market equilibrium. Writers as early as the mercantilists were concerned with the balance between nations, their relative strength, especially as measured by their balances of trade or payments. An internal balance of a country is distinguishable from its external balance with the rest of the world. The internal, according to Meade, has to take into account employment, inflation and wages; the external considers the **balance of payments** and related international variables such as foreign **exchange rates**.

See also: **cobweb, disequilibrium economics; neoclassical economics; new classical economics**

Further reading: Meade 1951; Weintraub 1974

ETHICS AND ECONOMICS

The relationship between standards of conduct and economic principles.
Hausman and McPherson (1993: 673) argue a fourfold case for economists attending to moral questions:

1 The morality of economic agents influences their behavior and hence influences economic outcomes. Moreover, economists' own moral views may influence the morality and the behavior of others in both intended and unintended ways. Because economists are interested in the outcome, they must be interested in morality.
2 Standard **welfare economics** rests on strong and contestable moral presuppositions. To assess and to develop welfare economics thus requires attention to morality.
3 The conclusions of economics must be linked to the moral commitments that drive public policy. To understand how economics

bears on policy thus requires that one understand these moral commitments, which in turn requires attention to morality.

4   Positive and normative economics are frequently intermingled. To understand the moral relevance of positive economics requires an understanding of the moral principles that determine this relevance.

Much of economics grew out of moral philosophy so it cannot be easily dismissed as an immoral or amoral science. Aristotle, Smith and JS Mill were both interested in well-being and in economic issues. In British universities the teaching of economics often sprang out of moral philosophy, for example, at Edinburgh and Cambridge. Leading economists such as WS Jevons and Alfred Marshall were partially motivated to study economics because the **poverty** question of their day raised issues of conscience for economists. Marshall, in his inaugural lecture in 1885 at Cambridge, declared that his aim as professor was to send out graduates with cool heads but warm hearts.

Much of the strident criticism of economics as a dismal, or possibly wicked science, springs from economic theories which assume that economic agents are self-interested. In the eighteenth century economic theory, especially in Smith's *The Wealth of Nations*, made self-interest central and provoked ill-informed criticism because of self-interest being confused with selfishness. David Hume separated questions of fact from those of value in his is/ought distinction, giving rise to the familiar separation of positive from normative economics. Unfortunate consequences were that much of formal economics was perceived as valueless and that policy recommendations were founded on an unexamined moral philosophy.

In economics there is a distinction between the behaviour of the individual person and of collective entities, especially firms and governments. If morality is about altruism then it can formulate rules for all of these acting as economic agents. An individual as consumer, saver or worker is faced with choices which can lead to goodness or badness. Firms are crucial economic agents in the allocation of resources. Through their production and investment decisions, present and future possibilities for living are determined. Also they have a major effect on income distribution through their wage and salary policies. A government in its fiscal, trade and investment policies is responsible for the ultimate incidence of the measures it enacts.

There are many theories of ethics and hence many interfaces between ethics and economics. Ethical theories include utilitarianism and intuitionism. Contractarians also enter the debate between ethics and economics. A moral position is argued from an alleged foundational contract which establishes rights: a familiar case of this approach is Rawlsian justice. Earlier exponents of a contractarian view included Hobbes and Rousseau. By adopting such a position, a way of dealing with income inequality and deprivation is established. Also, communitarianism aims to emphasise the social and collective rather than the individual. **Social capital** is regarded more highly than the free working of markets to achieve welfare goals.

In many branches of economics ethical issues are raised. Questions of fairness are raised in discussions of income distribution, international trade, competition and allocation of scarce resources. Also there is the established concept of exploitation. Marx associated it with the extraction of surplus value. Furthermore, in the study of monopoly exploitation springs from prices being in excess of marginal cost and thereby producing supernormal profits. Firms, governments and individual persons are all capable of exploiting each other.

As economics has become more technical it seems less obvious that it is engaged in ethical matters. Like engineering, it shows the effects of changes in a system, not stating whether the consequences are good or bad. To say, for example, that market prices tend to rise when there is a shortage of supply is merely a statement of fact. Whately stated that the object of **political economy** is a study of the nature, production and distribution of wealth, unconnected to happiness and virtue. He used the example of a treatise on shipbuilding which would be about construction and management, not the utility of a ship. This approach in effect is an assertion that economics is ultimately positive economics. In **neoclassical economics** the discipline becomes the use of a method and little more. Samuelson (1948: 75) precisely stated: 'The primary end of economic analysis is to explain a position of minimum (or maximum) where it does not pay to make a *finite* movement in any direction.'

See also: **happiness**; **homo economicus**; **utility**; **welfare economics**

Further reading: Hausman and McPherson 1993; Little 2002; Samuelson 1948; Sen 1989; Whately 1847

EVOLUTIONARY ECONOMICS

An application of the ideas of biological evolution to economic problems; a type of **game theory**; a dynamic approach to economics.

The theme of long-term economic change was central to **classical economics**. Both Smith and Marx were keen to apply the stages theory of human populations becoming more technologically sophisticated as they progressed from hunting to shepherding to agriculture to commerce and manufacturing. A central question was whether such change would lead to the no-growth situation of the stationary state. Ideas of evolution propounded by Herbert Spencer and Charles Darwin inspired economists in their analyses of the processes of economic change. The ideas of the survival of the fittest and the natural selection of species had their economic applications. Marshall used biological analogies to discuss the long-term aspects of economic problems after the short-term problems had been analysed in mechanical equilibrium terms. He introduced the idea of 'the representative firm' as an average **firm** which survived using the analogy of trees in the forest.

Schumpeter, in his analysis of **capitalism**, outlined how capitalism was evolving into corporate capitalism. In his consideration of economic growth he viewed the **entrepreneur** as the agent of change and innovation engaged in a process of creative destruction. Through the process of discovering new ideas and innovating, the economy would move from one macroeconomic **equilibrium** to another. These processes are largely endogenous.

Boulding described the process of social evolution as a human understanding of patterns which is transmitted as the knowledge to produce something. Production is thus based on a biological process which is systems of threats, exchange and integration.

Evolutionary theory can be applied to the more micro levels of the industry and the firm. Nelson and Winter use micro-level evolution to create a theory of the firm which attacks the equilibrium approach of the neoclassical economists. In the first stage firms behave according to routines in their pricing, production and investment; then in the next stage there is a search for methods of production; and finally in the third stage there is a process of selection in which the less profitable firms disappear. In a competitive struggle using imitation and **innovation**, the industrial structure emerges. Alchian uses a biological evolutionary approach to his theory of the firm, showing that firms survive through superior ability or fortuitous circumstance. Imitation and trial-and-error are crucial.

Evolutionary game theory shows how, in a process of learning, the fittest who win in one game go on to further games. This is a move away from the study of super-rational individuals. It is dynamic, including in the modelling the learning which comes from observing one's opponents. Non-cooperation is assumed to explain the development of markets, money, the price mechanism and other economic institutions.

Further reading: Alchian 1950; Boulding 1978; Hodgson 1993; Loasby 1991; Nelson and Winter 1982; Schumpeter 1954; Weibull 1995

EX-ANTE, EX-POST

A distinction between the planned and actual values of economic variables.

In the macroeconomic debates of the 1930s in Sweden careful attention was paid to this contrast. Gunnar Myrdal in his *Monetary Equilibrium* described the contrast in detail. Ex-ante calculus is a question of anticipations, calculations and plans driving the dynamic process forward; ex-post is an overall bookkeeping balance. With this conceptual tool he then asserted that in monetary theory it is necessary to explain how a disparity between savings and investment ex-ante becomes a balance ex-post. The Stockholm School used a period analysis to show how **savings** would grow to equal investment expenditures which were larger at the planning stage. The initial investment generates increased incomes. Out of each round of increased income, savings will occur which accumulate to equal the investment. **Expectations**, **interest rates** and **prices** will change through the movement to an ex-post equilibrium.

EXCHANGE RATE

The price of one **currency** in terms of another.

These rates can be 'nominal', i.e. the trading prices in 'forex', (foreign exchange) markets, or 'real' because the nominal rate has been adjusted for **inflation**. They can be entirely market determined or can be managed by banks, which make appropriate sales and purchases in currency markets to maintain the currency at the desired rate. Rates can be fixed, a 'pegged rate', as under the Bretton Woods system 1944–71, or float with changes in the market, or a 'dirty float' in which a central bank interferes from time to time. Countries can use the currency of another, for example, the US dollar, thus having no control over their exchange rates.

The exchange rate is the most important **price** of a **national economy**, as it reflects the relationship between that country and the rest of the world. A country with an exchange rate which is too high will find it difficult to sell its exports, thus risking a balance of trade deficit and provoking speculative attacks on the currency.

Purchasing power parity is an equilibrium exchange rate which will purchase the same amount of goods and services in each country. This approach, associated with Gustav Cassel, is widely employed to compare living standards across the world. It suffers from the fact that not all of the production of a country enters into international trade and there are non-market determinants of exchange rates.

See also: **currency**

Further reading: Taylor 1995

EXHAUSTIBLE RESOURCES

The fixed amount of some non-renewable resources such as minerals; features of the landscape giving rise to the formulation of rules for their exploitation.

This is a major aspect of **environmental economics**, sharing the principal concern that resources are fixed in amount so need to be protected and conserved. There can be a complete ban on their use or an orderly depletion of them to satisfy the demand for oil or some other mineral, either as a consequence of **taxation** discouraging excessive use or **regulation** overseeing the rate of depletion. Another response to natural resources **scarcity** is to advocate recycling, but that in turn is a poor attempt at a solution, as recycling needs much energy for transportation and processing.

Hotelling discussed in a foundational article the optimum rate of present production of such resources, given that we would not want to conserve all of the fixed stock of such assets for posterity, contrasting extraction under free competition and monopoly. He viewed the problem as one of profit maximisation, and formulated the rule that prices of such resources should rise exponentially at a rate equal to the interest rate. He treated such resources as similar to financial assets.

The fixed nature of such resources has led some ecologists to criticise severely the promotion of **economic growth**. Understandable as this is, it does ignore the fact that an element in economic growth is usually technical progress, which can include methods which economise on material inputs.

Information deficiencies abound. The extent of a mineral reserve may be unknown until further geological research, which in turn may wait until price rises make exploration financially viable. Prohibition can excite unscrupulous people to seek out the protected species or natural feature because of its scarcity and hence high black market price.

As non-renewable resources are depleted there is a diminution in national **wealth**. Just as income is a net addition to wealth and depletion a subtraction, so both should be recognised in interpretations of national income accounts.

Exhaustible resources are often owned by monopolies, public or private. They benefit from a fixed supply, in this case natural, not the consequence of contrived artificial barriers to entry. Monopoly status runs the danger of leading to inefficiencies. As it is costly to sink mines, or engage in other infrastructure projects to extract these finite resources, in less developed countries foreign multinationals are often engaged in extraction, thus leading to disputes about the aims of national governments and private corporations.

See also: **environmental economics**

Further reading: Hotelling 1931; Krautkraemer 1998

EXPECTATIONS

Estimates or views about the future which drive **investment** and other economic activities forward.

Economic actions are undertaken for their future effects. This is especially so in the case of investment. Some view of the likely income from creating physical capital is needed. Possible consumer preferences and incomes, government policies and the state of the world all have to be taken into account. In financial markets, views on the future course of prices are crucial to portfolio adjustment. Some kind of qualification or weighting is needed for the data accumulated to date.

The simplest assumption is that the future will be the same as the past, not an unreasonable opinion in the case of a static society with no technical progress and at peace with its neighbours. Today's world is more turbulent, with information technology showing how rapid is change. Industrial structures are repeatedly altered by mergers and other acquisitions. War is a commonplace in many parts of the world. Hence simple extrapolation is useless.

An expectation can be single-valued or multi-valued, as one can expect a precise outcome of definite proportions or a range of possibilities which might conform to a probability distribution. If expectations concern many aspects of a future state, then weights are added to establish the more likely predictions.

Irving Fisher, a leading American economist, had a practical attitude towards expectations, introducing the idea of 'adaptive expectations' which are based on past data extrapolated into the future, taking into account the margin of error, hence its alternative name of the 'error learning hypothesis'. Previously naïve or static expectations excluded random shocks. The **cobweb** was an early example of this. This approach to forecasting does depend for its efficacy on considerable economic stability. Cagan and Friedman used this approach to expectations in their study of **inflation**.

Keynes wrote much on expectations. In his *General Theory* he noted that entrepreneurs and investors have to take a view on what consumers are willing to pay. Short-term expectations, he asserted, were concerned with the cost of output and sales proceeds from using existing capital equipment; long-term expectations concern future incomes if investment is undertaken. Expectations will thus determine output and eventually employment. Past expectations now embodied in capital equipment are also taken into account. In the long term, expectations of prospective yields will partly be based on present facts about the capital stock and consumer demand, and partly on the future course of capital investment, tastes and effective demand.

Shackle, in his analysis of Keynes' views on expectations, pointed out that when we make decisions based on our views of the future we can be surprised by news so that we can discern little about the future. Some of our expectations will be fairly certain, others classifiable as potential surprises. Our expectations are subjective and cannot be fully rational, as we can only make guesses about the future decisions which will determine future events.

Myrdal, in his exposition of ex-ante and ex-post values of economic variables, regarded the ex-ante as containing expectations which drove forward economic activity.

Recently rational expectations has become the most discussed type of expectations. Muth started this precise and limited view of expectations. He argued that expectations depend on the whole state of a national economy and no information being wasted. It is assumed that individuals do not make mistakes in forecasting the future. All relevant information has been acquired and all profitable opportunities exploited. The outcome in terms of the future value of an economic variable is not systematically different from a market equilibrium. Expectations are not always accurate but errors will have specific properties. This attitude to expectations is used to explain why market speculators only benefit if there is new information. Rational expectations theory was used to attack the discretionary demand management policies of the 1950s in the USA and the UK, through its conclusion that people would anticipate policy changes and adjust their economic behaviour appropriately. Pesaran raised many doubts about the rational expectations hypothesis and testing it. He argued that the more is known by economic agents about the future values of economic variables, the lower the probability of the econometrician knowing the underlying mechanism of agents' decision making. Ignorance of the time lags in economic relations would make it more difficult to model rational expectations. Thus, he argues, there is a case for regarding the formation of expectations as lying between pure adaptive and full rational expectations models. Davidson argued that agents, if sensible, would reject information when forming expectations on the basis of probability.

Behavioural economics provides a different view of expectations, by taking insights from psychology on cognitive dissonance and regret to show that the status quo is preferred. It is a less precise and technical notion of expectations than adaptive or rational expectations.

Further reading: Cagan 1956; Evans and Honkapohja 2001; Muth 1961; Shackle 1949, 1973; Pesaran 1987; Davidson 1982/83

EXPERIMENTAL ECONOMICS

Attempts to test economic theory by simulating real life economic decision making.

This tries to overcome the central problem of the social sciences, namely that, unlike the physical sciences, it is impossible to repeat experiments in every detail. Economic events occur at points in time so are all unique. Economic agents change, availability of resources alters, knowledge and technology advance. This means that any simulated experiments ideally concern static **equilibrium** problems which ignore time. The essence of partial equilibrium analysis is to examine the relationship between two variables with the rest of the world controlled by the *ceteris paribus* (other things being equal) assumption. Other assumptions have to be made about the rationality of economic choice.

Wage negotiations, purchasing goods and services and investing are all suitable subjects for economic experiments. In some experiments volunteers are presented with a sum of money, then told prices of various goods to see how they will distribute their purchases. In a wage negotiation problem the financial realities of an employer and other relevant information will be presented to the two sides.

Experimental **game theory** is the most sophisticated of experimental approaches to economics. Experiments are used to provide an empirical basis for principles of strategic behaviour. Bargaining games with two or three persons have looked at the nature of discounting. Rewards in these games will depend on the payoffs. Deviations from a sub-game perfect equilibrium can be detected.

See also: **evolutionary economics**

Further reading: Castro and Weingarten 1970; Fontaine and Leonard 2005; O'Neill 1987; Smith 1989

EXTERNALITY

The third party consequence of economic actions, which can be costly or beneficial.

All transactions between buyers and sellers, between producers and consumers, and between employers and workers can affect wider society. An externality can also be described as a spill-over or neighbourhood effect. The early modern analysts of externalities were the Cambridge economist Pigou, with his contrast between private and social dimensions to economic variables, and the Chicago economist Coase, who continued with the analysis of pollution.

The 'external' has various contrasts dependent on which economic entity is compared with the outside. The individual is compared with society at large. What occurs internally within a **firm**, especially production, is compared with its impact on other firms in that or other industries. The bulk of economic activity occurs within countries, but has an impact on other countries and internationally through organisations such as the World Bank and the International Monetary Fund. However, the most popular use of 'externality' is in the microeconomic sense of what effect a household or a firm has upon others for good or ill. An externality is the context of a particular economic activity formed by it. An externality can be something specific such as an injury to a particular person, or more generally, a phenomenon or state of affairs such as pollution or a low level of crime.

The most popular use of 'externality' in environmental matters is the wider physical consequences of the behaviour of persons and firms. The separation of private from social costs and benefits allows an externality to be viewed as a social matter. An external cost in microeconomics is often regarded as waste or inefficiency.

Given the objection to externalities that the sufferers are not compensated for damage and loss caused by others, ways of making the polluter or other perpetrator pay are proposed. By changing a social cost to a private cost, the process of 'internalising the externality' occurs. A firm pouring waste into a river can be ordered to clean up the waterway: this internalises the social **cost** to the firm. Pigou pioneered the idea of taxation to discourage firms, especially polluters, producing negative externalities.

Meade, in looking at the external economies or diseconomies, distinguished the external as an unpaid factor of production, and as the creation of an atmosphere. The first is illustrated by the case of an apple grower who by increasing apple production also increases the output of honey. There is an unpaid factor because the apple farmer cannot charge the beekeeper. The atmosphere is a fixed condition of production, such as the rainfall of an area.

Because externalities work through different mechanisms they are tackled in different ways. They can affect prices, the quality of production, the exercise of **property rights**, and the scope for other economic activity. If an externality leads to a complaint, either through causing damage or conferring benefits others do not pay for, there is the principal choice between finding a remedy through a private action in the law courts or resorting to a regulatory body, if it exists. Where the social costs of private activities are severe, for example having coal fires in houses, the tackling of the externality can be achieved by regulation even to the extent of an outright prohibition.

Externalities can be beneficial. This was recognised by Marshall in his distinction between internal and external economies. Suppose a firm finds others of the same industry taking up location nearby, their growth will benefit the original firm, for example, through joint research, training of the labour force and enhanced lobbying ability to persuade government to improve the infrastructure. Actions which have beneficial side effects give rise to the free rider problem. A popular example is in wage bargaining, where through the actions of a trade union a pay increase is obtained which is applied to all the members of that bargaining unit whether or not they are members of the union.

Examples of negative externalities invariably use the case of two parties to an exchange mutually gaining something of worth but the rest of the community not. However, a government can cause negative externalities, especially in its **taxation** and expenditure policies. A particular industry can be subsidised, perhaps for the worthy reason of avoiding localised **unemployment**, but the subsidy has to be financed, thus imposing a reduction in post-tax income of taxpayers who are not in the favoured industry.

It can be difficult to make the concept of externality operational, as the effects can be long-term or so dispersed as to be not easily discernible. If land is not properly valued then the cost of pollution is unknown. Where simple general principles of measurement do not apply, a piecemeal approach has to be adopted, often by law courts experienced through the use of precedent to ascertain how severe a tort is.

The existence of externalities gives rise to policy responses. Governments can tax external costs and subsidise those with the potential to create external benefits. The goal of such **fiscal policies** is 'to internalise an externality', which amounts to changing the status and incidence of something from social to private. There are limits to this process, including the difficulties in identifying the creator of an externality, and also the capacity of the perpetrator to pay for what can be colossal and widespread damage. In the absence of a government policy to cope with a particular type of externality, the beneficiaries of and sufferers from externalities have to resort to a settlement under the law of tort.

Externalities arise because of interdependences. Households, firms, governments and the physical environment are constantly interacting to their mutual advantage or loss. This is more general than a causal process. The utility I gain is related to other persons' utilities. Therefore for a full analysis of externalities a general **equilibrium** approach must be attempted.

See also: **Coase theorem**; **environmental economics**

Further reading: Cornes and Sandler 1986; Meade 1952; Papandreou 1994

FAMILY, ECONOMICS OF

The study of the consequences of the existence and behaviour of the family.

As a major social institution the family requires the attention of the economist. So much of economics has been about the individual that this branch of the subject can examine the behaviour within and between such collective entities. It shares with the firm its potential for production and also, like the **national economy**, is a network of consumption and production activities organised according to principles which vary from a central dictatorship to considerable democracy.

There are reasons both social and economic for the formation, expansion and dissolution of families. The traditional family of parents and children has been superseded by a variety of groups, not always with children, who have the principal characteristic of residing together, or otherwise being bound together by obligations towards each other. There are economic advantages which create families. Individuals find it difficult to be self-sufficient, sometimes almost impossible in the case of a person with several dependants. Companionship also makes a family attractive. A brotherhood or sisterhood based on following a religion or another philosophy of life will also constitute a family. One of the advantages of family life is gaining economies of scale by joint production of the means of life. Also families become an important joint protection against attack. Expansion of a family can be by childbirth or by an invitation to outsiders to join. The diminution or dissolution of families occurs when family members choose to set up new families or find the economic and psychic costs of living with a particular set of persons intolerable. A major reason for family shrinkage is divorce, which can occur through incompatibility or bad behaviour.

The principal economic activity of a family is sustaining its existence. It can attempt to be self-sufficient or can place some of its members in the **labour** market. Any labour force participation by one member of a family has consequences for the rest. It can be a substitute for others' participation or the consequence of one member stimulating the others to work. As there is the possibility of home production, there is always the choice of staying at home or going into the labour market. The family is also engaged in producing a surplus, which means producing within and without the family to achieve a total output greater than the family's **consumption**. **Saving** will be motivated by having a reserve to meet emergencies, the wish to help descendants and to accumulate sufficient capital to obtain non-employment income.

Becker dominates the economics of the family through applying many tools of **neoclassical economics** to the subject. In *A Treatise on the Family* he analyses different types of family and single-person households. With the building block of maximising within a family individual **utility**, family income and gains from non-market activities, he describes the allocation of roles among family members according to their comparative advantage. He also recognises that **altruism** has a role. His account is a broad enough essay in demographics to include the efficiency of the marriage market, with persons of similar quality mating, and the determinants of fertility, including the reasons for investing in children and the costs of doing so. The theory is ambitious in applying to any stage of economic development and in translating the theory used for larger markets to so small a microcosm as the family.

See also: **altruism**; **household behaviour**

Further reading: Becker 1981

FIRM

A unit within an industry which produces goods and services.

Economics has paid much attention to the consequences of the organisation of firms and the motivation of their owners and managers. The simplest case is that of the sole trader who owns and manages a productive enterprise able to select as her goals from **profit** maximisation to maintaining a satisfactory level of profit and market share as their goals. A partnership with joint ownership of capital has to reach a consensus among the owners. A company or corporation is more complicated, as hired managers are often employed who can have different aims and practices from the ultimate owners.

A firm operates within an industry and a market which can be structured in different ways, the extreme case being monopoly with the firm being coterminous with the market or industry. The market structure determines the extent of freedom of the firm. Competition will severely limit a firm's pricing decisions and marketing strategy. The relative size of firms, and their absolute size, will have an effect on their power over customers and even national governments.

Firms grow at different rates, partly as a consequence of the growth of demand for their products and partly through their ability to raise finance to become larger organisations. There is a choice between internal expansion or external expansion through mergers and acquisitions. The latter will often be chosen because a faster rate of growth can be achieved and because there is no other way of gaining access to scarce managerial and other skills. Also it is easier to join together firms with established markets than expand an existing firm into an uncertain new market. Any limit to their growth is likely to depend on the ability to avoid managerial diseconomies of scale and the strictures of competition policy.

Firms can be organised internally according to different patterns. Patterns of activity such as production, marketing, research and finance are often used, but there can also be a greater integration of functions and a division of activity largely according to location of the parts of the firm. Whether a firm is one shape or another depends on management responses to likely productivity and costs. Four types of firm have been identified. The M-firm is multi-divisional, with operating divisions separated from decision making. The H-firm is the holding company with the parent company engaged in evaluating the performance of subsidiaries. The X-firm is a hybrid mixture of H- and M-firms. The U-firm divides a firm according to the main functions and is more suited to smaller than larger firms, as in the latter the cost of communications between divisions could be great.

Coase asked the fundamental question: what is a firm? He noted that within the firm it is management by order, not the price mechanism, which allocates resources. Within the firm there is vertical integration of the different stages of production. When many of the activities of an external market are absorbed within a firm by managerial direction, costs are saved, especially those of contracting. **Taxation** in a market, such as a sales tax, will be avoided if exchanges occur within firms. There will be a limit to the size of the firm set by the marginal costs of operating within a firm as opposed to in the external market. Coase also considers the nature of the employment relationship rather than the less intimate principal–agent connection. A firm can also be seen as a production function transforming inputs into outputs, as a legal entity, or a capability based on accumulated knowledge.

See also: **competition and monopoly**

Further reading: Coase 1937; Cohen 1975

FISCAL FEDERALISM

The financing of a government which functions at different levels, for example, national, state and city.

At each level there is a different capacity for making expenditure decisions, varying abilities to raise taxes and different claims, and to receive grants from other levels of government. The neatest form of fiscal federalism is where each level of government has specific functions and finances them itself from its own tax base. A scheme could be that the national government is responsible for defence, social security, foreign affairs and health, and receives the revenue from an income tax to pay for them. At the state level there could be responsibility for transport and industrial policy, with a corporation tax to finance this. At the city level, police and education are provided and financed by a sales tax.

Fiscal federalism becomes complicated when a level of government has too small an exclusive revenue to execute its functions: it then has to be in receipt of grants as well as its particular tax revenue. The problems of fiscal federalism remain as long as lower levels of government have some measure of autonomy. It is argued that some activities, such as road maintenance and education, are best run by local government but if a central government demands adherence to national standards and gives grants to ensure compliance, the multi-layered structure of the state will inevitably be questioned.

Further reading: Hughes 1987; Oates 1991

FISCAL POLICY

The stance of government in its spending and taxing policy. Associated with this policy is **debt** policy, the consequence of not raising enough revenue over time so that a government has to borrow.

As virtually all governments need tax revenues to finance what they choose as their functions, they have to make many fiscal decisions. There is the issue of the total tax burden − what proportion of national income a government wants to tax − either a low amount to encourage enterprise or a high amount to achieve a large welfare programme including income redistribution. Also it has to be decided what type of tax to use to raise revenue. The choice between raising revenue through direct, mainly income, taxes and indirect taxes on sales, goods and value-added will have crucial consequences for how much people work and spend their incomes. A fiscal policy will be neutral if it does not affect the consumption of one group more than another.

Fiscal policy will be different in times of war and peace. The task of financing armed forces and their equipment is so large during a war that there is a temptation to accumulate debt rather than pay for the increased expenditure through an equal amount of tax revenue. In times of peace the scope for pursuing social goals through fiscal policy will be limited if much has to be spent on servicing government debt. Fiscal policy in peacetime can be used to stabilise a **national economy**, taxing less and spending more during a downturn and doing the reverse in times of prosperity to balance the public finances over a cycle. An automatic stabiliser is a built-in feature of a tax system in order that changes in income are dampened down; for example, with a progressive income tax, post-tax income available for spending will rise slower than pre-tax income. If changes in taxes do not compensate for inflation then there will be 'fiscal drag'.

See also: **taxation**

Further reading: Peacock and Shaw 1971

FIX PRICE, FLEX PRICE

The contrast in speed of adjustment of various prices.

Fixed rigid prices can affect, or even prevent, the movement of a **market** to **equilibrium**. In Keynes' *General Theory of Employment, Interest and Money* it was assumed that money wage rates were inflexible downwards and that there was a minimum to the rate of interest because of the operation of the speculative demand for money. Myrdal in *Monetary Equilibrium* considers the relationship between the price stability condition for equilibrium and the degree of flexibility of prices. In Marshall's *Principles of Economics* the working of flexi-price markets is described.

The extent of flexibility has a mixture of determinants. In the labour market statutory provisions such as minimum wage laws and employment contracts prevent the rapid change of wages to market conditions. In capital markets the rate of interest has often been regulated under usury laws. In product markets prices can be fixed for a long time, either because of a firm's reluctance to alienate customers by altering prices, the cost of making catalogue changes, or the insistence of a government under a prices policy to change prices only in accordance with a set formula.

Further reading: Backhouse 1980; Hicks 1965

FREEDOM

The absence of restraint; the ability to do something. These two concepts of liberty were expounded by the philosopher Isaiah Berlin in a book with that title.

Economic freedom, the freedom to own property, run businesses and fix **prices**, is a basis of political freedom. Free enterprise is business in the private sector operating without state ownership and control. Without such economic independence it is impossible to have a free press and to finance political parties. Freedom to perform a range of actions does require resources, but if the resourceless are provided with means by the state they are limited by state policies and at any time could be destitute again.

Free trade means the absence of physical and financial barriers to the movement of goods and services; a freeport operates without such penalties too. To say that something is free is to recognise that its price is zero. Given scarcity, nothing is 'free', as every use has its opportunity cost: there is no such thing as a free lunch. A person who does not pay for a benefit is known as a free rider, for example, a worker who is not a member of a trade union but accepts the pay increases negotiated by the union. Non-union **labour**, often used to break strikes, is called free labour.

To a large extent, the Physiocrats in their reaction against mercantilism and in their doctrine of **laissez-faire**, and Adam Smith in his system of natural liberty, regarded the free economy as one which operated with little government activity to blunt the activity of an exchange economy.

See also: **Austrian economics**; **libertarian economics**

Further reading: Berlin 2002; Friedman and Friedman 1980; Peacock 1997

GAME THEORY

A study of decision making, including strategic behaviour, primarily to explain microeconomic behaviour. Although used in many social sciences, including psephology and defence studies, it has increasingly been employed in industrial organisation, labour and other branches of economics.

Neumann and Morgenstern attempted to apply a mathematical theory of games to fundamental economic problems, including rational behaviour, social exchange, competition and **utility** maximisation. They contrasted the maximisation of an isolated person such as Robinson Crusoe with an economy with many participants. They set out to devise a set of rules for rational economic behaviour suitable for all situations.

Although game theory is now conducted according to strict rules of mathematics and logic, there are earlier discussions of making strategic decisions presented in a literary way, as in Plato's *Symposium* and Hobbes' *Leviathan*. In them is the fundamental concern of the game theorist, the analysis of interdependent rational behaviour.

In the application of game theory to economics, the paramount concern is the examination of rational economic agents desiring to maximise their utility according to their preferences. Specific terms abound to analyse games. The agents are called *players*. The choice faced is between at least two *strategies*.

A game theorist begins with a statement of the identities of the players, their interests and the information available to them and a statement of the rules. A 'game' can involve several persons and consist of coalitions with rules for compensation. The gains might sum to zero for the players so any personal gain is at the expense of another participant, or result in an overall loss or gain. Games can be for entertainment or, more seriously, for the allocation of scarce resources.

Games are broadly divided into those which are cooperative and the more commonly non-cooperative games. Games can have *perfect information*, meaning that everything that has happened in the game to date is known to the player: if there is ignorance of the other player, the game has *imperfect information*. In economics most of the **information** is private to the player and unknown to the other players, excepting in perfect competition. There can be *simultaneous move* or *sequential move* games. The outcome of a choice to a player is measured in units of utility and called a *payoff*. The payoffs to the players can be presented in a matrix, with one player represented by the rows and other down the columns in a two-player game. These are *normal form* or *strategic form* games. Instead of a matrix there can be a *game tree* to produce an *extensive form* game which shows different choices branching out as lines from nodes. These *nodes*, the points joining the lines, can be *initial* to represent the first action, or *terminal* for the outcome. The nodes and branches coming from a single node are known as a *sub-game*. If a player takes an action but fails to execute it so the game proceeds down another path, there is a *trembling hand*. If there is a single optimal course of action then there is a *pure strategy*, but if several a *mixed strategy*. In making strategic moves the player can influence the other by commitment, which reduces the number of choices, threats or promises.

Economists use game theory to discover equilibria, stable states endogenous to a system. The most common **equilibrium** is the Nash equilibrium, which is a solution for zero-sum games where one player can only gain at the expense of the other. Where there is a non-zero game, there can be more than one Nash equilibrium. If one of the equilibria is removed in the solution, then there is a *refinement* to the Nash equilibrium. A *sub-game perfect equilibrium* occurs where there is a Nash equilibrium for the whole game and all sub-games. Nash took game theory into an important new phase in his study of non-cooperative games. Under Nash bargaining in a two-person game, a solution is produced in which a unique pair of utility levels is assigned to each bargaining solution. When equilibrium is reached no player has an incentive to depart from a chosen strategy. Nash generalised his results to include cooperative games.

Popular games have long had the same names. The most famous is the 'prisoners' dilemma', concerning whether it is better for each prisoner to confess or not confess. By cooperating, the two prisoners in a joint confession can maximise the outcome. Many special games have entered the literature. In the 'tit-for-tat' game there is cooperation in the first round but afterwards each player copies the action of the opponent in the previous round.

An obvious application in the economics of games is the study of pricing under the different market conditions of duopoly and oligopoly, where there are few players and strategy is crucial. Game theory is also important in public policy analysis and the study of environment systems.

Inevitably there are critics of game theory. It is noted that it is not essentially economic in content and makes uncomfortable assumptions of measurable utility and crude maximising behaviour. Rubinstein, considering the rhetoric of game theory, questions the applicability of the theory to devising actual strategies. The game is affected by the nature of the payoff, a utility number being different from an amount of money. The notion of strategy, central to game theory, is more than a plan of action as it requires assumptions about rivals' plans. Nash bargaining by using numbers wrongly suggests that it can generate quantitative results. Also the assumptions underlying the idea of a solution to a game are not clear.

See also: **competition and monopoly**; **neoclassical economics**

Further reading: Binmore 1992; Kreps 1990; Neumann and Morgenstern 1947; Osborne 2004; Rubinstein 2000

GLOBALISATION

The process of integrating the world economy through the trading of goods and services and flows of **labour** and capital.

As early as the time of the Roman empire 2,000 years ago, there was an extensive network of trade. The pace of globalisation increased in the nineteenth century through improvements in transport. With the expansion of **multinational corporations**, successors to the earlier mercantilist companies such as the English East India Company, a late stage of globalisation in which there was an international **division of labour** within companies effected by the creation of subsidiaries with different tasks. The internet has been a further force transcending national economic boundaries. Trade leads to **investment** flows, a greater number of economic connections between countries, then finally economic integration.

Globalisation requires a world infrastructure and peace in a substantial part of the world. It was because there was a Pax Romana that early exercises in globalisation occurred; the Pax Americana in recent decades has similarly facilitated the movement towards an integrated world economy and polity. Advances in transport technology and reductions in the cost of travel have allowed product and factor flows to quicken.

Globalisation transcends national boundaries and has the potential to frustrate national economic policy goals. This is especially acute in matters of **taxation** and employment. Some countries have high tax regimes so will be avoided by overseas investors. Also employment laws grant more rights to workers and their trade unions in one country than another. The tendency of globalisation is to locate economic activity where it is most beneficial, so national governments can face the prospect of becoming more and more closed economies if they do not produce a congenial business environment.

Opponents of globalisation fear that it spells the end to diversity. In particular, Americanisation through American management methods and the consumption of American products, especially food and drink, is seen as a threat to local production and culture. There is a convergence in economic systems with trade liberalisation and pro-market running of economies promoted. There is a fundamental collision between nationalism and globalisation. Whereas a nation state can devise laws and regulate its citizens, there is a potential for lawlessness in the global economy as the United Nations falls short of being a world government. Those suspicious of the business corporation fear there is no democratic control over powerful global forces. A new disorder has been created, a runaway world. Proponents of globalisation argue that the creation of an integrated world economy both helps poor countries as world specialisation raises **productivity**, and growth of incomes and trade. More prosperity also increases the possibility of transfers from the rich to the poor.

Globalisation is often related to empire building, as in the theory of imperialism advanced by Marxists, which attempts to explain why a country expands its economic activities across the globe. Because, it is asserted, there is a tendency for the rate of **profit** to fall, firms can only maintain their profits by overseas expansion. This is especially so with a firm that has originally maintained its profits by its monopoly position. Once the monopoly is weakened it is only by conquering new markets that the domestic competitive threat can be escaped.

Globalisation seems to be irreversible, for to try to turn back the clock would be, as in past cases of the adoption of protectionism, to lead to more costly production and less consumer choice. It is hard to forecast how far globalisation can go, as factor immobilities and stubborn consumer and political preferences can thwart a shift to an homogenised world.

See also: **development economics**

Further reading: Bhagwati 2004; Jones 1995

HAPPINESS

An examination of the sources of well-being and its relationship with economic activity.

There are three important approaches to studying happiness – the utilitarian, the socialist and the econometric. Early exponents of the utilitarian were Francis Hutcheson, who used the term 'the greatest happiness for the greatest number', and Jeremy Bentham,

who repeated the expression as part of a calculus of pain and pleasure. Out of this WS Jevons formulated his theory of exchange. The
second strand, the socialist, is evident in the titles of several early
nineteenth-century socialist books, such as John Gray's *A Lecture on
Human Happiness* (1825). Happiness would come through workers
getting the product of their labour, needing to work fewer hours to
obtain a reasonable livelihood. More recently, happiness has been
studied by the correlation of economic and psychological variables in
the third, econometric form of analysis.

Modern quantitative studies implicitly assert that greater income
and wealth produce greater well-being. The rich have more access to
education, health care, housing, travel and entertainment, which are
either ends in themselves or routes to personal satisfaction. Antago-
nists of this view can point to the well publicised cases of the bore-
dom and misery of the rich, especially their increasing withdrawal
from society into high-walled compounds, demonstrating that their
wealth has bought them loneliness. Surveys of levels of satisfaction in
different countries are linked to data on aggregate economic variables
such as GDP. Measures of unhappiness include the number of sui-
cides. Happiness functions are not necessarily continuous, especially
where increasing income is accompanied by more happiness only up
to a particular income level.

Economic studies of happiness have relevance in many parts of
economics. In **labour** economics the human condition cannot be
ignored, so satisfaction and happiness are related to types of wage
remuneration and industrial conflict. Throughout economic policy
making the goal is often the increased happiness of individuals, as in
democratic societies policy choice does influence the prospect of
being re-elected. Any analysis of decision making ignores happiness,
satisfaction and **utility** at its peril. Studying happiness is important in
explaining economic behaviour. The quality of work, the nature of
consumption and the choice of investments will all be conditioned by
happiness received or expected.

Happiness is considered as the aggregation of individuals' satisfactions, but there is the earlier idea of a state as a whole making a gain
or a loss. The early mercantilists viewed the goal of a state as being
better off than its rivals through trading so successfully as to build up
a large store of bullion. Other mercantilists wanted a nation to have
high levels of employment and personal welfare, anticipating modern
attitudes to this question.

Just as the concept of the GDP as a measure of **economic welfare**
has long been questioned, so has the idea of thinking of happiness as

having material determinants been severely scrutinised. Perhaps material welfare can be at most regarded as a necessary condition. Alfred Marshall, writing in his *Principles of Economics* in 1890, observed that the poor could derive the highest happiness from religion, family relationships and friends, but that grinding poverty would dull those pleasures.

Much of the debate about happiness is centred on what it is. Avoiding the extreme view of Jonathan Swift in *A Tale of a Tub* – that happiness is the state of being well deceived – many questions can be asked. Is happiness a commodity or a piece of property which can be bought and sold? Is it an outcome of resource allocation? Is it a state of satisfaction which is induced by drugs, wealth or leisure? Is happiness a subjective feeling, or a state of blessedness? Is it the product of **altruism** through happiness arising from absorption in an outside goal, or the pursuit of the welfare of others, or in promoting fairness? Is happiness associated with one type of personality rather than another? If the amount of happiness is a product of family, finances, work, friends, health, or personal freedom, can it be accurately predicted? Is it age-related so that happiness is related to the life cycle? Is happiness, like misery, an aberration from a long-term trend?

The controversies over the nature of happiness can perhaps be resolved by settling on the idea of 'well-being'. This is a dynamic concept which recognises the flourishing of individuals within a society. It avoids excessive individualism and has the dynamic of considering more than the moment by building the possibility of growth and improvement, which takes one back to Aristotle. Well-being is often distinguished from growth of GDP in that it embraces non-material rewards.

There is a loose identity between utility or subjective satisfaction and happiness in economics, but happiness is a broader concept. There can be such a thing as a happy society characterised by harmony, low crime, the existence of much **social capital**, fair **income distribution** and a good standard of income and health. Given the complexity of 'happiness', to seek it is more than to follow the principle of utility maximisation.

Robert Barro in the 1970s also created a 'misery index', which is the sum of the rates of unemployment and of inflation in percentage terms: when both are high stagflation occurs.

See also: **economic welfare**; **ethics and economics**; **utility**; **wealth**

Further reading: Bruni 2004; Easterlin 2001; Frey and Stutzer 2002; Ng 1978; Oswald 1997

HEALTH ECONOMICS

The study of the health care industry.

The industry has a large range of products both in the form of public health and personal health care. Public health measures include health education, which will reduce later the demand for health care, and protection of the public against epidemics and contamination from poor quality food and unsafe working conditions. Governments also have an important role in licensing health professionals and drugs. Personal health care consists of all those interventions, whether surgical, medical or therapeutic, chosen to deal with a particular disease, injury or other debilitating condition. Health systems differ from country to country according to the structure of production. There can be state-provided hospitals and clinics, facilities offered by commercial firms or charities. It is usual for there to be a mixture of ownership. All these types of provider will operate according to different principles, whether meeting need as decided by government with state medicine, making a profit through private production, or furthering a welfare goal set by a charity either concerned generally with helping the sick or dealing with a particular type of medical problem.

Supplying health care has parallels with production in other industries. It can be offered according to the principle of a state monopoly which reflects the tastes and priorities of government, or in response to the demand of potential patients in an open market. An unusual feature of this industry is the interaction of supply and demand, as the suppliers literally create their own demand by telling ignorant consumers what they need in treatment. The financing and delivery of health care have also given rise to much discussion. The provision of health care in countries such as the UK through a publicly run and financial service based on rationing has been criticised. Given this dissatisfaction with the efficiency of state-run health services, attempts have been made to simulate the market by having 'internal markets' in which parts of the massive organisation act as providers competing to satisfy other parts of the system. This requires careful costing and contracting.

Health care is labour intensive, and the labour force is highly skilled with many specialisms. Where doctors have little control over the allocation of their time, conflict with administrators can be great. As health care increasingly uses new types of equipment and more and more new pharmaceutical products, there is a constant struggle in the allocation of funds between spending on one input rather than the other. Because the pharmaceutical industry is research intensive, new drugs are frequently introduced to the **market**: these are initially expensive through their patent protection and the need to have high prices to recoup research costs.

Demand for personal health care grows rapidly. As per capita incomes rise, the demand for basic health care rises. At higher levels of income, demand moves from health necessities to stop acute pain and ensure survival to dealing with less urgent conditions, including allergies and psychiatric conditions, and lifestyle enhancement such as cosmetic surgery. Furthermore, much demand is unpredictable because of the occurrence of accidents and impact of viruses. This massive increase in demand, if delivered in treatment, needs financing. The ways of doing so include general **taxation**, hypothecated taxation, direct charging to the patient, or charging through a health insurance company. As with the provision of health care itself, the financing of it comes usually through a mixture of these channels of finance.

The provision of preventive and curative care is surrounded by emotive issues which make many argue that health care is a special case, a matter of life and death, so should be supplied differently from other goods and services, even freely. There is the assumption that health care is a 'good', but it can lead to a deterioration in health. Also there is the popular notion that a country has more health care if it devotes a greater percentage of its GDP to health care than other countries, but it might merely have a different wage structure, with health care workers relatively better off.

Further reading: Jones 2006; Sorkin 1975

HOLISM

The tendency of organisms to produce wholes greater than the sum of their parts, according to JC Smuts; a cooperative approach to economic organisation which rejects atomistic competition.

An early advocate of the holistic approach was Veblen, a founder of the US school of **institutional economics**. Unlike the partial **equilibrium** approach of **neoclassical economics**, holism sees each part of an economic system conditioned by the economic system as a whole. Individual entities are influenced by interrelationships of the whole system, thus collectivism is preferred to individualism. Economists such as Keynes have claimed that their theories are 'general', based on the relationships between economic aggregates, with varying degrees of success. Later, macroeconomics, which sought out its microeconomic foundations, had the flavour of holism. Also economic behaviour has to be viewed as an aspect of human behaviour as a whole, an echo of the concerns of eighteenth-century economics. Holism enables economics to be linked with the other social sciences, especially sociology.

Causal holism abandons the economic methodology of producing elegant models with predictive power in favour of description with many explanations. Instead of simple specific inputs leading to specific outputs, an output is the product of the system as a whole.

Further reading: Fleetwood 2002; Polanyi 1944

HOMO ECONOMICUS

An economic agent determined to maximise material gain.

As part of the Enlightenment project, economics was regarded as part of the study of human nature and 'economic man' became prominent. Adam Smith in his *Wealth of Nations* argued that the fundamental human propensity is to truck and barter. This makes possible an exchange economy, but this market activity is to advance one's own interest. This self-interested behaviour of a rationalising economic person is heavily criticised as it is wrongly thought that to be self-interested is the same as being selfish. The Biblical commandment 'to love your neighbour as yourself' suggests the importance of pursuing one's own advantage as the basis for being other-directed. Also it is in a person's interest to be productive and create **wealth** – distribution is another issue. Smith asserted that the desire for betterment is possessed from the cradle to the grave and is the driving force behind economic growth. In the **invisible hand** principle, the beneficial consequences of self-interest are stated. The asocial individualism of the economic man brings benefits.

In **neoclassical economics** the homo economicus with **utility** functions and goals seeks to maximise satisfaction, often only in the short term. Seeking the most cost-effective way of achieving one's ends is regarded as a form of instrumental rationality. The idea of economic agents as rational and engaged in maximising their utility has been attacked because of doubts about rationality and an awareness of the subtlety of economic motivation.

Further reading: Grampp 1948; Oakley 1994

HOUSEHOLD BEHAVIOUR

The actions of members of a household as suppliers of labour and savings and consumers of goods and services produced outside the household. This branch of economics makes use of **neoclassical economic** theory, feminist economics, the **economics of the family**, labour economics and **consumption** theory.

A starting point for the analysis of households is to consider them as bundles of assets or bundles of activities. The assets of a household are its holding of financial claims, physical wealth in the form of housing and other objects, and human capital. The stock of assets will be determinants of the health, education and business and labour force participation of the members of that household. The activities conducted by households collectively or individually by their members can be broadly divided into work or leisure. The work can be employment or self-employment. Neoclassical analysis considers the goals and production functions of households. In economic terms a household attempts to maximise its income from its resources, many of which are in the form of **human capital**. The activities can either be for the sake of the household itself or given to or traded with the outside world. What is own production for the sake of the household often escapes national income accounts.

It is important to ask if a household is just a special type of **firm** which combines residence with workplace, workers and dependants. If this line of conceptualisation is taken then questions of the initial financing of the household, its size and optimisation or other aims, are important. There are limits to the analogy, as few households can be regarded merely or predominantly as productive units.

A household has many choices to make, including whether to engage in market or non-market production, work or leisure, and criminal or legitimate pursuits. It must have an income which can come from work, gifts, welfare payments or theft. **Market** activity will be encouraged by the amount of remuneration proposed. For some occupations the labour supply will be inelastic with respect to the wage rate, as no other source of income is possible, but this is an extreme case. The attraction of market work will be different for the principal earner of the family than for the others. Non-market production in the form of housework is often undertaken because of the high cost of hiring cleaners, childminders, gardeners, decorators and drivers. Living off gifts is a way of life open to only a small proportion of the population, given the distribution of wealth. Welfare payment distribution is decided by social policy and in some depressed areas can be the major source of household income for many families. Criminal activity in the form of property offences has been much studied. There is a cost to individuals of such behaviour – getting caught so losing the chance of earning and acquiring a bad reputation – but a gain from acquiring valuable goods, often devalued by the low prices criminal fences will pay.

The study of labour force participation raises the question of why men, women and children look for work and become employed. These studies begin with an examination of the trade-off between work and leisure. Many important determinants have been identified, including the length of a person's education. Women have increased their participation, especially since 1960, and male participation has declined.

Paradoxically, the growth of macroeconomics from the 1930s triggered research into household behaviour which is substantially microeconomic. To understand effective demand its components had to be analysed, which began research into consumption. Aggregate **economic growth** is related to savings ratios, so savings requires special attention too. The consumption of households is offset against that of firms and governments. In the case of households there is more scope for the examination of psychological motives. All three institutions will be affected by their incomes, by interest rates and by expectations.

The economics of household behaviour is not to be confused with the practical subject of home economics, domestic science, which is concerned with the techniques of household production, cooking, cleaning and rearing children. There is some overlap between household economics and feminist economics, as the latter is concerned with the management of time and labour force participation.

Economics began as *oeconomica* in the writings of Greeks such as Aristotle and Xenophon. The view that *oeconomica* was concerned with household management was contrasted with *chrematistike*, the art of wealth-getting. Much economic activity occurred in those ancient households, both agricultural and manufacturing. Xenophon in his *Oeconomica* observed that men were engaged in wealth gaining but women in household management, perhaps the first gender analysis of occupations.

See also: **family, economics of**

Further reading: Kooreman and Wunderink 1997

HUMAN CAPITAL

The value of human beings as assets producing a stream of income. Through **investment** in education there is a private return to the educated person, as well as a social return as society benefits through the population being rational and cultured.

The earliest application of this capital notion was to slaves. It was common in Ancient Greece to list slaves in an inventory of possessions, and even friends could be included because they can be used. Later the appreciation of human beings as labour crucial to the productive process led to attempts to value human capital. One of the earliest measurers of human capital was Petty, who applied the technique of valuing land as so many years' purchase to valuing the population. A later economist to attempt human capital calculations was JS Nicholson. More recently Schultz produced estimates. Human capital is both an embodiment of natural ability and education: it is mainly the latter which is calculated, so either the cost of education or the present value of extra lifetime income through schooling is used. Usually human capital is now measured using cross-section data on occupational pay or financial data from educational institutions. The latter approach selects formal education as the principal element in creating human capital so the number of years of schooling times the average cost per year is calculated.

Both Cantillon and Smith recognised that the cost of education could be a reason for wage differentials. A rational person or parent would only pay for education if it would enhance a person's prospects in life. Human capital studies are used to justify investment in education. The private return to education stimulates enrolment in educational institutions; the social return persuades governments to subsidise it. However, such a policy can be self-defeating. There can only be a private return to human capital investment if educated people have differentially higher incomes. Educating more people increases the supply of persons available for better paid jobs, thus reducing the income differential and destroying the private return.

Decisions to invest in human capital can be taken by various persons. Parents are major investors where school and university education is privately financed. In advanced countries where the state provides free education, the amount and type of policy will be determined by the goals of education policy. But state provision of education can lead to the state's assertion of the right to keep the human capital it has created within the country, as was proposed to stop the brain drain by limiting the emigration of graduates, as happened in Soviet-type economies. **Firms** pay for training. This can be general or specific. General training will be of use in many firms (for example, word processing), so a single firm will be reluctant to finance the teaching of a transferable skill which can be used elsewhere, and will leave education to local colleges. Specific training, for example in the internal accounting procedures of a large firm, will be of exclusive use to that firm and hence more likely to be financed by it.

To concentrate on education as a creator of human capital is controversial, as there are other determinants of personal income, including inherited ability, the social environment and general health.

To regard persons as capital might be considered a degraded view of human nature. On the other hand, to assert that humans are valuable will discourage activities which depreciate the human capital stock, for example, expecting workers to be employed in an unhealthy environment for an excessive number of hours.

See also: **capital theory**; **labour**

Further reading: Becker 1964; Blaug 1975; Kiker 1974; Schultz 1971, 1972

IMPOSSIBILITY THEOREM

The problem under democracy of more than two individuals faced with several options making consistent choices when their preferences are different; also known as the general possibility theorem.

Arrow stated this problem of collective choice as that occurring when more than two choosers confronted by at least three possibilities seek a collective order which corresponds to all the individual orders of preference. It is impossible to achieve this as several conditions have to be met: a transitive ranking of preferences, the independence of irrelevant alternatives, the non-imposition of x above y in the collective order, and the non-dictatorship of any chooser in that no individual has the same preferences as the collective order. As there could be no satisfaction of these conditions, Arrow asserted that it was impossible to have a social welfare function. This impossibility of making a consistent choice is also called the paradox of voting.

This problem of aggregation of individual preferences into a social choice function is widely discussed throughout the social sciences, including international relations. The cases where the majority view solves the problem is distinguished from those where it does not. This formalisation of social choice is criticised for its assumptions, including that there is a transitive ranking of options independent of excluded possible options. The theorem refers to a particular social welfare function so has a limited role in **welfare economics**. To apply this type of decision making to democratic choice is difficult as voters lack the information to see what the different options actually are, and the world is more dynamic than Arrow assumes. Tullock examined the interdependence of the preference structures of individuals, and concluded that under majority voting a determinate and satisfactory outcome is usually achieved.

Further reading: Arrow 1950, 1962; Tullock 1967b

INCENTIVES

Inducements to make an economic agent perform, especially to work or to save and invest.

All factors of production have their minimum supply price; otherwise a factor would not enter, or remain, in a particular occupation. Workers need at least subsistence wages otherwise they would lack the strength to work and ultimately to survive. If capital does not receive a return comparable with alternative investments and enough to cover risk, it will not be supplied. **Rent** has to cover the incidents of ownership, especially maintaining secure possession. These are the basic incentives which ensure only the low-level functioning of an economy.

Incentive mechanisms also aim to improve performance, as when they are employed to encourage increased productivity. In wage systems premium pay, bonuses and share or stock options are designed to encourage greater effort. At the heart of the principal-agent problem is the devising by contract, or otherwise, of a mechanism to ensure the principal reaches desired objectives. Also either the principal or agent can have private **information**, which raises questions of moral hazard.

The extremes of poverty and the prospect of bettering one's condition induce greater performance. A barren or devastated area will provide a strong push to a population to emigrate. The chance of a better life is a major motivating factor. Smith, in his growth model, asserted that a desire for betterment which we have from the cradle to the grave will encourage saving and investment, setting a national economy on a growth trajectory. Hume argued that manufactures could be an incentive encouraging higher **productivity** in agriculture as farmers would have to work harder to buy them.

As **taxation**, especially income taxes, reduces post-tax income it threatens work incentives. A disincentive can be produced by high marginal rates of income tax as the net reward to supplying more hours of work can be unattractive to workers. But such tax rates could also be an incentive to workers with a post-tax income goal who will have to work harder if tax rates rise.

Apart from monetary gain, other benefits can incite greater activity. The charity worker with altruistic motives, the loving parent, the loyal friend will not expect a measurable reward. Even for employees in the traditional firm some incentives are non-monetary, especially through collectively provided agreeable working conditions in pleasant workplaces with flexibility of hours and management.

Incentives are usually regarded as positive in the form of a reward, but they can also be negative, as when there is punishment such as withholding resources until compliance is met, or criminal sanctions to desist in one activity to promote another – for example, to preserve an area as rural by penalising the builders. The most questionable form of incentive is an inducement to influence a member of a government to change an economic policy. This can be **corruption** or financial help for an associated activity.

See also: **labour**; **migration and mobility**; **taxation**

Further reading: Merrett 1968

INCOME DISTRIBUTION

The array of incomes within a national economy.

Different types of distribution include the factor distribution of incomes between land, labour and capital, and the personal distribution between groups in different bands of income. Changes in demand and supply, the durability of custom and the welfare policies of governments will be principally responsible for the differences in the incomes of individuals and households.

Factor distribution of income between land, **labour** and capital, especially 'labour's share', is quite stable over time, with over 60 per cent of **national income** going to labour in wages and salaries and the rest to **profit**, interest and **rent**. The distribution of incomes between and within occupations reflects the bargaining power of each group and the hierarchical and other reasons for differences in pay. Personal incomes are the consequence of labour market activity, ownership of income producing assets and **transfer incomes**.

Measures of inequality applied to income distributions include Lorenz curves, Gini coefficients and an examination of deciles and quartiles. These measures are the triggers for redistributive policies, especially fiscal changes. The shape of the income distribution reflects certain basic ideas – that labour should be rewarded for its work, that more difficult and skilled work should command higher remuneration, that owners of capital should be paid for its use and that the poor should get some help but not enough to be a disincentive to work. Income redistribution can be attempted at the pre- or post-tax income levels. If the former, there have to be rules for wage differentials and for capital ownership; if the latter, taxes, especially direct taxes, have to be high enough and progressive to effect a switch of income from the rich to the poor.

See also: **equality**

Further reading: Atkinson 1975

INCOMES POLICY

A set of government measures to restrain the growth of incomes, especially wages, in times of **inflation**; a macroeconomic policy to supplement monetary and fiscal policies.

In several economies, including the Netherlands, Sweden, the UK and the USA, this type of policy was employed, often as a short-term crisis measure. The policy could be addressed to annual pay increases, the wage bill as a whole, or all types of income, including dividends. A target for income growth was usually set: a popular percentage was the trend growth in **productivity** so that income increases would be financed by comparable output growth. To accommodate particular strains in the labour market threatening to defeat the policy, it usually allowed exceptional cases justifying higher than the norm increases, especially labour shortages, pay out of line with comparable groups and unusually low pay. To administer the policy and to vet claims for exceptional increases special institutions, especially pay boards, were set up. Sometimes an incomes policy was used in conjunction with a **prices** policy which monitored increases in product prices.

It was difficult to have an incomes policy as a permanent measure because of its conflict with the market determination of incomes. Employers short of labour in particular occupations and areas had every incentive to bypass the policy guidelines. Jobs would be upgraded or non-wage remuneration increased. Unions resented being presented with permitted maxima for pay increases and tried to exceed the target to impress their members. The benefit in the long term bequeathed by such policies was an education in the implications of pay rising too high. Also in some industries bad labour practices were bought out through permitting exceptional pay increases: this improved productivity for many years.

See also: **labour**

Further reading: Corina 1966; Fels 1972

INDUSTRIAL ORGANISATION

The study of the structure of industries, including the number and size of **firms** within them; a study of firms' behaviour in markets.

This analysis of industries is crucial to formulating and implementing competition policy, especially the US federal antitrust policy since 1890 under the Sherman, Clayton and subsequent acts. Industrial organisation (IO) does much to explain the nature of markets and the behaviour within them. As in other branches of economics, static, dynamic and evolutionary approaches can be employed.

A basic approach is to consider the extent of concentration of output, sales or employment in the hands of the leading firms of an industry, taking into account changing consumer tastes and technology. An industrial structure often emerges by changes in demand over time but it can also be devised as part of a planning process, an ideal structure would also have to recognise market changes. Depending on the extent to which an industry is monopolistic or competitive, different pricing methods and investment decision making will ensue.

The 'structure-conduct-performance' model roots the behaviour and success of firms in the structural nature of an industry. Under structure, attention is paid to barriers to entry, how much product branding is used and the absolute or relative concentration of firms. Production and pricing decisions of firms are examined under conduct. **Profits**, **efficiency**, **innovation** and the creation of jobs are the performance.

Inevitably such studies have sociological implications. How firms are organised and managed will determine attitudes of workers and of politicians governing a society. The impact on productivity of different forms of organisation is considerable.

Game theory has formalised this branch of economics, showing the strategic interactions between firms, especially in the cases of duopoly and oligopoly. Instead of having simple models based on firms motivated only by profit maximisation, a formal analysis of the broader behaviour of firms is possible. The empirical study of industrial organisation includes demand estimation, mergers, advertising and auctions. Institutional economists also look at the corporate system, the relationship between public and private sectors, the degree of centralisation in an economy and the consequences of industrial concentration. Industrial organisation is at the interface between economics and management science, entering into detailed studies of price discrimination, product branding, the markets for different types of good and the conditions determining the entry and exit of firms from particular activities and markets.

See also: **competition and monopoly**; **economic concentration**

Further reading: Aoki 1984; George *et al.* 1992; Needham 1978; Shubik with Levitan 1980

INDUSTRIAL RELATIONS

An examination of employers' organisations, **trade unions** and their mutual interchange in the course of work and in the negotiation of pay.

Industrial relations constitute a 'system' in that a set of rules is devised to regularise relationships between employers and workers. The rules are complex, as they arise through legislation, labour contracts and various customs and understandings. Some of these are expressed formally in documents; others are part of an oral tradition.

This branch of **labour** economics is necessary because of the imperfections in the principal institutions of the labour market and the many signs of friction. Unions, in particular, are criticised if they are too numerous or have overlapping jurisdictions leading to a competition for members. Employers' associations are rebuked for having few sanctions to keep their members in line.

Friction in an industrial relations system is manifest in strikes and other forms of industrial unrest which occasion either complete cessation of work or a reduction in workers' effort. Although most strikes are in connection with pay disputes, some strikes are the inevitable consequence of a lack of clarity in the rules in the system. The most powerful route to reforming a system is a new comprehensive statute, but it will only improve matters if it commands general assent from both sides of industry.

Included in industrial relations are systems of arbitration to reconcile conflicts between capital and labour. One type of arbitration is pendulum arbitration, under which the arbitrator either has to accept the employer offer or the union demand: as each side wants to win there is an incentive to be moderate.

See also: **game theory**; **labour**; **trade (labor) union**

Further reading: Clegg 1976; Hyman 1975

INFLATION

The persistent rise in the price level of an economy.

A monetary phenomenon which is usually measured by a change in the level of a consumer or retail **price index**. The rate of inflation is central to determining wages and interest rates. When the price increase reaches very high rates, even hundreds or thousands, as in Germany in the 1920s and recently in South America and Africa, this rise is called 'hyperinflation'. Such out-of-control inflation will make **money** lose its store of value function and serve as a medium of exchange only briefly. 'Inflationists', such as Hume or Thornton, however, recommended a short-term expansion in the money supply to increase output and encourage the employment of unused capacity.

Inflation has been classified according to its cause. Demand inflation is the consequence of excess demand in the economy as a whole, usually starting in the labour market and being transmitted to product markets. **Cost** inflation occurs when there is an increase in the price index in the absence of excess demand, often through trade union militancy or an increase in the cost of imports.

The Phillips curve originally plotted wage rate data against unemployment percentages (a proxy measure of macroeconomic demand). Further studies of this relationship separated short- from long-term curves, with the latter being vertical at the natural rate of **unemployment**. NAIRU is the non-accelerating inflation rate of unemployment.

Stagflation is the unpleasant combination of rising prices and stagnation in a national economy. Often inflation is the consequence of rising demand, but it can also occur when a stagnant economy suffers cost-push inflation through high import prices, as when oil prices rose in the 1970s, or trade union militancy.

See also: **price index**

Further reading: Jackman *et al.* 1981

INFORMAL ECONOMY

The set of economic activities not recorded in official statistics; the black or unofficial economy.

Criminal activities such as property thefts, drug dealing and prostitution would be outside the published figures, but a host of other activities also disappear statistically. To avoid **taxation** much ordinary economic activity, especially in construction and personal services, is kept from tax collectors' eyes. Another important reason for the non-recording of economic activity is the failure of some forms of production to be marketed, for example, subsistence agriculture and suburban gardening. Often statistics on the output of the smallest enterprises are not collected to reduce the cost of data collection.

Because the **national income** is measured by income, output and expenditure methods it is possible to see discrepancies between expenditure and income: if the latter is smaller than expenditure then income could be hidden. Direct inspections of assets by tax authorities can lead to investigations into the sources of persons' incomes. Also a change in the composition of the money supply, with more of it consisting of cash to meet changing demand, can indicate the growth of the informal economy.

An informal economy can be an economy at its earliest and most primitive stage before there has been extensive monetisation. Early economies with much self-sufficient agriculture have a small proportion of production passing through markets so most output is not directly measured. In these countries population and average consumption have to be multiplied together to estimate their own production.

The extent of an informal economy is a function of the degree of **regulation** of an economy. Where there is tight bureaucratic control there is an incentive to evade the eyes of inspectors but not always the means, thus reducing the chance of an informal economy.

See also: **corruption**; **national income**

Further reading: Schneider 2002

INFORMATION

The influence on the behaviour of economic agents of the data they possess; the study of the **market** for information.

Every component of economics is concerned with information because the markets, and their substitutes, have varying degrees of knowledge of what is actually the state of affairs. This is especially true of labour and financial markets.

Under perfect competition there is the assumption of perfect knowledge. This does not mean full information on the past and the future but sufficient information for firms to make decisions about entering and leaving a market. Classical economists were aware of information deficiencies. De Quincey, for example, questioned whether the 'competition of capitals', the increasing number of capitalists entering a profitable industry, would lead to a fall in the rate of profit: in his *Logic of Political Economy*, chapter V, he admits that individual tradesmen can be ignorant even of their own profits.

Problems arise because information is rarely complete and costless. Much information is kept private by economic agents to their own benefit. Some information is obtained at high, some at low, cost. The **cost** of searching for information is expected to have a return which will recoup the cost – for example, the search for a job will result in a higher income. There is the cost of collection and processing before information can be useful. Information can be deliberately generated or the incidental by-product of the working of markets. It is acquired differently according to the nature of the economic system. Under central planning, reports and surveys will attempt to establish the expected output and demands of the various sectors of the economy, then material balances will be drawn up to see if adjustments in demand and supply are necessary. In the capitalist economy, the market itself is spontaneously providing information, as Hayek repeatedly proclaimed. Movements in **prices** will show whether demand or supply are in excess, and these movements will be sufficient information to signal to producers the need to adjust their schedules. Hayek pointed out that there is a movement to **equilibrium** because economic agents acquire information from the situation they are in. The fragments of knowledge that individuals possess are spontaneously combined in a way that is beyond the capacity of a single directing mind. A perfectly coordinated economy is a full information economy.

Ignorance leads to a loss of welfare. Goods may be purchased at an unnecessarily high price because the full range of prices for the same good in a particular market is disguised from buyers. Wrong investments occur if the full array of data on different possible investments is unknown.

Akerlof began the modern discussion of the effects of information deficiencies. In his famous article on the market for lemons, he recognised the imbalance, or 'asymmetric information', in knowledge of heterogeneous goods with the seller knowing more than the buyer. With such uncertainty the buyer will assume that there are defects, so will be prepared to pay only an average price. This destroys the **incentive** to sell high-quality goods so they have to be traded elsewhere. Where there is an absence of trust, businesses will suffer.

Information is regarded as 'news' when fundamental information about key economic variables, such as unanticipated movements in **interest rates** or the **national income**, is reported, causing unanticipated changes in other economic variables.

A form of restrictive anti-competitive practice is the 'information agreement'. Instead of firms meeting and deciding market arrangements, there can be joint action on the basis of the circulation of information on costs and prices. Because of knowing such information on other businesses, the same prices can emerge as under a collusive oligopoly.

An 'information economy' takes into account the growth and operation of the internet and other forms of communication.

See also: **competition and monopoly**; **game theory**

Further reading: Akerlof 1970; De Quincey 1897; Hayek 1937; Hillier 1997; Macho-Stadler and Pérez-Castrillo 1997

INNOVATION

The application of an invention to production.

An innovation, essentially meaning a change, doing something different, can occur in products, processes and behaviour. Such new things can be self-generated by a person or organisation, or purchased from a previous innovator.

The extent of innovation is a product of the competitive pressures on a firm from rival **firms**, either domestically or internationally. Innovation will also be provoked by the state of the economic **cycle**. The taking up of a bunch of inventions can revive a stagnant economy, as partly happened in the 1930s when the motor car industry expanded.

Whereas the quantity of inventions is crudely measured by the number of patents, the amount of innovation is counted by the proportion of a type of capital stock embodying a technical change. Also the amount of product differentiation, reduction in costs and management structures are indirect indicators of innovation.

Further reading: Antonelli 2003; Freeman 1997

INPUT-OUTPUT ANALYSIS

The use of a matrix of columns and rows showing the flow of output between different industries, the rest of the world and final **consumption**.

This type of analysis, inspired by the idea of the circulation of the blood, was translated into economics by using the concept of the circular flow of income. Quesnay, a leader of the French Physiocrats, in his *tableau économique* of 1758, drew a diagram describing the flows of income between landlords, farmers and manufacturers. Modern input–output analysis is based on the work of Leontief, who started with a table for the USA economy of 1925.

The usefulness of such tables is seen in regional and national economic planning. They are extensively published by national accounting offices. They are static if they merely show the distribution of output to other industries and to final demand; a dynamic version will incorporate time lags in production, holdings of stocks and fixed capitals and the adjustment of output to excess demand. These tables have more application in the short run when the input–output coefficients can be assumed to be reasonably stable, but it is possible to revise input coefficients in line with technical change. Input coefficients can be direct, indirect or induced.

Further reading: Cameron 1968; Department of Economic and Social Affairs 1999

INSTITUTIONAL ECONOMICS

An approach to economics which is built on the examination of key institutions of the modern economy, especially the corporation.

A full study of institutions requires an examination, sometimes using anthropology, of traditions and customs in a spontaneous order, then an examination of more sophisticated institutions with bureaucratic rules and **property rights**, considering their governance, including through private contract, and their methods of working, including the types of incentive used and the form of allocation adopted.

At the end of the nineteenth century in the USA, prominent institutional economists included Ely (founder of the American Economics Association in 1885), Commons and Veblen. Commons turned from the study of **trade unions** to an examination of capitalism, trying to understand the changing industrial structure of his day. Veblen attempted to connect anthropology and economics, as well as looking extensively at the US corporation owned by absentees. By examining the emerging economic institutions of the modern American economy and collective economic action, these writers were able to challenge the emerging **neoclassical economics** of the day. Rather than use simple maximisation assumptions, they acquired a deep knowledge of the rules of those institutions. New source materials were used, including Supreme Court judgements, to show how economic decisions were made.

This approach to economics has been transformed by the new institutional economics, which embraces rather than despises neoclassical economics. Coase, Williamson and Demsetz have made leading contributions. The tradition of viewing economics in conversation with law, politics, anthropology and sociology as truly a social science continues. It makes uses of ideas such as transaction costs and property rights to provide a new approach to old problems.

See also: **contract theory**; **economic anthropology**; **property rights**

Further reading: Gruchy 1973; Tsuru 1993; Williamson 1985, 2000

INTEREST RATE

The price imposed by lenders for using borrowed money; the reward to lenders of capital. It is usually expressed as a percentage and paid in **money**. An 'own interest rate', according to Sraffa, is an interest rate expressed in terms of itself, avoiding the use of money, so there can, for example, be a steel interest rate.

Interest rates can be fixed by governments and monetary authorities or by the market. A neutral interest rate will have no effect on the real economy. Older theories of interest included the classical loanable funds theory, which stated that real factors of thrift and investment demand will bring about a unique rate of interest. Keynes looked at interest rates as a phenomenon of money markets. The demand for liquidity has to be taken into account. Levels of interest rates will take into account time, as a longer period means a greater sacrifice of liquidity, the risk of default by the borrower, the possibility of exchange rate fluctuations and the chance of inflation.

The term structure of interest rates shows the relationship between short- and long-term rates. A central bank by the open market operations of buying and selling treasury bills and bonds, can change the relationship between rates, partly to change the nature of borrowing, as long rates will determine investments in buildings and machinery but short rates will be crucial to financial market operations. Interest rates can be fixed for a stated period or floating in line with money market indicators.

The three ancient religions of Judaism, Islam and Christianity prohibited the imposing of interest, which was called 'usury' or 'use', as it was regarded as exploitative, especially to relatives who were borrowing because of their distress. Without interest, borrowers wishing to exploit an **investment** opportunity could be without finance and **economic growth** would be impeded.

See also: **banking**; **monetary policy**; **money**

Further reading: Robinson 1952

INVESTMENT

Additions to, or replacements of, the capital stock, either in real or financial terms.

Smith assumed that what was saved would be immediately invested, but the possibility of **savings** going into idle hoards was recognised by both Malthus and Keynes. Investment is undertaken in the expectation of a future return either as a flow of income or of other identifiable benefits, such as purity of air. The decision to invest will be made when the expected yield is greater than the cost of finance. The motive for **investment** is the obtaining of a rate of return sufficient to cover the risk of committing funds, higher than the cost of finance and as high as alternative uses of funds.

The purchase of financial securities is called investment as it is the alternative to **consumption** and is undertaken for the sake of future gain. In terms of the economy as a whole this kind of investment does not add to real national income if it is the purchase of existing securities, but by leading to the inflation of the money value of financial capital enlarges the national wealth.

Much investment is in physical things such as buildings and machinery, unlike human capital. Reputation is an important form of investment, increasing demand for a firm's output and allowing the charging of higher prices.

Sometimes current expenditure, which is consumption, is loosely called 'investment', causing endless confusion. This is done especially for education expenditures, as the aim is to add to the human capital stock, but part of this expenditure will always be consumption.

See also: **accelerator**; **capital theory**; **human capital**

INVISIBLE HAND

The mechanism by which individuals although pursuing self-interest unintentionally promote the public good.

It is an expression used by Adam Smith in his *Theory of Moral Sentiments* and *The Wealth of Nations*. In the former work Smith says that the rich are

> led by an invisible hand to make nearly the same distribution of the necessaries of life, which would have been made had the earth been divided into equal portions among all its inhabitants, and thus without intending it, without knowing it, advance the interest of society, and afford means to the multiplication of the species.
>
> (Smith 1976a: book IV, 1.10)

The expected achievement of the invisible hand in that passage is modest: it is only necessaries, not entire incomes, which are equalised, sufficient to maintain the population in subsistence. In the *Wealth of Nations*, in a discussion of investment, Smith argues by directing that industry in such a manner as its produce may be of the greatest value, he intends only his own gain, and he is in this, as in many other cases, led by an invisible hand to promote an end which was no part of his intention. Nor is it always the worse for the society that it has no part of it. By pursuing his own interest he frequently promotes that of the society more effectually than when he really intends to promote it. I have never known much good done by those who affected to trade for the public good.

(Smith 1976b: book IV, ch. II)

This attack on swaggering persons who claim to be promoting the public good severely questions their motives. There is no need consciously to seek the public good if economic agents following the principles of natural liberty go about their business.

Great debate has surrounded the concept. Rothschild notes some early uses of it, such as the bloody and invisible hand mentioned in Shakespeare's play *Macbeth*. The 'hand of Jupiter' is a parallel, as is the 'hand of God' in Christian theology. Baumol makes use of 'the hidden hand' of God. Theological parallels are sensible because the kind of specialisation linked by the invisible hand is very like St Paul's description of the different offices of the church having a favourable joint outcome. Ahmad identified four functions of this concept in Smith's work: to limit the size of the landlord's stomach, to curb the residual selfishness of the landlord, to optimise production and to preserve the natural order. Its chief significance, however, is to show that an economy following its natural course can have desirable outcomes without the interference of a government.

The invisible hand concept is used to justify a **laissez-faire** attitude towards the running of a **national economy**: instead of a government promoting public welfare, private individuals achieve the same. The concept is popular with Austrian economists such as Hayek, who linked the invisible hand to the idea of a spontaneous economic order. Critics point out that the existence of market failure means we should be cautious about unregulated **markets**. It is less certain that in oligopolistic markets and national economies with much economic concentration there would be separate producers independently pursuing their interests. The world is much more integrated now and more regulated by government.

See also: **Austrian economics**; **laissez-faire**

Further reading: Ahmad 1990; Rothschild 2001; Smith 1976a, 1976b

IS-LM MODEL

A formalisation of the principal elements of John Maynard Keynes' model of the economy constructed by John Hicks in his article 'Mr Keynes and the Classics' (he used SI-LL for the model).

The IS, or investment-savings, curve shows the locus of combinations of income and the rate of interest where investment equals savings. The LM curve, using the same axes, shows equilibria between L, liquidity or the demand for money, and M, the supply of money. This graphical description of an economy shows at the intersection of the IS and LM curves there is both an **equilibrium** in the goods market, represented by the IS curve, and in the money market, shown in the LM curve.

This apparatus has been used to show the relative efficacy of fiscal and **monetary policies**. Its flexibility and adaptability has given it prominence in most macroeconomics textbooks. Changes in fiscal policy can stimulate the economy: this is shown by a shift in the IS curve. Changes in the amount of money supplied by monetary authorities will shift the LM curve, with an increase in the money supply reducing interest rates and increasing income. The **elasticity** of the respective curves shows the relative potency of each policy. Where there is a steep, i.e. inelastic, IS curve **fiscal policy** will be most effective, but least where the LM curve is inelastic as there will be 'crowding out'. Crowding out occurs when there is a fiscal stimulus to an economy which raises interest rates, thereby cutting private sector investment and cancelling out public sector expansion.

The apparatus was used in the debates between Keynesians and monetarists to argue the relative merits of different policies. The diagram became so over-used that even Hicks regarded it as an albatross. The post-Keynesians especially disliked a reformulation of Keynesian macroeconomics which resembled too much the equilibrium approach of **neoclassical economics**.

Further reading: Hicks 1937; *History of Political Economy* 2004

KEYNESIANISM

The branch of economics devised by the followers of John Maynard Keynes; a development, rather than a literal repetition, of his thinking.

Keynes in his *General Theory of Employment, Interest and Money* contrasted his theory with the classical version of macroeconomics, especially **Say's law**, and undertook the creation of a macroeconomic model based on effective demand. There are elements taken from Marshall's economics in that a demand and supply analysis is transferred from the micro to the macro branch of economics. Certain concepts are bound together in Keynes' analysis, particularly the **multiplier**, the **consumption** function, liquidity preference and the marginal efficiency of capital. In policy terms, the use of **fiscal policy** to have deficit-financed public works schemes gave Keynesianism an identity; **monetary policy** is of less significance. For ever fixed in the public mind is that Keynesians are keen on discretionary fiscal policy, hence the popular contrast with monetarists who emphasised the pre-eminence of a monetary policy following simple rules as the best way to manage a national economy.

Klein, an early expositor of Keynes, argued that the *General Theory* was revolutionary in presenting a theory of effective demand, a theory of the determination of the level of output as a whole. In other words he made economics move on from a study of households and firms to aggregate relations in the national economy overall. Also full employment is not inevitable, as there can be a permanent **unemployment** disequilibrium. Many anticipations of every theme of the *General Theory* exist, as Laidler details. Robertson, for example, as early as 1915 in his *A Study of Industrial Fluctuation*, referred to output as a whole in his analysis. Despite Keynes being more in a continuous tradition than a revolutionary, he did introduce a formal model which revolutionised the teaching of economics.

Coddington identified three types of Keynesian – the fundamentalist, the hydraulic and the reconstructed reductivist. Different approaches choose between fiercely guarding the holy shrine and allowing linkages to other schools of economics, especially the neoclassical.

Leijonhuvud was keen to show how the revolutionary approach of Keynes had been tamed. He objects to the attempt to give the *General Theory* a neoclassical rewrite. Keynes was attempting to escape from a Walrasian general **equilibrium** world in which markets failed to clear to formulate his own analysis of the relationship between markets. Crucial to the analysis of Keynes, and not the Keynesians, was his consumption function.

It was the achievement of Patinkin to integrate value theory with monetary and employment theories. He introduced a real balance effect, the change in aggregate expenditure causing a movement in the price level which affects the purchasing power of money. The demand for real balances, the private demand for all consumer goods, the demand for all investment goods and for securities, in real terms, will be determined by real income, the **interest rate** and the price level (if the money supply is constant). It is a short period and general theory because pricing is applied to real balances, individual goods and goods in aggregate.

Keynesianism has been the parent of several new schools of thought, including neo/new Keynesianism and post-Keynesianism. The inheritors of the Keynesian creed have split into different camps, including the neo-Keynesians and post-Keynesians. Neo-Keynesians take from Keynes the ideas of sticky prices and wages and a possible failure to reach full employment, but use the methodology of **neoclassical economics** with the assumption that economic agents are rational. They use general equilibrium theory and emphasise the micro-foundations of macroeconomics. The view that markets are competitive is replaced by the recognition of varying degrees of monopoly power.

The Cambridge economist Joan Robinson referred to illegitimate interpretations of Keynes as 'bastard Keynesianism', insisting that both a static equilibrium and the process to reach it had to be distinguished. Hicks and Meade were associated with this illegitimacy through arguing that a given stock of capital could achieve full employment if real wages fell to an equilibrium position. In Britain the post-Keynesians were influenced by Kalecki's formulation of Keynes, especially his examination of the role of finance in investment with its implications for liquidity and effective demand. Also they emphasised the foundation of Keynes' *General Theory* in the Marshallian short period in which the level of money prices is related to the level of activity, and stressed the importance of demand rather than supply. They are opposed to neoclassical general equilibrium modelling, and argue that under **capitalism** there is no natural movement of an economy to full employment.

New Keynesians, starting with Keynes himself and Joan Robinson, and including Mankiw, in their work on fiscal policy emphasise the slowness of prices and wages to react thus impeding progress to full employment. They attack the New Classical School, especially its use of rational expectations. Building on Keynes' attack on neoclassical economics, especially on **unemployment**, and Joan Robinson's work on imperfect competition, the New Keynesians have linked micro- to macroeconomics in their interests, which include efficiency wage theories, capital market imperfections, **credit** rationing and **monetary policy**.

See also: **capital theory**

Further reading: Coddington 1976; Klein 1952; Laidler 1999; Leijonhufvud 1968; Patinkin 1956

LABOUR

The factor of production which cooperates with land and capital to produce goods and services. It is remunerated by wages and salaries in the case of employed labour, but by a hybrid income mixing wages and **profits** in the case of self-employment. Labour itself is conceptually similar to capital inasmuch as much of it embodies human capital, and like land in that much of it is scarce, earning economic rent.

The demand for labour is determined by the demand for its product. The supply of labour can be the supply of persons willing to work, the supply of hours or the supply of effort. The total supply of labour constitutes those employed, unemployed and self-employed, thus membership of the labour force depends on receiving wages or a salary or being engaged in job search activity. This supply depends on the growth in the population and the participation of that group in the labour market, hence reference is made to labour force participation (economic activity) rates.

The market for labour consists of employers and workers. It exists at the national level but also in local areas and occupations because of the heterogeneity of the labour supply. Labour markets can be difficult to clear and often are in a state of disequilibrium, as evidenced by the coexistence of **unemployment** and unfilled job vacancies. Poor clearing leads to frictional unemployment and is sometimes the result of high search costs. Governments subsidise the clearing of labour markets to reduce unemployment and increase output. The traditional way of doing this is to reduce labour market **information** deficiencies by setting up labour exchanges or job centres, with free advice on obtaining employment and a free notification of vacancies service for employers to use. Many labour **markets** are notorious for poor clearing. Workers can be very reluctant to move to another place, to retrain and to accept different working conditions. Employers can be slow or partial in advertising for the labour they need and have selection procedures which fail to obtain an optimal labour force. There can be interference in the setting of wages, as under **incomes policies**, so the wage level is kept below the market clearing price.

The interaction of employers demanding labour and workers supplying it determine wages and salaries. Labour costs are usually greater than the amounts paid in direct remuneration. The extra elements of cost include fringe benefits, such as pensions, and the expense of running collective facilities such as sports centres.

Wages come in different forms. At the macroeconomic level there is the wage rate, which is an average for the whole economy and is not specifically determined in non-planned economies but emerges as a statistical phenomenon. Given the segmented nature of the labour market, wage differentials abound. Cantillon and Smith suggested the principal reasons for occupations being paid differently. Wage differentials occur because of varying amounts of training, the pleasantness of the job, the degree of trust placed in the worker and the probability of success. Regional and industrial differentials also exist because of their relative prosperity. In internal labour markets, those within large firms, wages will be determined by hierarchical and other managerial rules; in the external labour market by competition between firms. As firms are not completely self-sufficient in labour, they will have to connect with the external market for first-time workers from schools and universities and where they have labour shortages. Existing workers recruited from the external labour market will be paid the 'key rates' determined competitively: these rates are joined together to form a wage contour for that group of firms. Wages under **collective bargaining** can be determined nationally or locally. What often happens is that the national level determines basic pay, often called the wage rate, and the local or even plant level, additional bonuses and other allowances which when added to the wage rate constitute earnings. The rate of growth of wage rates and of earnings can diverge so that there is 'wage drift', the number of percentage points difference between the rates growth and the earnings growth.

Outcomes in a labour market are often disliked. The wages and employment levels which emerge are regarded as sub-optimal. Because wages are below an acceptable welfare level, minimum wage legislation is introduced, partly to exercise a mild form of egalitarianism.

Whereas Keynes and the Stockholm School were concerned with the non-flexibility of wages, modern policy makers are obsessed by labour market rigidities. These rigidities are impediments to the flexible use of labour. Protective labour legislation and the welfare state and the nature of labour contracts, whether negotiated by trade unions or not, can make it difficult to change the use of labour. Without rigidities there would be less job security, more adjustments to pay, including pay reductions, and higher levels of labour productivity.

Labour has always had a special status in economics because the way it is treated determines the quality of life for most of the population. The length of the working day and the level of pay relative to subsistence are central welfare issues. Both classical economists such as Smith and marginalists such as Jevons regarded labour as disutility.

The labour market will always be difficult to analyse because of the heterogeneity of labour and the many cases of asymmetric information.

In **Marxian economics** concrete labour is what labour actually does, for example, weave cloth, and created use values, but abstract labour is devoid of the actual circumstances of work – a general property measured in the quantity of hours worked essential to capital accumulation and the creation of exchange values. Labour power is a worker's capacity to work, which is sold to capital.

The special roles of labour, as the recipient of most of the **national income** – a major element in **costs** and the basis of some theories of **value** – have prompted the idea of the standard of value being a labour standard rather than a gold standard. Writers as diverse as the early nineteenth-century socialist Robert Owen and the later John Hicks have suggested this.

Further reading: Addison and Siebert 1979; Cahni 2004; Ehrenberg 1997

LAISSEZ-FAIRE

Opposition to governments with extensive power to interfere in economic life.

The origin of the expression is attributed to Boisguilbert and Legendre, who objected to the mercantilist policies in the seventeenth-century France of Colbert. The Physiocrats were eager followers of this doctrine of little interference in the economy. It was argued that free internal and external trade would be of immense benefit. Also production would follow its natural course if capitalists could invest in response to prospective rates of profit. The eighteenth century, an age of enlightenment, attacked old superstitions and unjustifiable methods of living and working. The classical economists were only partial converts, despite often being associated with this anti-intervention stance. In matters of trade, banking and responding to poverty, they recommended a mixture of government action and private initiative.

Laissez-faire attitudes have long been regarded as brutal and uncaring. They seem to be based on the unrealistic assumption that people are naturally good and do not need the oversight of government to restrain bad conduct and order actions with good social outcomes. The critics of laissez-faire point to market failures; the advocates to the expense and shortcomings of government.

Further reading: Bastiat 1964

LIBERTARIAN ECONOMICS

A branch of economics especially associated with the Chicago School of economics which emphasises the role of **markets** and minimises the role of the state.

It is a descendant of Physiocratic **laissez–faire** and natural law economics. The Physiocrats resisted an imposed political order, as under a social contract, preferring nature to take its course. Natural law writers emphasised that through conscience rather than outside controls public conduct would be proper. Libertarian economics continues themes from classical economics and often uses neoclassical methods.

Early writers in this stream of economics include Ludwig von Mises, who wrote extensively about the dangers and mistakes of **socialism**. Later Austrian economists, including Hayek, showed the importance of understanding the spontaneous nature of a national economy freely using market mechanisms. Because of these mechanisms the economy can be self-managed.

The 'Chicago School', founded within the University of Chicago in the 1920s by Frank Knight and Jacob Viner, departed from Chicago's earlier institutionalism. They were concerned to apply neoclassical price theory to a variety of economic problems. The school was soon to attack **Keynesianism**. Later from the 1950s Milton Friedman and George Stigler, helped by Hayek in an adjacent department, initiated its distinctive libertarianism. Friedman extensively attacked government intervention through policies which constantly meddled, as did demand management, rather than follow a central rule as did monetarism.

The policy proposals of this school of thought are few and echo the recommendations of political liberals. It is important for there to be little **regulation** in the running of a **national economy** and for choice mechanisms to be reinforced, for example, by granting educational vouchers to parents so they can choose between publicly financed schools. Consumer sovereignty and individual choice are always paramount. These economists have a preference for monetary over **fiscal policy**, which is consistent with their view that the state should have minimal functions. Every activity of the state is examined to see whether there can be a market alternative, even for welfare programmes.

Inevitably the libertarians have been criticised for ignoring the modern desire to recognise that there are welfare needs which require state provision, for caring little for the environment, for disregarding the ill effects of **property rights** and for being willing to sit back as the mechanisms of markets turn over, not caring how many inequalities will be created. Much of libertarian economics is micro-economic because of its persistent use of price theory, with less interest in the macroeconomic issues raised by critics.

Libertarian economics has to be distinguished from anarchy, as libertarians always stress the importance of the role of law as one of the pillars of a minimal state: even libertarians who advocate privati-sation of policing still want it to exist in every country. It is also dif-ferent from the ideas of 'liberals', in the American sense, which overlaps with European democratic socialism

See also: **Austrian economics**; **capitalism**

Further reading: Tilman 2001

MACROECONOMIC FORECASTING

The use of aggregate data on the different aspects of a **national economy** to predict the future values of key economic variables, especially GDP, **prices**, wages, **productivity**, **money** supply, **con-sumption** and **investment**.

Stages in the creation of a forecasting model began with a process of abstraction, of reducing the vast diverse complexity of economic life to a few relationships between selected economic entities.

Early attempts to model the economy were made by Cantillon and Quesnay, the latter with his *tableau économique*. Of the classical economists, Ricardo was the most abstract through creating a model of value and distribution. The foundation of modern macroeconomics in the 1930s, and the associated development of **national income** accounting, made possible the formulation of basic equations to describe a national economy and the data to estimate their value.

Leading banks, research institutes and finance or treasury departments of governments attempt to create their own forecasting models. The simplest of sets of equations is the starting point before a cluster of more intricate equations is used. Issues which need to be constantly addressed include the linearity of functions and the justification for engaging in the extrapolation of time series. Crucial to the success of forecasting exer-cises is the correct specification of economic relationships and the iden-tification of causal mechanisms. 'Granger causality' is constantly assumed, i.e. using one time series of data to forecast another by introducing time lags of varying duration. Endogenous variables must be distinguished from those which are exogenous. An important tool of the forecaster is the econometrics of time series. Types of forecasting error have to be discovered so that predictions can be more refined.

A distinction is made between structural forecasting, based on economic theory, and non-structural forecasting, which is based on reduced form correlations. Stochastic models which use time series, the values of an economic variable at different dates, and the autoregressive method of relating past to current values, are distinguished from qualitative or quantitative non-stochastic models.

The success of monetary and fiscal policies is heavily dependent on the accuracy of forecasting. But also the underlying macroeconomic theory used can imperil the choice of model. More ambitiously, a macroeconomic model can attempt to identify the sources of **economic growth** in an economy and test long-range economic policy. There is also modelling of the regions of national economies.

Further reading: Klein 1970; Whitley 1994

MARGINALISM

A school of economics which succeeded **classical economics** and laid the foundations for **neoclassical economics**.

It is argued that there was a 'marginal revolution' in 1870, with three leaders: Stanley Jevons in Manchester, Leon Walras in Lausanne, and Carl Menger in Vienna. Several attitudes were shared by these writers. An interest in consumer **equilibrium**, in optimisation at the margin using the concepts of marginal cost, marginal revenue and marginal utility, characterised their work. There are sufficient precursors to these writers to question whether there was indeed a revolution. In particular Lloyd, Senior, Dupuit, Gossen and Jennings were aware of the concept of marginal **utility**, without considering the full range of marginal entities.

Jevons in his *Theory of Political Economy* (1871) consciously sought to challenge the doctrines, especially the labour theory of value, of Smith and Ricardo, by placing marginal utility in the central position of the theory of exchange. Combining the utilitarian analysis of pleasure and pain devised by Bentham and the mathematical method of differential calculus, he formalised the nature of exchange and set out the conditions for consumer equilibrium through equating marginal utilities of different goods. Also he applied marginal analysis to the supply of **labour** and theories of capital and interest. His contemporary Carl Menger, in his *Principles of Economics* (1871), also made use of obtaining satisfaction at the margin. He also rejected labour theories of value and showed how a consumer maximises satisfaction from a given income, without using mathematics more advanced than arithmetic. Walras, the third of the leaders, also produced an economics making marginal utility central and differential calculus the crucial tool, in his *Elements of Pure Economics* (1874). **Value** in exchange emerges spontaneously as a consequence of free competition. The analysis of exchange is elaborated to many commodities, laying the foundations for general equilibrium theory.

To look at the margin is crucial to decision making because it is in decisions to expand or reduce a commitment of resources that consumption and investment are affected. Marginal cost and marginal revenue are the most important of marginal concepts: the equalising of these two measures is the rule followed by a profit-maximising **firm**.

Marginal cost pricing is at the heart of the efficient allocation of resources. **Prices** then have the function of ensuring that there is social **efficiency**. What is good in theory cannot always be implemented, especially because it is difficult to identify the marginal unit of a complex system. Also if average cost is declining then marginal cost will be declining at a faster rate. This means that the revenue obtained when setting prices equal to marginal cost will be insufficient to cover fixed costs.

The marginal approach has the major advantage of looking at infinitesimal changes, so can be expressed using calculus. That was perhaps the main legacy of this school of thought. Mathematics was employed more in economics, enhancing the subject's status.

The opponents of marginalism are many. To some extent they are the descendants of the critics of utilitarianism. Others make the simple point that it has encouraged too stylised a form of economics to be useful as a guide to policy. Marxists dislike marginalism for providing a theory of value which is subjective and ignores labour as the source of value.

See also: **Austrian economics**; **neoclassical economics**

MARKET

The bringing together of buyers and sellers to effect exchanges at a mutually acceptable price. Markets can be based on any communications network, including a physical meeting, telephonic and internet contact.

Factor markets for **labour**, land and capital are distinguished from the product markets for goods and services resulting from the employment of those factors. A market is a buyer's market or a seller's depending on which side has an advantage: the buyer when there is a surplus of supply and the seller when there is scarcity.

There will be market clearing if the amount demanded exactly matches the amount supplied. Market failure occurs if the free working out of the forces of demand and supply does not achieve a welfare goal. In the public sector often there is a lack of a market because of the free provision of services, so that a market has to be simulated by, for example, surveying consumers.

The extent to which markets are used distinguishes one type of national economy from another. **Planning** is contrasted with the market as a method of allocation. The existence of markets is often heavily criticised. 'Market forces' are alleged to be harsh in their operation, caring little for the violent effects of adjusting to new equilibria, such as when unemployment results. On the other hand, the tolerance of inefficiency can lead to welfare losses. Experience has shown the triumph of the market over other forms of allocation, partly because it is less arbitrary than rationing, partly because of it being central to the capitalism which has become dominant in the economic systems of the world.

An 'efficient market', especially a stock market, has prices which reflect all information, in the weak sense of using all past prices, or in the strong sense of using all publicly available prices.

In some economies markets are few, especially where there is self-sufficient subsistence agriculture, or a plentiful public provision of services and control of consumption by government. Markets will emerge to make allocations more efficient and to challenge the arbitrariness of government.

See also: **efficiency**; **price**

Further reading: Aldridge 2005; Salanié 2000

MARXIAN ECONOMICS

Economic analysis suggested by Marx and developed by his disciples.

The economics of Marx grew out of earlier theories, especially the dialectical materialism he had absorbed as a philosopher from Hegel and the eighteenth-century stages theory, and the leaders of the classical

school, Smith and Ricardo. The principal themes of Marx's economics occur in volume one of his *Capital* (volumes two and three
were published posthumously through his literary collaborator Engels
creating a manuscript from notes). Building on Aristotle's distinction
between use value and exchange value, and using Ricardo's labour
theory of relative value, he developed his theory of value based on
socially necessary labour time then outlined the circulations of commodities and money as a prelude to explaining absolute and relative
surplus **value**. With such tools he was able to analyse the nature of
capital accumulation and its implications for wages and the working
classes. Capital is composed of constant capital, 'dead' labour embodied in commodities in the past, and variable capital which is current
labour. As capital accumulates the ratio of constant to variable capital
increases, leading to a falling rate of profit and to more intense
exploitation of labour. Workers are alienated through not owning the
means of production and its product, and lacking control over the productive process. There is exploitation of industrial workers through the
extraction of surplus value from them by means of lengthening the
working day beyond the time needed to produce subsistence.

Although there are parallels with Marx in much of **classical economics**, he did have some original approaches. His theory of crises
was an important contribution to trade **cycle** theory, despite being
carelessly scattered through *Capital*. A crisis, or upper turning point,
occurs every ten years. Only in monetised economies will there be
cycles, because the nature of capitalist production is to separate
buying from selling so that the proceeds from sales may be hoarded
rather than passed on in new purchases. Using contemporary economic experience, he examined many causal contributions to cycles,
including different growth rates between industries.

Much of his economic writing is critical in tone, reflecting the aim
to analyse and attack capitalism rather than provide an elaborate
blueprint for a new economy and society – apart from in his *German
Ideology*, where production in communities avoiding too much division of labour was advocated.

Historical experience of capitalism in the nineteenth century led to
the questioning of Marxism, especially its claim that there would be a
sequence of events leading to the collapse of capitalism. In the twentieth
century the concerns of this school of economists went in new directions, including studying the transformation problem, analysing monopoly **capitalism**, especially with the expansion of the **multinational
corporation**, and considering whether at the level of the state or
smaller community, including the firm, ideals could be realised.

In the second half of the twentieth century many economists, including Baran, Sweezy, Dobb, Joan Robinson and Meek, developed the ideas of Marx. Themes prominent in neo-Marxist works have been value theory, distribution, crises of capitalism and the international spread of capitalism through the multinational corporation. **Development economics** has used Marxian analysis, for example, in the dependency theory of Andre Gunder Frank, which divided countries into the centre and the periphery with the more important countries extracting a surplus from the poorer countries. As in Marx's own precursor Ricardo, there is a broad sweep in Marxian economics, an attempt to analyse long period changes; hence Marxian economics cannot be divorced from Marxian historiography and Marxian sociology.

See also: **surplus value**

Further reading: Frank 1978; Howard 1992; Junankar 1982; Marx 1976

MERCANTILISM

The economic theories and policies pursued by merchant pamphleteers in several European countries from the sixteenth to the eighteenth centuries.

They believed states should be strong through balance of trade surpluses and the accumulation of bullion. Just as merchants had as a central goal the obtaining of value-added by selling dear and buying cheap, so also should a nation endeavour to obtain a surplus from other countries. As pillars of the state the merchants expected privileges, especially monopoly rights to trade to particular countries with their exclusive trading companies.

Central theoretical concerns were the maintenance of a sound **currency**, trade restrictions, full employment, population growth and state establishment of industries. The mercantilists were interested in promoting the power of national states, which they thought could only be at the expense of others in a zero sum game. This static view of economic life was later superseded by a conscious attempt to promote **economic growth**. New industries were to be encouraged, and output expanded through full employment and measures to increase productivity. The rapid circulation of money was advocated, and a primitive quantity theory of money outlined.

Mercantilist writers in their vast scope stumbled across many economic concepts and theories. Perhaps the most inventive of all was

Petty. He pioneered demographic methods and manpower planning, advocated public works schemes to reduce unemployment, had a broad view of the functions of the state which included education and providing medical services, recommended a general expenditure tax, outlined a land and labour theory of **value**, used the idea of opportunity cost, asserted that the **labour** supply curve is backward bending, and made **human capital** calculations.

With the growth of the English East India Company after 1620 there was a loosening of mercantilist doctrine with the advocacy of a general **balance of payments** surplus, rather than a surplus in every balance, and a movement towards free trade. Leading mercantilist writers included Mun and Petty in England, and Steuart in Scotland. In French economics the mercantilism of Colbert was replaced by **Physiocracy**, in Britain by **classical economics**.

The fame of Smith's analysis of the mercantile system in *The Wealth of Nations* allowed his criticisms of the system to be a kind of definition of mercantilism: that it defined wealth to be gold and silver, opposed free trade and preferred the producer's interest to the consumer's. The nature of mercantilism was more complex and contradictory, especially the increased approval of free trade in the eighteenth century by mercantilists such as Josiah Child. Also, Hume was one of the economists who challenged the very heart of mercantilism by showing that the price specie flow mechanism made a permanent balance of payments surplus a futile goal.

In the 1980s in Western economies, the appeal of protection caused some economists to be labelled neo-mercantilists. With the decline of manufacturing industry in developed countries and the attendant unemployment costs from restructuring their economies, there was an attraction to promoting the welfare of individual states and being more isolationist. With transport and other forms of communication becoming faster and globalisation more of a reality, the desire to turn the clock back was attractive. In a sense neo-mercantilism occurred gradually with the expansion of public sectors extending and emphasising the power of the state.

Further reading: Grampp 1952; Heckscher 1935; Magnusson 1995; Viner 1937

MERIT GOOD

A good which has beneficial effects when consumed, with the consequence that governments are willing to subsidise its consumption.

Education, health care and the arts are prime examples. Such goods receive special attention because there are social as well as private gains from encouraging consumption. There are also merit 'bads', including addictive substances in the form of tobacco, alcohol and hard drugs.

To label goods and activities as worthy or unworthy of consumption does appear as paternalist. In democratic societies the list of what is approved can change, as in the case of prohibition in the USA where alcohol consumption was legal, then banned, then again legalised. As governments respond to medical research, for example by banning smoking in public places, the list of merit bads lengthens.

It is through the pattern of government spending and taxing that the promotion of merit goods is possible. However, because the demand for merit bads is often inelastic, fiscal authorities imposing indirect taxes on them can obtain considerable tax revenues, thus giving governments an incentive to encourage bad behaviour.

MIGRATION AND MOBILITY

The movement of persons between one place and another. Migration, a population shift between countries, can take the forms of emigration elsewhere or immigration, which is the inflow of people. Mobility, whether geographical, industrial or occupational, is a movement between one part of a national **labour** market and another.

Flows between countries have been exceptionally high during periods of rapid economic development, such as to North America during the nineteenth century, and in times of great turbulence when a refugee problem is created by the vicious action of national governments or civil war. Modern international migration has been largely of two types. The brain drain consists of highly trained scientists, teachers, doctors and nurses filling personnel shortages in rich countries. There is also the movement of unskilled persons, often to provide a replacement population taking over the less pleasant jobs abandoned by an indigenous population which has moved on to good, well paid employment. Gross flows always have to be distinguished from net, the phenomenon of emigrants returning home is very well established.

A distinction is made between primary migration and secondary. In the first flow of primary migration persons in a spirit of adventure, often with little information, go to another country: that movement is often quite slow. Subsequently there is a secondary flow of family and friends. There is a 'wave theory of migration' linking the primary to the secondary flows.

The determinants of migration have been neatly divided into pull factors making the destination attractive and push factors inducing people to leave. **Poverty** and persecution are the principal reasons compelling populations to move. The attractions pulling people to a new place include job opportunities, higher wages, plentiful high-quality land and a pleasant climate. These factors can be combined into models of migratory flows as a function of net differences. Real incomes, employment, and climate are measurable for inclusion in these models. To predict the magnitude of migration, gravity models have been used which estimate that the flow will be greater according to the size of the population in the original and final places and the closer they are together. Movements of people have also been analysed using Markov analysis. This calculates the probability of a person moving from one cell of a transition matrix to the next. Migration can be seen as a Darwinian process of the survival of the fittest, which was literally true in the arduous early voyages to America. There is the related concept of motility, which is the potential for mobility, estimated by extrapolating past trends or conducting surveys of intentions.

Moving to another place, another occupation or a new employer is a costly process. There are the monetary costs of travel, acquiring housing and learning the new skills required. Also there are the psychic costs of losing proximity to friends and relatives and even having to abandon communication in one's native language. These costs can be met privately or subsidised by new employers or governments. National governments are often interested in promoting flows within and from without their boundaries. Skill shortages and ageing populations can prompt schemes to encourage immigrants: such a population policy is more expedient than taking years to train the present population and increase the birth rate to remedy the perceived problem. A concern for **economic growth** will lead to **regional policies**, including subsidising moves to new areas where there are labour shortages.

See also: **economic demography**

Further reading: Giersch 1994

MONETARISM

A doctrine for the conduct of **monetary policy** based on rules rather than discretion.

This policy was partly an attempt to revive the **quantity theory of money** and partly an alternative to the discretionary demand management policies which failed to conquer inflation. Associated with the monetary policy were proposals to curb public expenditure and deregulate the economy. It had intellectual underpinnings in the works of the US economist Milton Friedman and his colleague Anna Schwartz, who analysed long time series to see the relationship between changes in the money supply and in economic activity. The policy conclusion was that **inflation** and economic **cycles** could be tackled by following the rule that the rate of growth for the **money** supply should be that of the trend growth of **productivity** for a national economy In order to make such a monetary policy a success, it was essential to have strict controls on public expenditure with few temptations for governments to borrow and expand the money supply.

Implementing the doctrine, as took place in the USA, the UK and many European countries, quickly ran into difficulties. Defining the money supply was difficult, and often the measure used as a target was evaded so a new definition was required. Also the demand for money functions was unstable as velocities of circulation were not as constant as thought. There was the difficult underlying question of the causal role of money, including whether the money supply changed passively to changes in economic activity, and what was the transmission mechanism for money affecting economic activity.

Further reading: Friedman and Schwartz 1963; Laidler *et al.* 1981

MONETARY POLICY

Those actions of a central bank on behalf of, or independent of, a government as part of its macroeconomic policy.

Originally monetary policy had few instruments, concentrating on interest rate changes and open market operations. Experience of **money** markets and their greater sophistication of products extended the range of monetary tools over time. The Federal Reserve Board of Governors in the USA from 1913 has extended its powers to set reserve requirements and set targets for the growth of monetary aggregates. The Bank of England since 1951 has experimented with many approaches, including setting rules for consumer credit, looking at liquidity as a whole and controlling the monetary base.

The goals set for monetary policy include the achievement of a target rate of **inflation** or target rate of interest, as well as the principal macroeconomic goals of low unemployment, growth in the Gross Domestic Product, the stability of the economy over time and the stability of the financial sector, output or price stability. An activist monetary policy can be destabilising because due to the time lags associated with monetary policy the ultimate outcome of using such a policy can be surprising.

A crucial issue is the extent of independence for monetary policy makers. Partly because of the possibility of there being a **political business cycle**, the idea of a central bank conducting monetary policy without government ministers interfering has become popular. It is difficult to have complete independence, as there is political interference through careful choosing of the members of monetary policy committees, in the setting of policy objectives and in the management of other macroeconomic policies which can defeat the exercise of monetary policy. Before the implementation of Keynesian demand management, most of macroeconomic policy was monetary rather than fiscal, with the interest rate a key tool. Changing fashions in economics reduce or diminish the importance of monetary policy. In the 1980s when monetarism was popular in Western countries, **monetary policy** was prominent.

See also: **banking**; **fiscal policy**

Further reading: Bofinger 2001

MONEY

The most liquid of assets; what is generally used for the discharge of a **debt**; a social institution facilitating exchange.

Money replaced barter because it was more convenient and portable and there were fewer search costs to establish 'the double coincidence of wants', that a person with a surplus could find another person with surplus which they mutually wanted to exchange.

A distinction is made between inside and outside money, a contrast between privately and publicly issued money. The latter can be possessed of intrinsic value, or be 'fiat money' whose value is accepted on trust because of the integrity of the issuing authority. Privately issued money can be less generally acceptable as there are fewer constraints on its general issue. Publicly issued money by a monetary authority can be excessive, especially when controlled by a high spending government with little concern about depreciating its own currency. Hayek argued for the privatisation of money; Smith in his real bills doctrine asserted that an excessive issue would be redundant, as bills of exchange corresponded to real transactions in an economy.

As long ago as Aristotle in book V of his *Nicomachean Ethics*, the threefold functions of money as a unit of account, medium of exchange and store of value were noticed. There is little dispute that money is useful for aggregating the values of different things, for example, apples and steel, using the same standard or yardstick. A variety of types of record-keeping rely on being able to use monetary units. Also there is much evidence of its success as an instrument of exchange, but it has had less success as a store of value.

Money is a medium of exchange but held between exchanges, assuming a store of value role. Clower asserted that money buys goods but goods do not buy goods, 'cash in advance'. This means that bonds cannot be used to buy goods. Demand for money is related to consumption of goods and to the nominal rate of interest. Clower asserted that the distinction between money and non-money commodities is crucial to creating monetary theory and is possible because of some commodities being means of payment. A commodity which is money can be traded for all other commodities.

Money can be neutral in the sense that a change in its quantity has no effect on the real economy. Money can be an illusion; for example, it can lead to false evaluations which promote unintentional switches from consumption to investment. Money is said to be a 'veil' obscuring the real processes of an economy: an increase in the supply of money, therefore, could affect prices without changing output. Money can be regarded as passive, expanding or contracting according to the needs of trade. However, the view that one can separate the real from the money economy has been challenged. David Hume argued in his essay 'Of Interest' that in the short term the increase in the money supply could stimulate output and employment in an underemployed economy. Also the amount of money will affect the rate of interest, which in turn will influence the level of investment.

Discussions about money often become debates about the demand for and supply of money. Keynes set out the three types of demand for money – transactions, precautionary and speculative. These arise from money having different functions. Because money is a medium of exchange it is used to effect transactions; because it is a store of value it can be kept as a precaution to meet unusual demands for cash. The demand for money is the demand to hold it as cash rather than to convert it into less liquid assets. The speculative demand for money is the holding of cash because investors do not expect to be able to make a capital gain as bond prices are believed to have reached a peak. Money can be held because our plans and contracts are incomplete, providing it is adequately performing its store of value function

The money supply is variously measured depending on how sophisticated the monetary system is in providing a range of assets with the characteristics of money. The most primitive supply is coinage, or even commodities such as shells; then follow paper money in the form of banknotes and bills of exchange, then bank deposits transferable by cheque and a range of modern financial instruments such as certificates of deposit. It is difficult for a central bank or other monetary authority to control the money supply, as not always is the whole range of types of money regulated and more financial instruments are invented. If control of the money supply is very tight then disintermediation might occur, i.e. instead of borrowing and lending being effected through the use of a bank or other finance house there are direct relations between borrowers and lenders, for example, by corporations lending through the issue of commercial bills.

Why do we need money, rather than have a substitute economic institution? The functions of money partly give an answer, because as a unit of account it makes possible contracts and the measurement of the **national income**. As a medium of exchange it enables more complicated commerce involving more people than physical barter ever did: hence the possibility of a single coincidence of wants when money is introduced. Saving is possible if money preserves its value long enough over time to be a store of value so that it can be a medium of exchange at a later date.

Recent theorists of money include Kiyotaki and Moore, who acknowledge the problem of the double coincidence of wants which money can solve. They argue that the trade which money facilitates can be between goods available at different dates, rather than physically different at the same date. Because of a lack of trust there is a limit to the commitment an economic agent can make to accept another's inside money at a later date. Wallace divided models of money into a category governed by physical characteristics and the ability to achieve some allocations, and another which produced **utility** directly or indirectly by freeing resources.

Further reading: Clower 1967; Hayek 1976; Kiyotaki and Moore 2002; Wallace 2001

MULTINATIONAL CORPORATION

An international **firm** which produces in several different countries; also known as a transnational.

Firms of this character have evolved from companies which exported much of their output. The time came when it became sensible to produce abroad rather than incur transport and related costs. Distant locations can have the attractions of lower labour **costs**, easier taxes and fewer regulations inhibiting the right to manage. Also there can be a profitable transfer of technology from an advanced economy. Corporations which have sprung from the USA, UK, Switzerland, France, Sweden and Japan principally, have reached an individual size in terms of total income larger than that of some **national economies**. The different subsidiaries spread across the world are linked by the internal market within the corporation, with exchanges of components and services taking place at 'transfer prices' which do not always reflect full costs.

Multinationals give less developed countries access to technology, networks of customers, modern management and finance difficult to obtain locally. The companies themselves through the geographical diversity of their locations have been able to cope easily with the shift in manufacturing from North America and Europe.

Criticisms of these corporations are many, both by critics in the country of origin of the corporation and in the countries where its subsidiaries operate. The very size of multinationals and their participation in financial markets challenges the power of national governments who have a declining ability to set their own economic policies. Through shifting employment from one location to another, sometimes to avoid industrial strife and incessant demands for higher pay, from developed to less developed countries, these corporations can create **unemployment** in particular places. They can compromise the finance of national governments, for example by avoiding **taxation**. Tax revenues from corporations will fall through use of accounting devices which make profits appear mainly in countries with low tax regimes, so that governments which have a high tax policy will find their corporate tax revenues diminishing. Multinationals which have expanded through mergers and acquisition can change the character of the national economies in which they invest by following a global specialisation policy. This can lead to important functions such as finance and research being abandoned in the country where the subsidiaries are located. For example, Scotland, like Canada and France, resents being turned into a branch economy.

Given the controversial behaviour of these corporations, many institutions have attempted to regulate them. **Trade** unions have attempted in the course of **collective bargaining** to increase job security. National governments have sought to use competition policy to prevent predatory practices and have tightened their fiscal management to obtain a fair tax revenue. Some governments are too small to control huge commercial concerns, so have used Organisation for Economic Cooperation and Development codes of conduct.

However, many attacks on these firms reek of economic nationalism and hypocrisy. Direct investment overseas can be a response to **regional policies** which have offered many inducements to persuade multinationals to locate in those countries. Also critics ignore the fact that they have brought investment to countries which otherwise would have found it difficult to raise finance domestically.

See also: **firm**; **transfer pricing**

Further reading: Caves 1996; Humer 1993

MULTIPLIER

A measure of the expansion of employment or income; the ratio of an increase in income to a change in aggregate demand.

Kahn's 1931 article describing the employment multiplier – the ratio of the secondary employment in industries which have expanded to the primary employment in the industry which has initiated the change – started the formalisation of the multiplier. The ingenious Colin Clark made many estimates of **national income** and of the multiplier, which were cited in John Maynard Keynes' *General Theory of Employment, Interest and Money* (1936).

Other useful versions of the multiplier emerged. The **investment** multiplier relates the income increase to net investment. The foreign trade multiplier is the ratio of the increase in income to the increase in investment and exports which have stimulated it. The balanced budget multiplier shows that a government with its expenditure and revenue equal can stimulate the economy because it has raised **taxation** from households with low marginal propensities to consume and transferred it to a government with a high marginal propensity to consume. The credit, or **money**, multiplier is the ratio of the increase in the money supply to a change in the monetary base of liquid assets. Multipliers can be calculated for a region or the whole of a national economy.

Further reading: Kahn 1931

NATIONAL ECONOMY

The totality of economic activity of the households, **firms** and government of an independent country.

Economies are variously classified as young or mature, developed, less developed and underdeveloped. A taxonomy of national economies, based on ideologies, whether socialist or market, is also possible. Until the end of the 1980s there was a vivid contrast between the Soviet-type economy based on central national **planning** and the market or mixed economies outside the communist bloc.

Traditionally a national economy had autonomy over the conduct of its economic policy, but countries which have joined regional blocs such as the European Union have steadily transferred their independence to a central supranational body.

The total value of a national economy can be valued as a stock of assets, the national **wealth**, or as a production flow over a period of time as in the **national income**. National income accountants calculate the latter and also create input-output tables showing the flows between different incomes, final consumers and the rest of the world. The 'size' of a national economy is often measured by its gross domestic product (GDP); the size of a country by its land area or population.

The formal economy known to the government statistician and tax collector is contrasted with the informal/underground/black/shadow economy. Such a parallel economy exists sometimes to conduct criminal acts such as theft and tax evasion. Official statisticians deliberately exclude some activities because of measurement difficulties, as with household production, and non-monetised activities.

See also: **economic system**; **informal economy**

NATIONAL INCOME

The total of incomes accruing to the residents of a country in a given time period, especially a quarter or a year, as a result of economic activity.

In the 1940s, in the USA Kuznets and in the UK Stone were major writers on the methodology of national income accounts. The attempt to manage the economy more precisely, which the changes in macroeconomic in the 1930s argued were possible, would never have occurred without the systematic and consistent collection and presentation of this aggregate data. Earlier in economics many writers, using the analogy of the circulation of the blood, such as Petty, Richard Cantillon and Quesnay, wrote of the circular flow of income.

National income can be measured variously as the sum of incomes, expenditures or outputs, because an economic activity produces an output which when sold constitutes expenditure, which provides incomes for factors of production. Estimates of national income can be at factor cost (what the factors of production – land, labour, capital and the entrepreneur – receive), or at market price (what the consumers pay) which is in excess of national income at factor cost by the amount of indirect taxes net of subsidies.

There is always debate about what to include in national income as some activities are not openly declared, especially criminal activity, work in the black/informal economy and income attributed to owner-occupiers of property. Where there is extensive household production, as with self-sufficient agriculture, proxy measures of income based on population size and average consumption have to be estimated.

Further reading: Beckerman 1980

NEOCLASSICAL ECONOMICS

An individualistic approach to economics emphasising the rationality of economic agents and using equilibrium methods.

The school's debt to **classical economics** is slight. The working of competitive markets, the self-interested economic agent, the notion of a decentralised economy and the **invisible hand** are favourite borrowed concepts. Differential **rent** theory expounded by Ricardo used a marginal idea with many echoes in the neoclassical school. An examination of the prose of writings of the two schools shows the classical to be more literary and discursive with much appeal to history; neoclassical economics often has few preliminaries before a model is set out: issues of ethics or philosophy are avoided in this positivist economics.

Beginning with the 'marginal revolution' of the 1870s, in which a new approach to economics emerged in parallel with Jevons in Manchester, Leon Walras in Lausanne and Carl Menger in Vienna, neoclassical economics soon acquired its distinctive features. But some marginal concepts, especially marginal utility, were present in earlier writings, including those of Senior and Dupuit. An interest in consumers maximising their **utility** and firms maximising their **profit**, and economic decision making subject to rationality rules, became central. Jevons insisted that economics was essentially mathematical because it deals with quantities, and was one of the pioneers of the use of differential calculus. Marshall in his *Principles of Economics* (1890) built up a supply and demand analysis which provided a method for much of neoclassical economics.

Economic agents, especially firms and consumers, have the task of maximising their utilities. The concept of equilibrium is dominant. In neoclassical models the establishing of an **equilibrium** is a primary task: without it the fundamental analysis would fall apart. Utility of a subjective, individualistic kind is a repeatedly used idea. Without mathematics there would be little of this modern form of economics.

Neoclassical theories of production and distribution were expounded supremely in Samuelson's *Foundations of Economic Analysis*. He considered equilibrium systems and comparative statics before expounding dynamical theory. He also presented the theory of maximising behaviour, a pure theory of consumer's behaviour, and a **welfare economics** including a social welfare function. The book demonstrated how powerful a few mathematical tools borrowed from calculus and algebra can be.

Neoclassical economics extensively applies demand and supply theory to a range of economic problems, such as scarce resources, **discrimination**, patents and foreign exchange markets. A standard checklist of the themes of neoclassical economics – the theory of the firm, consumer behaviour, human capital theory, the economics of the family, general equilibrium theory, marginal **productivity** theory, switching and reswitching in capital theory, the Heckscher-Ohlin-Vanek **trade theory**, the use of models based on **rationality** and approval of **monetarism** – shows how much the school has come to dominate the economics faculties of universities in developed countries.

This school of economics in today's economic literature has its critics. Opposition is focused on several issues. The extreme formalisation captures little of the nature of the modern world, and the constant search for an equilibrium appears a vain quest. Although attempting to provide a value-free positive economics, neoclassical economics is not as neutral as it seems. It does not accommodate any socialist-type views. There is little attempt to take into account the distinctiveness of modern institutions, including the corporation. Unlike Marxian analysis, neoclassical economics firmly separates economics from social considerations. Because neoclassical economists are heavily critical of government action, believing in self-regulating mechanisms for national economies, and blaming trade unions for being monopolists, they are accused of being ideological and capitalist in their sympathies. As resources, technology and preferences are assumed, critics argue that essential bits of economics are ignored, including the concept of entrepreneurship as it is a disequilibrium phenomenon. It is assumed that economic agents act independently on the basis of full **information**. An 'as if' methodology is employed, using the assumption that economic agents are solely engaged in maximising an objective subject to constraints. The maximisation hypothesis central to neoclassical economics is questioned for a lack of testability, and for it not being contrasted with competing aims.

When neoclassical economists take to macroeconomics, they are fond of two approaches, which overlap with supply side advocates – recommending cuts in real wages to increase employment and predicting that the price level will increase in proportion to a rise in the money supply. An aggregate production function is used to explain supply. The models chosen are usually short-run and general equilibrium in character. At times neoclassical economics appears to be only a technique for applying a maximising model.

The neoclassical dichotomy is the separation of the value of capital from the value of money. The neoclassical synthesis disliked by the post-Keynesians was a formalisation of the Keynesian macroeconomic system started by Hicks and Modigliani. The central ideas of Keynes could be expressed in a set of simultaneous equations which tended to produce a full employment equilibrium and assumed the neutrality of money.

See also: **evolutionary economics**

Further reading: Henry 1990; Hicks 1937; Modigliani 1944

NEO-RICARDIAN ECONOMICS

A reformulation of the economics of David Ricardo by Piero Sraffa in his *Production of Commodities by Means of Commodities* (1960).

Although this school of economics has its roots in the works of economists such as Joan Robinson and Kalecki, the school more recently has been associated with Sraffa, Pasinetti, Garegnani and Harcourt. It challenges the assumptions and methods of neoclassical economics, especially attacking equilibrium analysis. It is concerned with the creation, distribution and accumulation of the 'economic surplus' in the economy after subsistence needs have been met and depreciated capital replaced.

Wages, quantities of capital and profits, the basis of real **prices**, are unchanging, until there is a change in technology. Sraffa produced a model with a resemblance to an input–output model, without specifying input coefficients, classical in tone with outputs moving in a circular flow to provide the inputs of other industries. This commodity-production model expressed in physical terms determined prices and **profits** under the conditions of a capitalist economy. Sraffa used a 'standard commodity', a weighted composite of commodities in the system, to solve the problem of obtaining an invariant standard of value. The quantities of goods produced are given without reference to the scale, composition and **elasticity** of demand. This makes it difficult to determine what should be produced. His foundational work was written in the 1920s but not published until 1960, so it ignored developments such as activity analysis.

See also: **Keynesianism**

Further reading: Näslund and Sellstedt 1978

NEUROECONOMICS

A study of the relationship between neural processes and economic decision making: an account of the processes of thinking in economics.

Economics has made psychological assumptions. For example, there is Smith's assumption that we all have a desire for betterment; and the neoclassical assumption that we prefer pleasure to pain. But neuroeconomics, by linking an examination of the nervous system to economics, can provide a more deterministic account of decision making. A modest form of neuroeconomics is to add to other explanatory variables an observation based on the nervous system. Instead of decision making being viewed as a deliberative act, the study of the brain enables it to be considered as a seemingly unconscious process. The mapping of the brain produces an understanding of reward systems, intertemporal choice and the practice of rationality. Glimcher's examination of the activity of neurons provides a basis for the predictions of a Nash equilibrium. Economic concepts can also be useful in neuroscience, for example, by showing the power of ideas like the **division of labour** and a constraint.

Further reading: Camerer *et al.* 2005; Glimcher 2003

NEW CLASSICAL ECONOMICS

A macroeconomic theory assuming that economic agents make rational market decisions based on optimisation and that **markets** clear. Its leaders are Barro, Lucas, Sargent and Wallace.

To the classical assumption that markets clear is added the assumption that buyers and sellers have rational **expectations** using all the **information** available. Because of this view, the school is sometimes called simply the Rational Expectations School. This gives new classical models consistency and allows the optimisation of future events. Within a general equilibrium framework private individuals maximise their utilities, as occurs in Lucas' 1972 article which has a model structural in nature and not affected by policy changes.

New classical economists prefer rules rather than discretion, and recommend tax cuts and the control of the supply of **money**. They object to **Keynesianism** and reactive economic policy which adjusts to economic events. The popularity of this school of economics has been linked to the **laissez-faire** attitudes of the 1980s and later. Rather than debate a trade-off between **inflation** and **unemployment**, the proponents of this type of economics pointed out that governments are unable to change unemployment from its **equilibrium**. The price level is swiftly affected by anticipated **monetary policy** because there is no systematic relationship between such policy and output or the velocity of circulation in the quantity theory of money. Lucas' 1973 article on the Phillips curve found a positive correlation between output and inflation in the 'Lucas supply function'. He assumes that the money market and labour market have cleared, reflecting labour and product market rigidities. Aggregate demand policies tended to move both inflation and output in the same direction.

Barro and others of the school believed in Ricardian equivalence, that is, that if government spending is kept constant and a fall in present taxation is matched by the present value of a future tax increase, or vice-versa, there will be no impact by government on the equilibrium real interest rate and consumption. This means that they can disregard the method of government financing.

Another concern has been the **real business cycle** which shows that fluctuations in an economy are caused by technology shocks, not the exercise of monetary policy. Lucas has used the natural rate hypothesis (unemployment will in the long run be stable at the equilibrium rate where labour demand equals labour supply) to affirm that monetary policy cannot affect the levels of unemployment and output.

Further reading: Barro 1989; Lucas 1972, 1973; McCallum 1989; Stein 1982

NEW POLITICAL ECONOMY

An examination of the economic effects of political mechanisms.

Its concerns include **regulation**, **rent**-seeking, the political business **cycle**, redistribution and the international interdependence of **monetary policies**. Much of this subject has an overlap with **public choice** theory. Because of its political roots, NPE has generated literature stimulated by economic events such as the development of the European Monetary System, Bank of England independence, **globalisation**, sovereign **debt** crises and the collapse of communism.

This attempt to explain economic policies does not chain itself to a social welfare function approach. It seeks out the sources of power in a society, as does any political scientist, and shows how policies emanate from such sources. Insights from politics literature, especially on voting and lobbying, are connected to economic discussions of reputation, credibility and commitment.

Despite the wide range of the new political economy school, it will always be criticised for lacking a central and unifying theoretical core as it focuses so much on specific problems at specific times. Its methodology does not fully place policy analysis within a general equilibrium framework. Also there are complaints that quantitative testing is difficult because of the existence of too many explanatory variables. The recognition of the political limits to economic policy helps to avoid too purist an economic analysis.

Further reading: Drazen 2000

NON-PROFIT ENTERPRISE

A **firm** with goals other than the attainment of maximum or satis-factory profits.

These can exist in the private sector as charities, clubs, mutual insurance societies and households. In the **public sector** they can be government departments, but are especially public corporations. It is generally not expected that the aim of governmental and quasi-gov-ernmental organisations will be the pursuit of profit. As the aim of production in the public sector is the supply of **merit goods**, the provision of enough at a desired level of quality will be the goal. Britain's nationalised industries, for example, when set up in the late 1940s were expected to break even, rather than maximise profits, over a five-year period: in practice some made persistent deficits and others increased their profitability.

There is a suspicion that the making of profits is a form of exploitation. Also there is a distrust of markets, partly because they trade at prices too high for poorer consumers. The conventional firm, if blamed for these reasons, can link up with non-profit enter-prises, partly to enhance its reputation, by offering professional expertise and services including transport and marketing.

Without the goal of making a **profit**, such an organisation is tempted to let **costs** mount up and efficiency diminish. Investment decisions are more difficult as profits are not available as a guide to the allocation of funds. However, given the altruistic nature of these enterprises it is possible to employ high-quality workers at less than market salary levels, because the mission goals of the NPE are trans-parently worthwhile. If efficiency is important, it is safer to let such enterprises flourish at the small and local level.

PHYSIOCRACY

The doctrine of a group of eighteenth-century French thinkers, known as the *économistes*, who rejected mercantilism in favour of **laissez-faire** economics.

They held as a central doctrine that agriculture alone produces a net product so that manufacturing is sterile. The early leaders were Dupont de Nemours, François Quesnay and the Marquis de Mir-abeau. The last great member of this school was Turgot. Their early writings appeared in the French *Encyclopédie*. Quesnay produced a *tableau économique*, a representation of the circular flow of incomes as a consequence of annual advances, which was an important acknowl-edged precursor of the input-output table.

In opposition to the idea of a social order based on a social con-tract, they asserted that there is a natural order, giving rise to making agriculture the basic activity of an economy and advocating a mini-mum of government activity to contradict natural processes. They developed **price** theory to explain allocation, advocated **taxation** only on land, as it alone produced a net product, and were opposed to tariffs which were impediments to domestic trade.

They inspired classical economics; Adam Smith visited Quesnay on his grand tour in 1764. Smith believed strongly in natural liberty but criticised the view that only agriculture is productive.

Further reading: Meek 1962

PLANNING

The organisation of economic activity by a central bureaucracy rather than by a diversified market.

National governments have undertaken planning in either the command or indicative forms. Their motivation has usually been the desire to accelerate the rate of growth. Huge economies, such as the USSR, emerging from being economies with large agricultural sec-tors, used planning to force the pace of industrialisation. Developing countries in Africa and elsewhere after 1945 were often urged to put planning at the centre of their growth strategies. Countries which were developed but lagging behind their neighbours also played with planning, as did Britain in the 1950s.

In the USSR, five-year plans with the force of law set targets for separate industries and their subordinate organisations from the 1920s. As well as those plans there were additional annual operational plans. Many difficulties were encountered, including the problems of using **prices** which did not reflect relative **scarcity**, the impossibility of meeting simultaneously a large number of targets and the lack of worker incentives.

Indicative planning started in France in 1946. Instead of planning by government order, the government had the role of indicating through influential economic forecasts the course of the economy, thereby inducing the investment to fulfil these created expectations. Commissions were set up for major industries and for cross-industrial interests such as research. Parliament participated in choosing overall planning targets. The employment of fiscal **incentives** encouraged firms to undertake the planned **investment**. In 1960s Britain, both Conservative and Labour governments made short-lived attempts to improve the British economy by this approach. A National Economic Development Council, with subordinate bodies for major industries, was set up. It was tripartite in nature with business, trade union and governmental representatives. The ill-fated Department for Economic Affairs drew up the National Plan in 1965. The failure of the plan after nine months reflected traditional planning problems: it is difficult to have national economic planning for an open economy, to attempt planning for growth whilst being on a fixed **exchange rate** (because deflation is often needed to maintain the currency at its par value), and to produce a plausible plan by aggregating the forecasts of individual industries.

See also: **comparative economic systems**; **market**

Further reading: Bergson 1980; Heal 1973; Meade 1970

POLITICAL BUSINESS CYCLE

The fluctuations in national economic activity induced by politicians who attempt artificial stimulation of the economy to encourage voters to perpetuate them in office.

Nordhaus produced a model to formalise political choices between economic objectives, looking closely at the trade-off between **unemployment** and **inflation**. He argued that a political party when in office would start with austerity, then employ generosity towards the date for re-election. These short-term attitudes of democratically elected governments would threaten social investment. Solutions to this induced instability could be **planning**, extending the period between elections, making more **information** available to voters so that they can understand the behaviour of politicians, **incomes policies** which abolish the unemployment–inflation trade-off, and the removal of policy-making to an independent body – as happens when central banks have control over the setting of interest rates.

In this opportunist approach it is asserted that an incumbent government will use monetary policy to stimulate the economy and create a feel-good atmosphere to induce voters to re-elect them. The partisan approach contrasts a left-wing political party with a right-wing party. They differ in their attitudes to the trade-off between inflation and unemployment. Left-wingers prefer a higher level of economic activity and are more tolerant of inflation. Also, rational **expectations** models of the political business cycle can be based on expected inflation.

Challenges to this view of the political process include evidence on how long-sighted governments actually are in their policies, how ineffective government policies are in creating cycles, and how sophisticated the electorate is as a consequence of living under the political business cycle.

See also: **new political economy**

Further reading: Alesina *et al*. 1997; Hibbs 1977; Minford and Peel 1982; Nordhaus 1975

POLITICAL ECONOMY

An early synonym for economics, later an attempt to integrate economic and political science.

The mercantilist writer Monchrétien de Wattville in his tract on political economy of 1615 qualified 'economy' with the word 'political' to expand the notion of economics from the Greek idea of household management to include the state. Many economics writers have described their surveys of economics as principles of political economy, including Steuart, JS Mill and more recently Meade. They expounded a large number of economic theories, including some on **value**, trade, **money**, population, wages, economic systems and the scope for economic policy.

To Adam Smith, political economy was intended 'to provide a plentiful revenue or subsistence for the people' and 'to provide the state with a revenue sufficient for the public purposes' (*The Wealth of Nations*, book IV). This was to narrow political economy to **public finance**. More recently the subject has become a forum for discussing radical economic policy proposals, a neo-Marxism which puts income distribution centre-stage and uses a historical method to see economic issues within the context of an entire socio-economic system. There is a deliberate attempt to integrate politics and economics, with government assuming a role much greater than in Smith's time. The nature of **capitalism** and the aims and practice of political parties are explored. There is considerable interest in **public goods**, **externalities** and monopolies. The different ways various types of government allocate scarce resources is studied. Modern political economy is in sharp contrast to mathematical economics, which strives to produce a value-free economics.

See also: **new political economy**

Further reading: Lindbeck 1971; Meltzer 1991; Sherman 1972

POVERTY

Being devoid of resources; worse off than a reference group because of illness, physical and social location, or a lack of economic opportunity.

Absolute poverty means a state of destitution in which people have no food, shelter or possessions. This extreme state occurs often in civil wars and after natural disasters before relief is brought. In more normal times absolute poverty occurs when income is insufficient to obtain sufficient food and water for survival.

Supporters of egalitarianism use a relative poverty concept, arbitrarily choosing a point in the income distribution, for example, the lowest decile, or even the median, below which all are poor. It is argued that being poor is not merely being short of food but finding it difficult to participate in society, including having the standard range of consumer durables and being able to afford entertainment. A deprivation index such the Townsend Material Index combines data on **unemployment**, overcrowding, non-car ownership and low social class – the indicators of relative poverty.

Poverty has many causes, including mismanagement of a **national economy** so that there are recurrent recessions and the attendant unemployment. Also the patterns of wage differentials and the relationship between wages and profits can produce a large number of persons with low incomes. Lack of education has often been seen to create an impoverished stratum of society, as Marshall recognised, in his examination of the poorest section of society, 'the residuum'. There can be a passive acceptance of poverty because it has long been experienced by a whole community and no one has urged the sufferers to complain. For spiritual reasons poverty can be sought as a way of life, as in religious and other communities in revolt against materialism and consumerism.

A poverty trap exists for persons returning to the **labour** market after living off welfare payments, as there is a high marginal tax rate on those who change from one type of income to another.

See also: **equality**; **income distribution**

Further reading: Banerjee *et al.* 2006; Lister 2004; Townsend 1979

PRICE

The amount of **money** or something of worth which has to be sacrificed to obtain one unit of a good or service.

In **value** theory, *value in use* is separated from *value in exchange*, the latter being the prices which emerged from markets. Prices were temporary aberrations from the long-run fundamental value of goods. As demand fluctuates, prices move around a fundamental value based upon the **cost** of production. In the development of economic theory, market value, or price, received more detailed attention. It was appreciated that markets are subject to varying degrees of competition and monopoly. Nineteenth-century writers such as Samuel Bailey and JS Mill related price determination to different types of markets, thus making a price a market phenomenon.

Prices have many functions. They provide a method of allocation which will result impersonally from a competitive market process, measure of total income and a signal to producers who will gain information merely by watching price movements. Prices also point to the changes occurring in a national economy.

Types of price abound in economics – natural prices, market prices, product prices, shadow prices and factor prices. Originally prices were necessary to facilitate barter or monetised exchange, and resulted from buyers and sellers coming into contact with each other and agreeing their exchange rate. They were relative prices; later they were expressed in money when physical barter was abandoned. Adam Smith used the concept of natural price, a central price to which all prices gravitated, which was the sum of the natural rent, natural wage rate and natural profit. There is a crucial distinction between product prices, the prices charged for goods and services to final consumers, and factor prices, the cost of employing the factors of production. Given that many prices are based on the cost of production, especially if the labour theory of value is believed, product prices and factor prices have an intimate relation: with a time lag, they change in the same direction.

A profit maximising **firm** will fix the price for each product such that at that price and output the marginal revenue will equal the marginal cost. A *price* is synonymous with average revenue, as total revenue equals output multiplied by price and average revenue equals total revenue divided by output. A whole structure of prices can be devised to reflect a different state of demand in each sub-market. This price discrimination is possible if the sub-markets can be effectively separated from each other, such as by time of day with different prices for peak time travel, or by age as when concessionary rates are available to young and old consumers, or by geographical location. If the firm is a profit maximiser then it will set the prices in the sub-markets such that the marginal revenue in each sub-market will be equal.

A variety of approaches to pricing can be followed. Marginal cost pricing, advocated to maximise efficiency, requires setting prices so that they are equal to the corresponding marginal cost. Often this cannot be practised as collecting data on marginal costs is difficult. Prices can also be fixed by administrative action. 'Full cost pricing' entails adding to average total cost a margin for net profit, or adding to average variable cost a gross profit margin which will both finance fixed costs and leave a return for the firm. This type of pricing involves guessing at the nature of the **demand curve** so that the sales at that price level can be predicted and average cost calculated. Also changes in demand will require marginal adjustments to prices, questioning whether the formula should be abandoned.

Prices can remain the same for decades under central **planning** because to change them frequently would make the fundamental calculations of the plan very difficult. But some pricing has to be attempted as a numéraire is required to aggregate inputs, outputs and other economic quantities to show the relationship between productive units, sectors and the national economy. Even in the market-orientated economies of the West at times of war (especially the Second World War) and of inflation (notably the 1960s and 1970s), governments attempted to fix prices within the framework of a prices policy. This required the collection of cost data and the invention of a formula to transform costs into prices. Inevitably the prices which were set would be difficult to maintain for very long under changing market conditions. Governments can attempt to stabilise prices by more modest methods than a national prices policy; for example by investing in buffer stocks, accumulating when prices are low to stimulate their price and selling them when prices are high to bring prices back to customary levels.

The effects of a change in price can be split into an income effect, as a rise in price reduces real income, and a substitution effect, as a price rise can reduce consumption in favour of the consumption of another good, and the opposite for a price fall. For a normal good, a fall in price raises the quantity demanded as these effects are both positive. For a Giffen good a price rise leads to an increase in the quantity demanded because the income effect is greater than the negative substitution effect.

Because prices change, speculation is possible. The motive of the speculator is the hope of gaining from future trends in prices. Speculation can be studied as an exchange of information, or as an exchange of risks.

See also: **competition and monopoly**

Further reading: Dorfman 1967; Hirshleifer 1980; Wiles 1961

PRICE INDEX

A measure of inflation.

This is calculated by measuring the total cost of buying a bundle of goods and services representative of the consumption of an average consumer of a particular national economy at different dates.

Price indexes are created to serve different client groups and therefore can be of different types. There is a sharp distinction between consumer and producer price indexes, with the latter anticipating changes in the former. Also there are indexes for forms of consumption especially prone to rapid increases, such as house prices. Originally the main purpose of constructing an index was to see if real wages were stationary, declining or increasing. Wage bargainers use such an index as the starting point in pay negotiations.

The relative amounts of each item consumed appear in the index as 'weights'. An index will show the movement of prices between a base year, the starting year for an index, and the current year. The Laspeyres index uses the weights of a base year; the Paasche employs current weights. As price increases can reduce expenditure and price decreases encourage more spending, the pattern of **consumption** will change with the consequence that current weights are different from base weights. This means that both of these indices present a false picture of price movements. The Fisher ideal index took the square root of the product of the results from the two indices as a compromise.

Early endeavours to produce a price index were made by William Fleetwood, George Poulett Scrope and, more importantly, Stanley

Jevons. Price indices are produced for the retail and wholesale trades and for different types of consumer.

Further reading: Fisher 1972

PRICE-SPECIE FLOW MECHANISM

A description of the relationship between the **balance of payments** and **prices**; an adjustment mechanism under the gold standard.

This idea has been attributed to David Hume, Isaac Gervaise and Richard Cantillon. Hume in his essay *Of the Balance of Trade* wrote

> Suppose four-fifths of all the money in GREAT BRITAIN to be annihilated in one night, and the nation reduced to the same condition, with regard to specie, as in the reigns of the HARRYS and EDWARDS, what would be the consequence? Must not the price of all labour and commodities sink in proportion, and every thing be sold as cheap as they were in those ages? What nation could then dispute with us in any foreign market, or pretend to navigate or to sell manufactures at the same price, which to us would afford sufficient profit? In how little time, therefore, must this bring back the money which we had lost, and raise us to the level of all the neighbouring nations? Where, after we have arrived, we immediately lose the advantage of the cheapness of labour and commodities; and the farther flowing in of money is stopped by our fulness and repletion.

In opposition to the original mercantilist view that a country should and could have a permanent balance of payments surplus, these writers stated that the price consequences of a trade balance would cause it to swing between surplus and deficit. As a consequence of a balance of payments surplus there would be an influx of silver and gold which would push up the price level. Then the higher prices would make it more difficult to export, so the balance of payments would swing to deficit, specie would flow out and prices would fall.

PRIVATISATION

The movement of assets, usually by sale, from the public to the private sectors.

This can take the form of the sale of state-owned industries, social housing stock and parts of the infrastructure such as bridges, roads and cemeteries. As early as Adam Smith, the sale of state-owned forests, then one of the few government-owned assets, was recommended. In the USA over a billion acres of public land was privatised in the 1790–1820 period. In the UK in the 1980s nationalised industries created forty years before, including telecommunications, gas, electricity and an airline, were sold to the public. In the transitional economies of Eastern Europe in the 1990s, many state-owned assets passed into private hands. The scope for privatisation has increased because of the accumulation of industrial assets by states in the twentieth century.

Various motives have prompted this change in the ownership of assets. As part of a budgetary strategy, the acquisition of further short-term revenues through asset sales was attractive. Also, given the poor commercial record of some publicly owned concerns, government expenditure in the form of subsidies to the loss makers could be reduced. The greater commercial discipline which was possible in the private sector increased profitability. Managers were able to direct their enterprises without constant interference from government ministers. The policy aims of a **firm** are narrower than those of a government as they are not subject to so many lobbies and are not expected to have social objectives central to their activities. There is the added discipline of having to be exposed to stock market criticism, including the possibility of take-over by another firm.

Critics of privatisation often exposed the faults of the mechanism of privatisation. For privatisation to succeed a share price had to be chosen which would both realise substantial revenue from the sale and avoid shares being left with the underwriters. In Britain it was claimed that nationalised industries were sold too cheaply, thus depriving the public of annual revenue and squandering the future wealth of the state. On the other hand it was argued that those who bought the new shares were better-off people who had suffered higher taxes in the past through the inefficiencies of nationalised industries so they were, in a crude sense, receiving some compensation.

Also the structure of the privatised industry had to be decided. Prior to nationalisation they would often be competitive industries; subsequently they were organised as state monopolies. To make the industries more marketable there was a case for allowing them to retain their monopoly rights, but this raised new concerns, thus a demand for **regulation**, especially to avoid reduction in the quality of service, including safety, and the unnecessary raising of product prices. However, an industry which was organised as a single corporation because of the belief that it was a natural monopoly should continue with monopoly status.

Inevitably an industry which has drastically changed its ownership will be subjected to official and informal audits. The criteria used to judge whether a privatisation has succeeded include the growth of output, market shares of domestic and foreign markets, returns to assets employed, levels of employment and remuneration, commitment to research and development, and levels of consumer satisfaction with the goods and services produced. Where the privatised concern remains a monopoly, anxiety about exploitation of consumers through high prices suggests the need for price controls, for example, only allowing product prices to rise by the general rate of inflation less an arbitrary number of percentage points.

Privatisation of publicly owned housing stock was criticised for creaming off the better houses for sale to tenants so that persons unable to purchase any house could only rent inferior property. Also local authorities with a responsibility for the homeless found they had to work with a smaller number of houses. The sale of transport systems and other major parts of the infrastructure raised fears of price increases and misuse of subsidies granted to private firms to maintain high-cost services on social grounds.

Further reading: Gayle and Goodrich 1991; Littlechild 2000; Thompson *et al.* 1986

PRODUCTION FUNCTION

The relationship between inputs and an output.

Such functions have been central to **economic growth** theory and important in the theory of the **firm**. They are central to understanding returns and costs. They show the extent to which a form of economic activity is labour- or capital-intensive. The structure of costs follows from the nature of the function.

The best known is the Cobb-Douglas function which shows physical output as the product of labour and capital inputs, assuming constant **returns** to scale and the elasticity of substitution between labour and capital is 1. Different types of production function occur when the assumptions are relaxed. There can be the constant elasticity of substitution function with that elasticity being greater than one, as suggested by Arrow *et al.* 1961.

The production function will indicate whether increased amounts of inputs result in constant, diminishing or increasing returns/products. Classical economists, especially Smith, Malthus and Ricardo, were aware of production functions in their discussion of diminishing and increasing returns. Usually agriculture was thought to have diminishing, and manufacturing increasing, returns.

See also: **cost**; **economies of scale and scope**; **efficiency**; **returns**

Further reading: Arrow *et al*. 1961; Douglas 1948; Heathfield 1971

PRODUCTIVITY

The amount of output resulting from employing one unit of a factor input, especially **labour** or capital; the output from the joint employment of several factors, hence total **productivity**.

There is always the problem of separating the productivity of one factor from another, as changes in the use of one factor often coincide with more or less of another factor being employed. Thus measuring labour productivity is difficult because it is hard to conceive of a constant amount of capital. It is easier to measure productivity for occupations with a physical product; productivity of government employees is crudely measured with averages.

Schemes to increase productivity include improving the motivation and work methods of workers and economy in the use of labour, often through changing capital-labour ratios. **Incomes policies** have used the idea of productivity to set out rules for approving non-inflationary pay increases: if productivity is expected to increase then a pay increase can be self-financing. Fixing overall pay increases to the trend rate of productivity growth in the economy, say 2.5 per cent, will avoid inflation.

The classical economists, especially Smith, attributed productivity increases to the use of the **division of labour** principle as it economised in the use of labour. A later writer, Denison, in *Why Do Growth Rates Differ?* emphasised the importance of education as a force for productivity growth.

See also: **division of labour**

Further reading: Denison 1967; Jorgensen 1995

PROFIT

The portion of the **national income** awarded to the owner of capital; the residual income after **rent**, wages and interest are paid if other factors of production have priority; the return for bearing risk.

The reasons for justifying the payment of profit as a consequence of owning capital have long been debated. Adam Smith related profit to risk; Nassau Senior to the abstinence of the person who refrains from **consumption** in order to save and invest.

In **classical economics** there was the strong belief that the rate of profit had a tendency to fall. Smith in the *Wealth of Nations* argued that the 'competition of capitals', i.e. more capitalists entering a market, would push down the rate of profit. Ricardo in his *Principles of Political Economy and Taxation* set out a model for a national economy in which with the population expanding and having to rely on increasingly inferior ground, the real cost of food and of wages would rise, thus squeezing the rate of profit. Thomas de Quincey in his *Logic of Political Economy* built on hints of Smith to expound three reasons for disputing this tendency. He challenged the view that capitalists knew enough about profit rates to respond to high profits by entering an industry. He questioned the notion of diminishing returns in agriculture assumed by Ricardo. Also, by using the rate of interest as a proxy for the rate of profit, he noted that it fluctuated rather than following a secular downward trend.

Some regard the existence of profit as proof of exploitation, following on from Marx's idea of **surplus value**. Others think of profit as a signal helping the investor to choose a project. The profit margin is the difference between the cost and selling price. Taxes on profits, or excess profits, have attacked high profits, partly because of their association with private monopoly power. To make profit more acceptable, some firms have instituted profit sharing schemes to top up wages and salaries and increase the identification of an employee with the employer, and some organisations have been set up on a non-profit basis.

Further reading: Parker 1991

PROPERTY RIGHTS

The rights accruing to persons, corporate bodies and governments over material objects, claims and funds.

Locke linked the idea of possession of land to the labour of cultivating it in his *Two Treatises of Government* (second treatise, chapter V).
He distinguishes what is common to the human race, the earth and
inferior animals, from the property of one's person as a result of
labour and the work of one's hands. By removing the fruits of nature
out of the common ownership my labour makes it my property. Land
cultivation justifies private property. There are private possessions
because it is the condition of human life to labour and have materials
to labour upon.

Smith, like Hobbes before him in *Leviathan,* argued that humans
join together in society to obtain common security. In *The Wealth of
Nations* as population grows land is appropriated and the landlord
class emerges spontaneously. In book V when discussing justice,
Smith asserts that in the earliest society of hunters there will be
equality and **poverty** but in the second stage, that of shepherds,
there will be inequalities of wealth, with the richer having authority
to command the subordination of the other shepherds. Thus private
property as an institution and its attendant rights result naturally from
economic development. Private property replaces common property
when animals are owned by individual shepherds. David Hume in *An
Inquiry Concerning the Principles of Morals*, section III, part II, fervently
expresses his support for private property rights, that men's possessions should be separated for the sake of the interest and peace of
society: they are crucial to the development of commerce.

Honoré (1961: 113–20) listed these as rights to possess, use,
manage, receive an income, to alienate to another owner and continue as owner without expropriation. Private property rights can
always be overridden by a government. As the scope of government
has expanded in the interests of reducing income inequalities, cleaning the environment, planning economic development and providing
accommodation for its own activities, private property rights have
been curtailed. '**Externalities**' and 'social **costs**' are repeatedly used
to justify invasion of what is private.

A property right gives the exclusive right to determine how a
resource or asset is used, and to receive the incomes and services
flowing from it. Some property rights are not directly exercised by
their owners, especially in the case of companies and corporations in
which hired managers direct the use of the firm's assets. Under a
system of private property rights the uses of property reflect private
preferences, not governmental priorities.

If property rights are loosely regarded as control over resources
then managers in governmental and corporate organisations have

some of these rights. Also there are job property rights, because through contracts and legislation employees have entitlements vested in their jobs and employers are limited in their control, for example, through discrimination legislation.

Demsetz argued that property rights are fundamental to exchange, as what is exchanged is two bundles of property rights. What these rights are, he argued, amount to the rights to harm and benefit others. As property rights exist only when there is a society, there are both internal and external costs and benefits. To internalise an externality there has to be a net benefit. Single-person ownership has the advantage of making it easier to negotiate property rights with others, but there can also be multiple-person ownership through a publicly owned company/corporation which could have the benefits of cost reduction.

Coase's approach to the problem of environmental pollution shows how powerful the concept of property rights can be. It can deal with problems of social cost without the need for regulatory bodies under a system of governmental interference.

For economic development to occur in the present state of the world it is essential to establish the title to land. Without that there cannot be permission to invest and no hope of returns. Further, it is difficult to obtain **credit** without the collateral provided by property ownership. Art, care and industry Hume saw to be the consequence of individual property rights. Without the security of at least a long lease, improvement is not worthwhile.

Increasingly as the role of government has expanded there has been an interference with property rights. Privacy is invaded, for example by allowing aircraft to fly over land; uses are limited to avoid social spill-overs; **rents** are controlled and, under planning law, transferred compulsorily to others whatever the owner's wishes.

See also: **tragedy of the commons**

Further reading: Alchian and Demsetz 1973; Barzel 1997; Demsetz 1967; Forubotn and Pejovich 1972; Honoré 1961; Hume 1975; Locke 1988; Soto 2000

PROTECTION

The policy of charging tariffs on imports and imposing other restrictions, including quotas, to close an economy from outside international competition.

The principal reasons for imposing a tariff include raising indirect tax revenue, reducing the domestic consumption of foreign goods and services, maintaining economic independence, retaliating against the tariffs of other countries and encouraging infant industries. The last is often regarded as the only acceptable justification for protection, but although it is plausible to protect a young industry until its output increases and unit costs fall, often infant industries cannot shake off the help a tariff affords to stand on their own feet. Protection was a feature of the Soviet-type economies which traded with each other but did not have free trade with the rest of the world. A measure of protection can insulate a national economy from trade shocks and make economic planning easier.

Extensive protection can have a devastating effect on world trade, causing a widespread slump in national economies. This occurred through the passing of the Smoot-Hawley Act in 1930 by the US Congress. Repeated negotiations were necessary to restore free trade. Later the General Agreement on Tariffs and Trade which led to the World Trade Organisation substantially eliminated much protection.

Consumer protection is more innocent. By restricting the activities of businesses it provides minimum quality standards for consumers and their protection from injury.

Further reading: Gray 1985; Vousden 1990

PUBLIC CHOICE

An application of economic theory to politics in the form of analysing non-market decision making.

The voting mechanisms used in committees and in whole countries where there are referenda to make a collective choice have different designs and outcomes. The simplest expression of the collective will is when a decision is unanimous. It can take time to reach unanimity, especially if incentives have to be devised and individuals persuaded into complete agreement to a proposition. If unanimity is unachievable then a simple majority of half of the voters plus one can be sought. There will be gainers and losers, so questions of redistribution and compensation arise. The median voter rule states that the pivotal voter when preferences are arranged in a continuum will decide the outcome. There will be an equilibrium if the preferences are single-peaked, i.e. with only one maximum. Other voting systems can follow the plurality rule of choosing who or what is ranked first by most voters. The Condorcet system is pairwise elections following a majority principle. The Borda count gives m candidates points ranging from 1 to m. The candidate ranked first in the preferences of a voter gains m points, the second $m-1$. The winner has the largest number of points. Instead of voting orally or on paper, preferences can be shown by conduct, especially exit, such as when high levels of taxation induce electors to move (the Tiebout hypothesis).

It is assumed that voters are rational so they compare the expected **utility** flows from each option. Also they act according to self-interest.

The founders of present-day public choice theory are James Buchanan, Gordon Tullock and Anthony Downs. Buchanan did not regard governments and legislatures as full of altruistic people but as coalitions of self-interested individuals. Schooled in American politics, he was well aware that **regulations** and tax laws are formulated in pursuit of private interest, not the interests of the public as a whole. Instead of investigating the old theme of market failure, government failure concerned him. Rent seeking and **wealth** trading is the activity of legislators, not the selfless promotion of public welfare.

A classic text of this branch of economics is Buchanan and Tullock's *The Calculus of Consent: The Logical Foundations of Constitutional Democracy* (1962). They began by analysing the US constitution, recovering the intentions of James Madison, its author, and examining different voting rules. They distinguished ordinary politics which made decisions in legislatures from the different level of constitutional politics which sets the rules for ordinary politics; ways in which the voting system, for example through logrolling, can be used to benefit particular interest groups. What the state ought to be concerned them. They realised that Smith's **invisible hand** is successful in dealing with private goods but not with collective goods. An inspiration for them was Wicksell in his dissertation of 1896 and its implications for collective choice. They were concerned with majority voting leading to decisions unfavourable to a substantial portion of a population. Realising that it is difficult to get unanimous agreement, they recommended qualified majorities or very large majorities, far in excess of 50 per cent plus one.

Downs, in his *An Economic Theory of Democracy*, argued that the public is largely ignorant of political issues – it would be costly for them to learn – and their votes have little impact, so it is rational to abstain from voting. Voters minimise the cost of acquiring **information** relevant to making political choices, with the consequence that the democracy does not operate at maximum efficiency. Governments come to represent the interests of producers, not consumers. Governments are not altruistic but eager to obtain income, power and the prestige of holding office. Also to get elected it is important to appeal to the median voter. Tullock has been concerned with rent seeking, looking first at groups who benefit through possessing a monopoly or trade protection at the expense of the public at large.

Public choice theory exposes government failure, rather than examining the more researched notion of market failure. It is part of the twentieth-century critique of **socialism**. Also it has enriched the study of decision making.

See also: **social choice theory**

Further reading: Buchanan and Tullock 1962; Downs 1957; Mueller 2003; Peacock 1992; Tullock 1967a

PUBLIC FINANCE

The study of the sources of finance and the nature of the spending of all levels of government and their agencies.

Public finance is one of the most ancient branches of economics. Xenophon in his *Ways and Means of Increasing the Revenue of Athens* wrote perhaps the first work exclusively on this subject. Increasingly public finance has been interested in the provision of **public goods** and responding to the existence of **externalities**.

Initially governments financed themselves by obtaining free services under a feudal system, by plunder and by collecting simple taxes. Indirect taxes on goods, especially on imports, had the simplicity of being easy to collect and less easy to evade. Income tax became a permanent feature of the tax structure later – in Britain briefly in 1435, 1450, 1798–1805 and then from 1842, and in the USA in 1913 after the passing of the sixteenth amendment to the US Constitution. Some governments can finance themselves if they possess assets such as oilfields which can be leased, but it is generally through taxing and borrowing that finance is raised.

The spending undertaken will depend on the functions of government and of the level of government. A minimal state with few activities other than defence, law and order, and a few public services will require little tax revenue in peacetime unless it has accumulated a large national **debt**. In the early twentieth century the spread of democracy and the introduction of a welfare state with some measure of redistribution of incomes and of services made government expensive. New taxes were devised to raise the required revenue, for example, on deceased persons' estates and on activities such as emitting carbons.

Public finance uses different techniques to achieve its goal of financing programmes at minimum cost. Cost effectiveness studies and programming budgeting have emerged as modern methods.

See also: **fiscal federalism**; **fiscal policy**; **public choice**; **public sector**; **taxation**

Further reading: Buchanan 1975; Rosen 2005

PUBLIC GOOD

A good or service which is collectively provided and collectively consumed; not a private good. They are both non-rival and non-excludable.

Unlike private goods, public goods have non-rival **consumption** in that one person's consumption does not reduce another's. They are non-excludable in that all the individuals in a group have the good or service provided for them – whether or not individuals approve of the use of nuclear weapons as part of their national defence they still get their alleged protection.

Mistakenly, education and health care are sometimes thought of as public goods but they are mostly consumed by individuals. Lighthouses used to be exemplars of public goods but there are cases of private lighthouses which collected dues when ships went into the nearest port. Defence and public health measures are the most clear cut examples, as a government collectively provides them and they are consumed by the community at large rather than by private individuals.

Public goods are contrasted both with private goods, such as food and clothing, and with club goods available to a group. A global public good is available to all the peoples of the world, for example, some forms of knowledge.

See also: **clubs, theory of**

Further reading: Head 1974; Loehr and Sandler 1978; Samuelson 1954

PUBLIC SECTOR

The array of organisations consisting of national, regional and local governments, together with agencies and other organisations financed by those levels of government.

Ownership or control brings enterprises within the ambit of this sector. The public utility is a popular type of public enterprise. A suspicion of the exploitative and fraudulent nature of some private sector firms leads to a call for the government to be engaged in commercial activities. In the nineteenth century in Britain many local governments ran utilities, hence the expression 'gas and water socialism'. The fear that large companies have an undue power in a **national economy** leads to the call for public control over the 'commanding heights' of the economy. If this change of ownership occurs then the list for nationalisation usually includes energy, transport, steel, health care and postal services.

As inclusion in the public sector is supposed to increase public welfare it is usual to have different styles of management, price and wage fixing and accountability than prevails in the private sector. The public sector becomes the most regulated part of a national economy. Running some public services such as health and education without setting market **prices** runs into many problems of allocation and rationing. For national income purposes a measure of output is necessary which, if the service is free, has to be estimated as equal to the sum of the inputs.

Dissatisfaction with the performance, especially financial, of the public sector encouraged the privatisation of much of the public sector of some countries from the 1980s.

Further reading: Lane 1993

QUANTITY THEORY OF MONEY

A theory relating the quantity of money in a **national economy** to the **national income**.

Mercantilists made use of this idea, especially John Locke. Later the theory was formalised by Irving Fisher as $MV = PT$ where M is the stock of money, V the velocity of circulation, P the general price level, and T the volume of transactions. It was assumed that M was determined exogenously, V was fixed by the slow moving commercial habits of the population and T was also stable. This meant that the price level would move up and down through changes in the money supply in the same direction. It is a tautology, stating that if the velocity of circulation and volume of transactions are constant, an increase in the quantity of money will be inflationary.

Later Pigou and his Cambridge contemporaries in the 1930s reformulated the basic equation as $M/P = kY$ where the left-hand side shows the real stock of money and the demand for it being the 'Cambridge constant' k multiplied by real income.

Friedman in his restatement of the quantity theory, although accused of merely adopting the Keynesian liquidity preference theory, asserted that he was demonstrating that **money** does matter and lacks neutrality. Mises, then Friedman, posited an 'optimum quantity of money' which is the amount of money in existence at a particular time, so changing the money supply is non-optimal.

Further reading: Blaug *et al*. 1995

RATIONALITY

The quality of economic behaviour based on reason.

To be rational requires agents to be deliberate rather than instinc-tive in their actions. It is necessary for them to be able to understand and process data relevant to the choice between alternatives. Also a rational agent has to be able 'to get it right', for example, not be unreasonable by inflicting pain and income loss on herself. Over time the rational person will follow a course of action leading to some definable outcome. It is difficult to be rational when simultaneously one has several goals and an array of strategies. Rules can be devised for acting appropriately in such circumstances.

Rationality is an element in individual decision-making models, not the actions of collective entities. Rationality is often used as a starting point for an economic model. Within the framework of an ends and means analysis, rationality is a tool to choose the means and achieve the ends. In economics the broad idea of rationality is given a narrow instrumental sense. To work towards the goals of efficiency, equity, growth and stability shows rationality.

The central assumption is that individuals will consistently pursue courses of action which will result in the maximum gain to them. The gain can be expressed in expected wealth or expected utility. Rationality can exist at several levels: the abstract or theoretical, decision making, the practical performance of tasks, the creation of a framework of rules or even the constitution of an economic system in its search to provide maximum economic welfare. Rationality is regarded as conforming to a standard. This gives it perhaps a normative quality, but more commonly the standard is a set of logical requirements of consistency and coherence.

In **neoclassical economics** these elements are formally combined. It is assumed that representative individuals act from self-interest, have complete **information** and are deliberate in their decision making. In the hands of many modern theorists, rationality is reduced to a study of the self-interested individual's attempt to maximise utility, but rationality is appropriate also when altruism is analysed. An altruistic social goal can be rational, as can helping other individuals when there are associated goals for the giver.

Simon, an early exponent of rationality, discussed the 'economic man' with stable preferences who will calculate how to reach the highest state preferred. He noted that classically we can define rational choice procedures in three ways. The maxi-min rule of choosing the option with the worst payoff; the probabilistic rule of maximising expected values; the certainty rule of choosing the option with the largest payoff. Many bold assumptions have to be made about information available, that payoffs can be measured and that such calculations occur. Unlike human decision making, which is often sequential, the rational economic agent can make all these estimations of payoffs before a choice is made. For decision making within organisations Simon preferred the idea of 'approximate rationality' seeking a satisfactory aspirational level. Information is gathered and a sequence of choices is made. Limited information leads to limited rationality but the model is dynamic. Bounded rationality is where human reasoning is exercised within some constraints. Decision makers are themselves limited in knowledge and ability to process options. In fact computational ability becomes more of a constraint than the rationality itself. This is an unambitious account of what rationality can achieve. Bounded is contrasted with perfect rationality. The usefulness of this approach is that rationality is reduced to the more manageable notion of information processing.

Rationality in decision making has taken the form of situational analysis. Karl Popper devised this approach as the logical response of individuals to the objective situation in which they are to be found. The simplest case is of the single response, the single exit from a situation. More complex modelling has considered multiple exit situations. Neoclassical economics makes use of this approach.

A problem with models assuming rationality is that a goal expressed in terms of **utility** raises problems of utility measurement. Given the popularity of thinking of utility in terms of revealed preferences, to be rational amounts to being consistent in choosing the better rather than the inferior option. Rationality, however, has been much employed in the theory of consumer behaviour, where cardinal utility and perfect certainty are assumed.

Inevitably the assumption that behaviour is of the extreme maximising type is questioned, and the gentler assumption of satisficing, of searching for a goal that is satisfactory rather than the best, is asserted as more representative of human psychology. The quest for efficiency might be abandoned for an easier life.

Traditional models of rationality are challenged by the view that much decision making is not the consequence of deliberate weighing up of a situation but the slavish following of rules. Inasmuch as the rules are carefully thought out, there is more chance of being rational by following what has been carefully devised.

A popular use of rationality is in the idea of rational expectations, which take into account all information. This is a central feature of New Classical Macroeconomics. In **game theory** rationality is crucial: in fact without rationality there would be virtually no game theory. Practical rationality enters into Bayesianism. Through using probability calculations it is possible to test the rationality of beliefs. Thus persons having the same information concerning an uncertain proposition would arrive at the same probability.

See also: **expectations**

Further reading: Lipman 1995; Oakley 1999; Simon 1955

RAWLSIAN JUSTICE

Justice viewed as fairness, a theory outlined by John Rawls in his *A Theory of Justice*; the core of an economic game in which society makes judgements about social welfare.

The first principle is that everyone is entitled to as much liberty as is compatible with the liberty of others. Also any social and economic inequalities have to be to the advantage of all; positions and offices will have unrestricted access as there is **equality** of opportunity. Under a veil of ignorance of their social position, everyone decides the original position and cannot pursue self-interest. This veil will guarantee an impartial pursuit of the common good. Using a 'maximin' principle he argues that resources should be given to the worst off so that they are as well off as they can be. This approach is in the tradition of social contract theorists going back to Hobbes, Locke and Rousseau; he argues that there is a hypothetical agreement that there will be equality. Those least well off would be disproportionately favoured.

The cost of Rawls' type of justice could be the destruction of economic incentives. If the worst off get a better deal then there is little point in striving. Paradoxically in helping the disadvantaged, in the next period those advantaged now become disadvantaged. If there is a veil of ignorance then there is no self-knowledge and possible difficulty in forming rules for a just society. Also, as with many schemes for redistribution, there is for Rawls the problem of the measurement of **utility**.

See also: **equality**; **welfare economics**

Further reading: Howe and Roemer 1981; Kukathas 1990; Rawls 1999

REAL BUSINESS CYCLE

Fluctuations in economic activity which have arisen from technological change rather than from monetary shocks or changes in expectations.

John Muth and Robert Lucas invented this idea. Originally the idea was concerned with fluctuations in the agricultural sector. Real business cycle models have been used to mimic changes in the US economy. RBC models provide explanations of macroeconomic fluctuations by aggregating the decisions of representative **firms** and households that have rational **expectations** and maximise objective functions subject to technology and resource constraints. The emphasis is on examining random changes in productivity, part of the process of technical progress, which cause movements away from trend real income growth: these changes are not evolutionary nor are they inevitable. These technological shocks, which shift production functions, are expected to lead to changes in output, hours of work and productivity. It is difficult, however, to discover empirical examples of these shocks as they are expected to affect all sectors and all factors of production. Kydland and Prescott in their statistical analyses noted some surprising facts, such as prices rising in recessions and falling in booms, and real wages rising in expansions of the economy.

Critics argue that the RBC models are of limited usefulness as they fail to explain real asset prices and major downturns such as in the 1930s. To place technological shocks at the centre of explanations of cycles inevitably excites the criticism that a plethora of specific explanations for specific ups and downs, such as major policy changes, are wrongly dismissed. Some technological shocks are too small to explain some fluctuations in general economic activity.

The identification of a particular cycle often leads to recommending particular counter-cyclical policies. It is more difficult to create them to cope with real business cycles as they have random causes.

See also: **cycles**; **new classical economics**

Further reading: King *et al.* 1988a, 1988b; Kydland and Prescott 1990; Long and Plosser 1983; Lucas 1980

REGIONAL POLICY

A set of measures to improve the economic performance of a relatively poor region within a **national economy**.

A regional problem requiring a policy response is often defined as a state of low income and high **unemployment**. There are many determinants of regional problems. National wage bargaining can prevent the poorer areas from having the lower wages which would attract an influx of capital. The exhaustion of natural resources, especially in mining, can permanently reduce the economic opportunities for an area. The existence of a regional problem suggests a disequilibrium within a national economy: thus the task of the policy maker is to devise measures which will bring about interregional convergence in key economic indicators.

Often labour mobility and capital mobility fail to bring about the equalisation of factor rewards predicted by classical economics. Given the sluggishness of factors of production to respond to changing economic conditions, regional policy measures have been characterised as taking work to the workers through capital mobility, or taking the workers to work, labour mobility.

Regional policies have been devised both by national governments and supranational organisations such as the European Union. A policy can concentrate on providing the conditions for economic revival, on improving the infrastructure so there is a transport network, sufficient housing and an educated workforce. Key firms can be set up to encourage others to follow and together set up a 'growth pole'. Fiscal inducements can be offered to counter the costs of relocations. Local **taxation** can be waived and investment allowances against corporate taxation given. Individual workers can be helped with transport, training and housing expenses.

Further reading: Vanhoove 1987

REGULATION

The control of **firms, markets** and households by governments and their agencies.

Regulation always has aims. It can be in furtherance of macro-economic policies such as monitoring prices to help with the control of inflation through monetary and fiscal policies. It can be to advance health and safety through banning activities, or allowing them to occur only with safeguards. It can be part of a move towards the creation of a utopia.

Regulators do not trust people. Behaviour has to be checked, activities have to be inspected and more and more information collected on human actions. In all countries there is an overall policy choice between the loosest of **laissez-faire** controls to a level of observing and controlling the public which leaves little personal freedom, that only commands public support when there is national danger such as an impending invasion or natural disaster.

Regulation takes many forms. There can be the collection of information so that persons will behave better as they know they are observed. Activities can be outlawed, such as home production of alcoholic spirits: prohibition needs to be backed up with inspection. Regulation can be detailed interference in management, stating who can be employed on what terms, what investment can be undertaken and how prices should be set for which markets.

Some of the oldest forms of regulation were of corn markets, where the police would monitor dealing for its fairness, as high corn prices could provoke civil unrest. Regulation is all-pervasive in the command, planned economy of the old Soviet type, but other types of economy have resorted to regulation in time of crisis, such as in the USA in the early 1930s; in wartime when resources are scarce government regulation is common. Regulation is also popular for some industries, such as public utilities, where a commission determines prices and the quality of service. As a form of government control it is easier and cheaper to implement than taking industries into public ownership.

The ideological stance of a government will determine the range of regulated activities. Health concerns, including the consequences of smoking tobacco, sensitivity to environmental issues and objections to an unequal income distribution, have been prominent in justifying new objects of regulation.

The costs of regulation are many and can be severe. The regulated have to bear compliance costs. Resources which could have con-ferred direct benefits on the population are used to run inspection and enforcement offices.

Regulatory capture occurs where those regulated distort the reg-ulatory process to their own benefit. A common example is where **firms** in an industry persuade the regulators to restrict competition for the benefit of the industry.

Further reading: Armstrong 1994; Posner 1975; Stigler 1971

RENT

Payment for the temporary occupation of land or buildings on it; a surplus income accruing to a factor of production.

The payment of rent for the use of land is justified as a reward to the owner for the risk of damage by a tenant and for the cost of defending it from someone wishing to take possession or to damage it. A landlord has possession under the **property rights** established by the state where his land is located. In **classical economics** Smith insisted that rent is a component of natural **prices**; Ricardo that it was a consequence of product prices so that there was a reverse order in the determination of rent.

James Anderson, Malthus and then Ricardo used a differential rent theory. This asserts that as land can differ in location, especially its position relative to an urban area, or be of varying fertility, its yield varies too. Cultivation will continue until it reaches the marginal land where the costs of labour and capital to obtain a crop just equal the value of the produce. On the land of better quality or location than the marginal land, a surplus revenue in excess of costs − rent − will arise. With population growth more and more land is brought into cultivation, with rent increasing on the superior land. The theory can be challenged empirically, for example, the order in which land of new territories is cleared: for defensive reasons the less fertile land on hill tops may be put to agriculture first.

'Rent' can be generalised as 'economic rent', as a return which arises from the factor of production being in short supply. There is the 'rent of ability' arising from a person having rare talents, for example, in sport or entertainment. The more inelastic the supply, the greater is the economic rent. Usually employment incomes can be split into transfer earnings – what that person would obtain from the next best employment – and economic rent.

Much attention is now paid to rent seeking behaviour, which is obtaining an income other than through the processes of trade or production, typically through having monopoly rights, or obtaining special privileges from government as when tariff protection is granted to an industry. Seeking an income this way is often despised for allowing private individuals to benefit at the expense of society at large; in extreme cases it amounts to corruption.

Further reading: Krueger 1974; Tullock 1967a

RETURNS

Output relative to factor inputs.

In descriptions of production the rate of flows of inputs and consequential outputs can be compared to see if they are the same or different. If output is rising faster than inputs, there are increasing returns, if slower, diminishing returns but they are constant if they change at the same rate. A pure return to a factor is calculated when a variable input changes but the fixed input remains the same in quantity and quality. In **classical economics** the principal example of returns is the application of a variable amount of a composite of labour and capital to a fixed amount of land. Diminishing returns occurred through soil exhaustion. Adam Smith assumed there would be diminishing returns in agriculture where division of labour would be impossible, partly because of the seasons, and increasing returns in manufacturing.

To understand increasing returns an analysis of methods of production is necessary. The more efficient use of capital equipment, including maximising the hours of use through a shift system, leads to higher productivity, increasing returns.

The nature of the returns will explain the shape of average total **cost** curves. The familiar textbook case of those curves being U-shaped, falling to a minimum then rising again past the optimum production level, is a description of increasing returns giving rise to diminishing returns. The widespread evidence of increasing productivity in many industries suggests that the predominant type of returns is increasing returns. Agriculture, once the exemplar of diminishing returns, has become more and more productive.

See also: **economies of scale and scope; production function**

Further reading: Young 1928

RISK AND UNCERTAINTY

Risk is an outcome which can be calculated through measuring probabilities; uncertainty concerns the unknown future.

There are many types of risk. If it is systemic risk, then it is associated with a political event such as a change of government or a war, and has a broad effect on many types of asset. If a specific risk is unsystemic, it has a narrower effect, as when the profits and price of a company's shares are affected by a loss of market. Specific risks are political or financial. If associated with the state of a particular nation it is a country risk; if the consequence of policy changes it is political risk. Financial risk can occur through anything which directly affects the finances of a firm; hence credit risk, interest risk, foreign exchange risk and market risk due to the volatility of trading.

Economic agents can have different attitudes towards risk: loving it, being averse to it or being neutral. To minimise the losses which can result from risk, insurance can be used so that risk is pooled through premiums being paid to fund the payout to losers who suffer the hazard which is the subject of insurance. But there are problems with insurance. There can be adverse selection when the insured do not disclose all the facts relevant to the risk because they are in a high-risk category, so that the premium charged by the insurer can be too low. The characteristics of the persons insured may be more likely to lead to claims than those of the population in general. To avoid adverse selection problems, insurance can be designed for different sub-groups. Being insured can make a person indulge in wilder behaviour, thus giving rise to moral hazard; for example, a bank with insured deposits could care less about the amount of loans it permits. There will be a divergence between marginal private cost and marginal social cost. Risk is concerned with objective probabilities and uncertainty with subjective probabilities. Possibly uncertain events which can be grouped can be assigned an objective probability. Knight associated risk calculations with a mechanical view of economics which was too precise. Risk deals either with a priori probabilities such as rolling a dice, or statistical probabilities based on relative frequencies such as in life insurance. Because an **investment** often has an unknown outcome, part of the return will have a risk premium. This was recognised as a necessary inducement to investors as far back as Adam Smith and JS Mill. In the capital asset pricing model of Merton and others, risk is measured by the variance in the expected return. Uncertainty is concerned with estimates where the instances cannot be classified validly. With uncertainty, the future is entirely unknown so it cannot be measured and be covered by insurance. **Profit**, the residual of revenue after costs have been deducted, occurs because of uncertainty: it is a reward for uninsurable hazard. Keynes, writing in 1937 about his general theory of employment, associated risk with Benthamite calculations of a consequence of an action and his work with the uncertain situations when the future is unknown. Shackle challenged the Keynesian view and argued that uncertainty is a complex phenomenon, not merely a world where probabilities cannot be calculated.

Heisenberg formulated in 1927 his 'uncertainty principle' that there cannot be an absolute accuracy of measurement of the simultaneous relationship between a pair of related measurements. The greater the uncertainty, the less exact the measurement. The major case of uncertainty is in financial markets, where many prices and rates of return cannot be estimated precisely. There is natural uncertainty when a process is essentially random. Model uncertainty occurs because of the assumptions, scope and structure of the model. Data uncertainty arises from measurement and classificatory errors. This kind of uncertainty is also known as 'epistemic'. In game theory there can be strategic uncertainty because of the information being private.

Subjective expected **utility** probability was developed by Ramsey and others. Subjective beliefs are revealed by the bets actually made, rather than intuition. Savage refined this attitude towards uncertainty by combining a personal utility function showing the utilities from different outcomes of an uncertain event and a personal probability analysis. The sum of the utilities multiplied by the probabilities is calculated. In practice it is difficult to find individuals with consistent views of risk.

Decision theory has the problem of uncertainty central to making a choice. A lottery is a principal example of such decision making. It is concerned with expected values and standard deviations. The axioms of the theory are that the preferences are ordered, transitive, continuous, substitutable, monotonic (neither increasing or decreasing) and decomposable. Modern views of uncertainty assert that it is based not only on randomness but also on beliefs and behaviour. The cultural norms of the society will obviously affect decision makers.

The sharp distinction between risk and uncertainty has been challenged. Friedman argued that human beings can attach probabilities to every conceivable event. Also it is difficult to argue that risk is always based on what is objective and uncertainty on what is subjective: Knight rejected the view that everything is unique or absolutely the same.

Further reading: Keynes 1937; Knight 1921; LeRoy and Singell 1987; Lupton 1999; Ramsey 1931; Savage 1954; Schmidt 1996; Sharpe 1964

ROBINSON CRUSOE ECONOMY

A self-sufficient economy of an isolated individual, first described in Daniel Defoe's novel *Robinson Crusoe* (1719).

Crusoe has been depicted as the model of self-interested man. Marx in *Das Kapital* regarded Crusoe as a pre-capitalist man producing goods because they are useful rather than profitable. Crusoe's different activities can be regarded as different modes of human labour. Crusoe keeps a record of the **labour** time expended on average for producing specific quantities of products. Marx regarded such an economy as 'simple and transparent'.

Crusoe can also be regarded as both a consumer and a producer, making choices between work and leisure. His economy is an extreme case of isolation from the rest of society and the world, with an isolated individual having to make all economic decisions. This picture of a simple life is extensively used as a starting point in explaining the theory of production. The process of rational **utility** maximisation is also shown in this parable.

Further reading: Grapard 1995

SATIABILITY OF WANTS

The limit to **consumption**.

Bentham, Senior and several economists of the early nineteenth century, noted that there is a law of diminishing marginal **utility**.

This means that when successive units of a particular good are consumed by one person initially the next unit consumed may provide greater satisfaction, but a point in this continued consumption will be reached when each successive unit consumed pleases the consumer less than the previous one. Because of this satiability of wants, greater amounts of a good will only be purchased if the price is lower, a reason for the downward sloping normal **demand curve**: Marshall in his *Principles of Economics*, book III, chapter III, describes this phenomenon.

This law is evident in **consumption** patterns of households. Given there is a limit to the demand for goods such as food, as income grows there is a switch from the consumption of necessities to taking comforts then resorting to luxuries. Later there is a switch to consuming services rather than goods, as was predicted in Petty's law.

The phenomenon of satiability has been used in defence of income redistribution. Those with large consumptions gain little satisfaction at the margin so would lose little through a fall in income, but the poorer with meagre intakes could still be gaining utility if income were transferred to them.

SAVING

The portion of income not consumed; the portion of income set aside for future **consumption**, and **investment**.

Savings can be undertaken by an individual person, by firms and by governments. For individuals, saving is difficult when incomes are low. A life cycle has been identified, with little saving until middle age then much saving for retirement until saving drops again. Firms often accumulate savings as they wait for investment opportunities, or because of a cautious policy of gradually distributing dividends to shareholders so that there will always be reserves to prevent a fall in dividends. Government saving is related to cycles in the economy. A government intent on maintaining the stability of an economy will have deficits, negative savings, in recessions but savings in times of prosperity when public sector debt can be reduced. There is the paradox of thrift, namely that saving is a virtue but there is a limit to being virtuous as the fall in demand will push the economy downward. In the macroeconomic theory debates of the 1930s there was much debate about saving, as it had to be clearly defined to be incorporated into a national accounting framework.

Saving can be voluntary or forced, a phenomenon recognised by writers as early as Thornton, Bentham and Malthus. A shortage of consumer goods makes people save by default, possibly by a switch in resources to producing capital goods. **Inflation** can reduce the amount of real consumption. To explain how an ex-ante imbalance between saving and investment becomes an ex-post balance under the operation of the **multiplier**, it was argued by JM Keynes that at each round of income generated, saving would be induced. In the Soviet-type economy the high rate of investment reduces consumption and forces household saving. In Britain during the Second World War, under budgetary policy the government extracted saving from taxpayers, as recommended by Keynes in his *How to Pay for the War*. Shareholders can be forced to save by the boards of directors of the companies they own as a result of a board decision to leave part of post-tax corporate income undistributed.

The optimal rate of saving is discussed in contexts such as **economic growth** theory. The Ramsey saving rule is that 'the rate of saving multiplied by the marginal utility of money should always be equal to the amount by which the total rate of enjoyment of utility falls short of the maximum possible rate of enjoyment' (1928: 543). Optimum saving as a proportion of the national income is the inverse of the **elasticity** of marginal utility.

Further reading: Ramsey 1928

SAY'S LAW

The assertion that a **national economy** at the aggregate level in its natural state is in **equilibrium**.

The law of **markets**, as its originator, the French economist Jean Baptiste Say, called it, originated in his reply to a pamphlet by William Spence concerning the loss of trade between England and France during the Napoleonic Wars. Say argued that there can never be a general glut of production, for we do not buy goods with money but with the proceeds of a sale. 'Supply creates its own demand', so an economy in equilibrium will be at full employment.

The most fervent contemporary expounder of the law was James Mill in *Commerce Defended* (1808). He admitted that there could be excess supply of a particular commodity but not of all commodities. If there is an excess supply of one good then there must be a deficiency in the supply of another because overall the economy is balanced annually. His son, JS Mill, in the second of his *Some Unsettled Essays on Political Economy* ('Of the Influence of Consumption on Production') distinguished the law for a barter economy from a version for a monetised economy. The great problem is that when the economy becomes monetised prices are expressed in money, not other goods, and the proceeds of a sale can be hoarded and not used to buy other goods. He believed that the law held if produce were distributed without miscalculation.

This was opposed strongly by Malthus and later by Keynes. Malthus argued in his *Principles of Political Economy*, section III, that commodities are not always exchanged for commodities, and that Say was ignoring the principles of supply and demand through not tracing the effects of a glut on lowering prices and supply. Demand could fall through saving being preferred to consumption, or through workers preferring indolence to the work which would increase income. Keynes argued, in book I, chapter 2 of his *General Theory of Employment, Interest and Money*, that the fallacy underlying Say's law is that there is a connection between deciding to abstain from **consumption** today and deciding to provide for future consumption. From the proposition that the demand price for output as a whole equals the supply price stem the classical doctrines on thrift, laissez-faire, unemployment and the quantity theory of money.

Further reading: Kates 2003

SCARCITY

The limited nature of most resources.

Scarcity has been called The Economic Problem. In **classical economics** the assumption of a fixed amount of land is prominent, for example, in Ricardo's theory of **rent** and in Malthus' principle of population. Robbins, writing in the 1930s, defined economics as 'the study of scarce means which have alternative uses' reflecting scarcity. In an uncontrolled market scarcity is identified by the levels and movements in prices. Because of scarcity, everything has an opportunity **cost**. In economics trade-offs are frequently encountered as more of X is at the expense of less of Y. Lines downward sloping from left to right illustrate scarcity and trade-offs in a diagram with X and Y axes. Scarcity is a state of demand exceeding supply. This gives rise to problems of allocation, which are usually resolved by free use of the price mechanism or by rationing.

Socialist critics of conventional economics dislike the notion of scarcity, hence their opposition to Malthus' population principle in which subsistence limits population growth. Some types of scarcity can be eliminated by increasing supply: for example, exploration to discover further oil deposits, or training workers to reduce a skills shortage. Changes in fashion can reduce demand and consequently cause a profusion of unwanted goods. Traditionally land was regarded as the scarce factor fixed in amount, but any factor, including skilled labour and financial capital, can be scarce. Concern about the scarcity problem has been revived through the growth of **environmental economics** and the study of **exhaustible resources**.

See also: **exhaustible resources**; **rent**

SEARCH THEORY

An account of the behaviour of buyers and sellers in seeking to clear markets.

The leading example of search is in the **labour** market where workers search for job opportunities and employers for workers. Stigler pioneered a neoclassical marginalist approach to search, stating that search would continue in a labour market until the marginal benefit from search equalled its marginal cost. A worker often has to pay the costs of search – travel, buying appropriate clothes for interviews, preparing the curriculum vitae and engaging in correspondence. The costs of search are a form of investment to the person incurring them: either a worker or an employer through meeting search expenses expects to obtain a positive rate of return. A shortage of labour will encourage an employer to spend more on searching greater distances for workers and to subsidise their private search costs. There are strong arguments for subsidisation of search costs by employers and retailers in order to adjust demand to supply. Governments provide **information** to reduce the search costs of households; for example, in providing free job centres so that there will be lower unemployment, and in producing literature on food to improve health.

In a sense, in all product markets there is the constant search which buyers and sellers participate in together. Search theory has also been used in the study of **money**.

Further reading: Stigler 1962

SEGMENTED LABOUR MARKET

The description of the **labour** market as a set of separated sub-markets.

This theory, initiated by JS Mill and JE Cairnes, asserted that the labour market is fragmented into non-competing groups separated by barriers to entry. Mill used it to explain the lower wages of women.

Labour is essentially heterogeneous in nature because of wide variation in skills, education and native abilities. A labour market can only be understood in a very generalised way if a detailed analysis is not undertaken. Where the market is artificially divided to express prejudices about workers' personal characteristics, for example their race, then **poverty**, wage differentials and **discrimination** arise. Differences in income are found to have little justification and are clearly the consequence of devices to restrict supply to sub-markets. The segmentation might occur because of prejudice, custom, or the practices of educational establishments and training institutions.

Because the sub-markets are sealed from each other, wages and employment vary from part to part of the total market. The sub-markets with barriers to entry will have restricted supply, which will increase prices/wages and reduce output/the number employed. By legislation artificial barriers can be outlawed, but physical barriers, such as those separating local markets, will remain.

See also: **discrimination**

SELF-MANAGED ENTERPRISE

A form of producers' cooperative.

Workers' participation in management in its mildest forms can range from consultation to their representation on boards of directors. The extreme case of 'industrial democracy' is where the management is conducted by the workforce as a whole, with the workers on the board of directors and responsible for all financing, personnel, production and marketing decisions; also known as autogestion. It was a leading feature of the former Yugoslav economy and also extensively practised, even in modern manufacturing factories, in the Basque region of Spain. This type of enterprise has its ancestry in communist or communitarian ideals.

Ideally, the absence of a tension between management and workers will increase productivity and lead to fairer wages. But problems abound for such enterprises, as many workers might be reluctant to be involved in management. Also, as workers prefer any value-added to be distributed in higher wages rather than assigned to investment, the enterprise will become undercapitalised over time, unless departing workers can sell their equity shares; but if they do, then the enterprise becomes a kind of joint stock company with outside shareholders.

Further reading: George 1993; Vanek 1972

SOCIAL CAPITAL

The infrastructure of a country; the benefits accruing from social interaction.

This form of capital in the traditional sense, sometimes called overhead capital, referred to the infrastructure which made possible the functioning of a society and an economy. Roads, railways, ports, schools, hospitals and other public buildings are the principal examples. In some senses this is an informal kind of socialism, of benefit to a community but with light central control.

Recently the concept has been extended to consider the informal networks of society. It describes the cooperation of groups in joint productive activities. This form of capital includes intangibles such as traditions, neighbourliness, networks of friends and non-commercial organisations, and excludes physical and human capital. Unlike the private capital of households, it is held for the benefit of other individuals. It shares with other types of capital durability and the yielding of substantial returns. Social capital reduces the cost of communication by making much of it informal. It also makes the observance of contracts easier, as a major form of social capital is trust. Where there is trust, transaction **costs** and monitoring costs will be lower.

Further reading: Becker 1974; Field 2004

SOCIAL CHOICE THEORY

The rationale for making decisions for society at large when individuals have different and incompatible preferences.

To make any judgement about the state of a whole society requires inquiry into social choice, taking into account the number of persons and number of possible states. This raises an adding-up problem which has to be faced in many areas of economic policy and which in any pursuit of the public interest has a long ancestry. Sen considered different dimensions to social choice, including committee decisions when committee members have different views, social welfare judgements about whether there will be a net benefit to society, and normative indications for a society such as the meaning of national income.

Early sketches of social choice theory originate in late eighteenth-century France, when there was a conscious effort to institute democracy. Using sophisticated approaches, Borda and Condorcet began the modern analysis of this problem. Following Borda's method, if there are n options and each voter ranks her choice from the least desirable 0 to the most (n − 1), the option with the highest score is the winner. Under the Condorcet approach, if the candidates are paired, the voters have to choose; of every pair the winner will have been successful in all the votes. Another approach is the median voter theorem, that the choice of the median voter is the equilibrium voter, providing that there is only one peak in the distribution.

Bentham tried to decide upon the social good by adding together satisfactions into the total **utility** for the whole community. There are questions of the measurement of utility, essential if there were to be aggregation from the individuals' utilities to the total utility of a community, and also whether to consider distribution of utility within a community as well as the total. Interpersonal comparisons of utilities are difficult if it is strictly asserted that utility is a personal subjective state, except in cases of extreme wealth and poverty, unless proxy measures of utility and comparisons of groups are tolerated. Sen suggests 'informational broadening' (1999: 366).

To have a fair outcome, consistency has always been required in this area of economics. Several problems have been identified. There is the difficulty of following a principle of majority rule in decision making, in that the majorities from difficult votes can be incompatible, which is often the case when voters delegate to political parties with large programmes the expression of their preferences. There is also, in Arrow's expression, the 'impossibility' of reconciling the preferences of individuals. The conditions for a social welfare function were set out and debated.

Bergson made an early attempt to create a social welfare function, setting out conditions for an increase in economic welfare so that an increase in the national dividend or income would on average not affect the poor more than the rich or vice versa.

Arrow has four elements in his proof of the impossibility of social choice. First, the universal domain criterion states that a vote is rational only if it corresponds to one of the set of ordered preferences. Second, Pareto **efficiency** pronounces the voting system irrational if the winning choice is not the preferred choice. Third, non-dictatorship demands that the outcome cannot be dictated by a single person. Fourth, there is independence from alternatives which are not the subject of the vote.

Sen in 1977, in his assessment of Arrow, raises the problems of deficiencies in **information** in the representation of interests, and the difficulties of regarding binary choices as basic to social preferences.

Libertarians argue that there is a need to incorporate individual rights into social choice theory, as explained by Wrigglesworth. This right must be exercised by the person concerned. Society is better off by recognising that right, but the right might lead to so much damage that it should not be exercised, for example, promoting racial hatred and that the right is just.

Further reading: Bergson 1938; Sen 1977, 1999; Wrigglesworth 1985

SOCIALISM

A creed based on collectivism; a cooperative form of organisation for a community or an entire country; an alternative to **capitalism**.

This ancient idea can be traced at least as far back as Plato's *Republic* in which the elite guardians lived in common. The monastic life was a later form of sharing. In the nineteenth century schemes of socialism abounded. Saint-Simon attempted a form of scientific socialism in which national economies would be run by experts, a possible inspiration for twentieth-century Leninism in Russia. More idealistic community schemes are associated with Robert Owen, Charles Fourier, William Thompson and John Bray. Later in the nineteenth century a debate between revolutionary and gradualist socialism began. JS Mill favoured the latter, as did the Fabian Society founded in 1884.

Central to most of socialism is the desire to have all means of production under the control of a collective entity, whether a government or a voluntary community. Also, a replacement for the alleged anarchy of the market and the **poverty** of much of the population is sought. This quest is justified in terms of producing a fairer **income distribution** and less arduous working conditions.

However, it is difficult at the state level to be both democratic and fully socialist, as a multitude of political parties and political dissent destroy unity. A critical free press is also a threat to socialism. At the state level, various forms of **planning** have been advocated and practised to replace the individualism inherent in the market.

Socialism at the level of the small community has often been practised. Famous examples include the Israeli *kibbutzim*. Often these seek a utopia with equal incomes, an abolition of the **division of labour** and the pursuit of a set of religious or quasi-religious goals. This concept has ancient roots with divergent recommendations. Plato in his *Republic* wanted common ownership, but unlike many of his successors, he advocated division of labour because of its promotion of **productivity**. Thomas More, in his *Utopia* (1516), was deliberately writing of an imaginary place in that 'utopia' in Greek means 'no place'. In his ideal community there was common ownership, and compulsory labour limited to six hours per day, alternating between work in the country and in the town every two years. Labour and goods would be allocated by elected officials. Movement around the country and the style of dress would be strictly controlled. Eating would have to be in common. Later, many writers, including Thomas Reid in his *Practical Ethics*, flirted with the idea of utopias.

Before Marx, socialist theories and proposals abounded in Britain and France. Major themes of these socialist pioneers included the view that **labour** was the only source of wealth, that capitalists exploited the productive/working classes, that there should be greater or complete **equality** of incomes, that there is an inverse relationship between wages and profits, and that production should usually avoid the division of labour. Agrarian writers, such as Spence in a lecture on 'The Real Rights of Man' in 1775 at Newcastle upon Tyne, advocated the common ownership of land. Charles Hall in *The Effects of Civilisation on the People in European States* (1805) powerfully anticipated later authors. He argued that what people produce should belong to them and that workers receive only one eighth of the national income so lose to those who do nothing. If resources are used to produce manufactures for exports, fewer resources are available domestically to provide necessities for the poor. He recommended a redistribution of land. Saint-Simon in his writings in the 1820s, including *Catechisme des industriels* (1823–26) advocated a 'scientific socialism' of industrial associations run by scientists and economists. Detailed schemes for running socialist communities abounded. Owen in his *Report to the County of Lanark* (1820) devised a blueprint for new communities of 300 to 2,000 men, women and children with a mixture of agricultural and manufacturing work. Fourier, especially in his *Social Destiny of Man* (1840), drew up utopian schemes which based production on human passions, including the desire for change of activity. In his ideal community, or 'phalanstery', of 1,600 persons there would be no division of labour but inequalities of incomes in the form of dividends. The Irish writer William Thompson in his *An Inquiry into the Principles of the Distribution of Wealth Most Conducive to Human Happiness* (1824) proposed mixed manufacturing and agricultural communities of 500 to 2,000 inhabitants. Owen was rare amongst these writers in putting his ideas into practice in communities in Hampshire, England and Indiana, USA, suffering heavy financial losses from his investments.

State capitalism, especially associated with the Soviet-type economy, required that the state own all the means of production and operate the economy like a large multi-divisional **firm**. Marx in *The Communist Manifesto* saw in the first stage of revolution the proletariat, the wage earners, centralising all the means of production in their hands and becoming the ruling class, using many of the methods of capitalists. But this state would wither away through the abolition of classes, so no class could oppress another. As the state is run by workers for their benefit, there is no need for independent **trade unions**. Market processes are not used for allocating goods and services, but planning undertaken by administrators rationing what is available.

The socialist calculation debate considered how an economy under socialism would be organised and if it would be more efficient. Mises argued that proper pricing would be impossible if the state owned the means of production. Hayek argued that too much **information** would be needed under planning so it would be impracticable.

Further reading: Stiglitz 1990

SPATIAL ECONOMICS

A study of the consequences of the existence of physical space between economic agents.

The physical separation of productions gives rise to transport and transaction **costs**. They can create barriers to entry and lead to local monopolies, which were common before good roads and railways linked towns. The presence of distance reduced the amount of **information** circulating about alternative suppliers, and enabled firms to practise price **discrimination** against consumers.

Early theories of location were those of von Thünen and Lösch. Thünen in 1826 described a city in an isolated state bounded by wilderness. He drew a series of concentric rings on homogeneous land, enclosing different agricultural activities, with perishable goods being produced closer to the city. The city at the centre of the rings would have the most population and hence most demand for produce. Land closer to the city would be more valuable. There are echoes of the differential theory of **rent** which can be based on fertility or location differences. Outlying producers would have to pay their own transport **costs** to be competitive in the central market. Christaller developed a theory of central places: places with central functions which achieved their status through accommodating institutions of administration culture, religion, health care, entertainment, culture, commerce, finance, and transport network hubs. The distribution of central places will depend on markets, traffic and the degree to which places are separated. The optimal location for production is defined by Weber as the place of minimum transport costs. More complex theories have a broader concept of cost, recognising the diminishing importance of location to some modern industries and economic activities. Marshall was an early pioneer of the idea of external economies for a **firm** arising from its location in a cluster of similar producers.

Many economic theories have a spatial dimension. In the theory of the firm there can be spatial monopolies because of transport costs separating suppliers, and spatial oligopolies where dispersed firms compete for the same group of customers. In the theory of distribution, spatial issues often arise. An important type of wage differential is geographical or regional. In the theory of rent there can be differential rent because of either fertility or location. Because regional and local governments have tax-raising powers, a tax burden will vary from place to place. In the Tiebout hypothesis it is argued that there will be fiscal mobility, so that individual taxpayers will move to that area which has the preferred combination of publicly provided facilities and taxation levels.

Policy responses to the existence of transport costs usually consist of subsidising remote consumers, for example, by charging the same price for postage stamps irrespective of delivery costs and the same fare per mile for public transport so that the profits made from short trips cross-subsidise the longer hauls. There can be central or local government grants to help the locationally disadvantaged. **Regional policies** aim to equalise the incomes and economic prospects of persons at different locations.

Technical progress has reduced transport costs. The creation of the internet and advanced electronic and telephonic communication have made physical location of little importance. Increasingly there can be footloose industries able to locate anywhere without disadvantage.

See also: **migration and mobility**

Further reading: Christaller 1966; Hoover 1948; Tiebout 1956; Weber 1929

STABILISATION POLICY

The combination of monetary, fiscal and other measures to reduce the amplitude of cyclical swings in a national economy.

This policy concern can be traced back to the Swedish economist Knut Wicksell, who argued that there would be a cumulative process away from **equilibrium**: if the market rate exceeded the natural rate of interest the economy would decline but there would be expansion if the market rate were less. A disequilibrium could be rectified by adjustments in banking policy to change the rate of interest.

In the mid-twentieth century, demand management, partly under the influence of the Keynesian revolution, in the form of frequent discretionary changes in national tax rates, **interest rates** and other tools of government, was used to keep economies on their desired track. Difficulties abounded in this attempt at 'fine tuning': data were often late and full of inaccuracies; there were time lags in recognising the need for action, taking action and obtaining the desired results; and there was a paucity of capable forecasting models. Subsequently other fashions in stabilisation policy emerged, especially when **monetarism** was in vogue, along with policy rules such as aiming to have a steady rate of growth of the money supply. Central bank independence has attempted to make monetary policy independent of government so that stabilisation policy will be based more on economic expertise than on political decision.

The most difficult task of stabilisation policy is when an economy has virtually collapsed with hyperinflation, a worthless currency and a stock market crash. An organisation such as the International Monetary Fund can only recommend a drastic revision of public finances, including large cuts in public expenditure, and a reformed **currency**, perhaps even a new one.

Further reading: Stiglitz *et al.* 2006

STOCKHOLM SCHOOL

A group of Swedish economists of the 1930s who provided a distinctive dynamic theory of macroeconomics and policy proposals to revive depressed **national economies**.

The principal writers were heavily influenced by Wicksell, who set out the conditions for price stability and monetary **equilibrium**, describing the cumulative processes of contraction and expansion caused by divergences between the natural and money rates of interest. Myrdal, Ohlin and Lindahl were leading members of the school. Myrdal in setting out the conditions for monetary equilibrium made the ex-ante and ex-post distinction. Lindahl wanted to determine time functions or curves based on the initial values of economic values and the conditions determining the fluctuations in those values. He analysed plans which express economic motives. In the process of **planning** different changes have to be recognised: those caused by altered anticipations, economic events, immediate and distant influences on planned actions, and those which are so fundamental as to require a new plan. Unlike their theoretical competitors in Cambridge, England centred on John Maynard Keynes, they used period analysis, thereby avoiding comparative statics. Independently Ohlin, for example, developed key concepts such as the multiplier by tracing the effects of investment over several periods and the speed of inventory adjustment; also he considered the consequences of different methods of financing public works.

Their policy recommendations, especially those aiming to cure **unemployment**, were closely related to the Social Democrats' programme, including public works. Lindahl, in his discussion of the balancing of the budget, recommended that there should be an ordinary budget consisting of current revenue and expenditure and an extraordinary budget stating loans and capital expenditure. The current budget would allocate money to the extraordinary so that public works could be carried out. Taxation would rise and fall with the prosperity of the economy.

Further reading: Jonung 1991; Lindahl 1939; Myrdal 1939; Ohlin 1937

STRUCTURAL ADJUSTMENT

The responses by the **labour** force and other factors of production to changes in demand or supply, often resulting from an external shock to a national economy.

As a consequence of a decline in one industry or area and an increase elsewhere, structural **unemployment** occurs in the old, and shortages in the new parts of an economy. A frequent response is to have training schemes to help the labour force to adjust. Much of **regional policy** is concerned with structural adjustment. The private costs of structural adjustment are often subsidised by unemployment allowances and other welfare payments. The biggest problem of adjustment is where a country has predominantly old industries, especially in manufacturing and mining, which cannot meet international competition.

A major shock, for example a change in the price of imported energy, can necessitate massive changes, such as adopting different technologies and reducing the level of activity in industries with a high demand for electricity or oil. Awareness of global warming is leading to calls for changes in the construction of buildings, type of travel and many forms of production.

Structural adjustment programmes are a major part of the work of supranational organizations. The International Monetary Fund often demands free trade, a currency devaluation and balanced government budgets. The European Union has sought a restructuring of agriculture through setting aside land and preventing over-production.

STRUCTURE OF AN ECONOMY

A set of relationships between parts of an economy.

Every **national economy** is built up from micro components, from **firms** and households. What is occurring at the macro level can only be understood by examining these micro foundations, because economic agents exist at that micro level. With the growth of government there is also a governmental sector as well as households and firms in an economy. As these three types of sector all produce for themselves and others and consume from each other, there are bonds which tie them into one structure.

The predominant way of analysing an economy is the matrix cellular method in which the rows and columns of a table are used to indicate how one component of an economy, for example, a region or an industry, is related to the others. If this structure is stable then it can be used for predictive purposes. The best known description of this kind is Leontief's input-output matrix.

An economy can also be described as a building with foundations supporting a superstructure, as when identifying key sectors and basic activities. Deep structures can be identified by statistical and econometric techniques to discover underlying relationships, as in identifying different cycles in a national economy. Economics, like linguistics, can view deep structures as unifying theoretical constructs. These biological, architectural and statistical tools illuminate how an economy functions.

Structures can be described by activity, listing the proportions of output or employment in each activity. The state and private sectors can be contrasted and the distinction between producing goods and producing services noted. Structures can be static or dynamic: if the latter, one part of the structure can drive forward change in the other parts. A structure is especially dynamic if many of the sectors have an investment character. Some structures are hidden, as is the case with corporate ownership which is too interrelated and changing to be obvious. The informal or unofficial economy is a disguised structure where the separate 'firms' are concealed and the relationships between the informal and formal sectors scarcely known.

Economic policies will affect the way in which an economy is described structurally. In the Soviet-type economy there was a division between defence and non-defence industries, with the former receiving for reasons of international politics preferential access to resources. The characteristics of labour will provide a basis for describing an economy. Because a worker has a particular occupation, industry and place of work, it is natural to speak of the occupational, industrial and geographical structures of an economy. Imbalances in any of these structures will suggest policy responses in terms of training and regional policy.

National economies have traditional or modern structures. The extent to which the modern prevails over the traditional has a crucial effect on the overall economic growth rate. By abandoning an agriculturally dominant structure for industrialisation, growth rates have soared in many Asian countries.

See also: **dual economy**

SUPPLY-SIDE ECONOMICS

A popular school of American economics in the 1980s, also known as Reaganomics.

It emphasised the importance of low taxation to provide **incentives** to workers and investors. A well-known tool of this type of economics was the Laffer curve, which asserted that tax revenue would rise to a maximum at a particular level of a tax rate, thus making high tax rates pointless for a government. There have been empirical tests to determine if the tax revenue-tax rate curve is of the predicted shape: it is for some individual taxes, but it is not universally true.

This approach sought a regime of low **taxation** and a reliance on monetary policy to run the national economy. It was a reaction to the Keynesian-dominated approach which enthroned effective demand as central to managing an economy. In a sense it was a revival of Say's law.

Although largely concerned with macroeconomic policy, by examining incentive mechanisms supply-side economics rooted government policy in microeconomics. Taxation proposals were linked to a call for deregulation of industries to further increase post-tax incomes.

See also: **taxation**

Further reading: Bartlett and Roth 1984; Minford 1991

SURPLUS VALUE

A term in **Marxian economics** which measures the amount of exploitation extracted from workers by capitalists.

Under merchant **capitalism** surplus value arises through a merchant selling goods for more than they cost; under industrial capitalism, by lengthening the working day absolute surplus value in excess of the subsistence needed for workers is created. There can also be relative surplus value by labour **productivity** reducing the amount of labour needed to produce subsistence, thus leaving a margin for the capitalist. Instead of the **national income** being distributed as wages, rent, interest and profit, it can be simply divided into wages and surplus value. It was asserted that in the early stages of economic development surplus value is mainly absolute in nature; later it is chiefly relative.

The rate of surplus value, or rate of exploitation, is measured by the ratio of surplus value to variable capital (the wages fund). Other methods of measuring exploitation include seeing if workers have wages at least equal to their marginal products.

See also: **Marxian economics**; **value**

Further reading: Walton 1972

TAXATION

The array of charges levied by governments.

Taxes are direct if levied directly on persons, as is an income tax, or indirect, such as a sales tax if the immediate object of taxation is impersonal. A personal income tax can start after a tax-free allowance, and can be different for lower and higher bands of income, or be a flat tax with the same rate for all levels of income. If the amount of tax taken rises at a faster rate than the taxpayer's income, it is progressive. The average rate of tax is the proportion of total income paid in taxation; the marginal rate of tax the proportion of the last unit of income levied as tax. If the marginal rate of tax on the last unit of income is high, there can be a disincentive to supply labour, although a higher marginal rate can be an incentive if the taxpayer has a post-tax income goal. Indirect taxes can be lump sum or ad valorem, i.e. related to the value of what is taxed. These taxes are often regressive; since they are fixed in amount they absorb a higher proportion of the pre-tax income of lower income groups.

Treasuries and finance ministries have imaginatively discovered many things and activities which could be taxed: incomes in all their variety, capital holdings and gains, imports, sales, value-added. Taxes can be collected directly by government employees, or indirectly when the permission to collect taxes is sold to a 'tax farmer' who has a right to tax providing an agreed sum of revenue is handed to the government.

Adam Smith (1976b) set out the 'canons of taxation':

I The subjects of every state ought to contribute towards the support of the government, as nearly as possible, in proportion to their respective abilities; that is, in proportion to the revenue which they respectively enjoy under the protection of the state.

II The tax which each individual is bound to pay ought to be certain, and not arbitrary. The time of payment, the manner of payment, the quantity to be paid, ought all to be clear and plain to the contributor, and to every other person.

III Every tax ought to be levied at the time, or in the manner, in which it is most likely to be convenient for the contributor to pay it.

IV Every tax ought to be so contrived as both to take out and to keep out of the pockets of the people as little as possible over and above what it brings into the public treasury of the state.

The first of these maxims raises the issue of fair taxation based on ability to pay, which is ambiguous because this attempt at equality can be based on absolute sacrifice, relative sacrifice, or marginal sacrifice. Also Smith is suggesting a benefit tax, whereby the amount paid by the taxpayer should be equal to the benefits received from the state. The second, by requiring certainty in a tax system, avoids much **corruption**, as can happen when a state contracts tax collecting out to a tax farmer. The next maxim relieves some of the burden of paying taxes, as the payment of taxes when income is received, for example, at harvest time, avoids the need to borrow to pay taxes. The fourth maxim concerns the efficiency of the tax system. As the goal of taxing is to meet the demands of the state in executing its functions, it should not be collecting taxes excessively to pay the costs of administration.

Tax incidence is concerned with identifying the ultimate payers of a tax. Partial **equilibrium** analysis shows the incidence on individuals; general equilibrium analysis shows the effect of a tax on the economy as a whole. The tax can be shifted forward to the consumer by raising **prices**, or backwards to the producer, leading to a fall in demand for final and intermediate goods. Ricardo, in his *Principles of Political Economy and Taxation*, provided a detailed analysis of the incidence of a wide range of taxes, including whether national wealth had been diminished by the heavier taxation levied during the French Revolutionary and Napoleonic Wars. Liability to pay taxes under legislation is statutory incidence; economic incidence shows the effect of taxation on economic behaviour, especially the supply of labour and of savings.

The relationship between **economic growth** and levels of taxation is of perennial interest. The structure of taxation between one type of tax and another will affect incentive mechanisms and hence productivity and growth of GDP. Scandinavian countries appear to have enjoyed both. Singapore and Hong Kong flourished with little taxation. In principle, heavy taxation will be opposed because of its interference with personal liberty. A government's priorities will not necessarily be the same as individual taxpayers'. Nozick called taxation 'forced labour' for the government, so the idea of a Tax Freedom Day has emerged. If the total tax burden is 50 per cent of national income, this day will occur in the middle of the tax year.

Taxation has long attracted reformers. To encourage work and saving, a shift from direct and indirect taxation has been advocated at least since Hobbes who, in *Leviathan*, proposed an expenditure tax. Reform can be a process of simplification, of reducing the number of taxes and the rate structure so it is clearer to the taxpayer what is due. The steepness of progression can be modified in case marginal tax rates penalise effort. There can be tax competition between countries in order to attract highly qualified labour and capital: a low tax regime is called a 'tax haven'. To avoid competition of this kind schemes of tax harmonisation are negotiated between countries, as has happened in the European countries on indirect taxation.

See also: **fiscal policy**; **public finance**

Further reading: Salanié 2003; Seligman 1895

TECHNICAL PROGRESS

Changes in methods of production and products over time.

Technical change is only possible as a consequence of inventions being turned into innovations. An invention is crudely measured by a patent statistic; an innovation can be measured by a diffusion rate. Some inventions can be attributed to individuals or groups of experimenters; others emerged back in the mists of time. Their significance varies according to impact on the body of knowledge of a science and the production possibilities created. They can be new production methods, materials or techniques of analysis. Innovations occur through enterprising people and organisations embodying inventions in their capital stocks and procedures. Often as a consequence of competition there is an imperative to try new ideas. Also individuals in pursuit of higher incomes and governments intent on promoting economic growth will be keen to adopt technical innovations.

Technical change is the product of research and development activity. It can be the output of individual researchers, university departments, or industrial or government research laboratories. The distribution of research activity will partly be determined by the pattern of government expenditure and partly by the incentives to undertake scientific inquiry. Patent protection is the method of assigning the gains to owners of intellectual property, but can incur legal expenditure which is too high for individuals. The prospect of monopoly profits encourages research activity in industries such as pharmaceuticals. The structure of industry is important. In a perfectly competitive industry earning only normal profits, research activity is only worthwhile at the level of the industry. Oligopolistic industries have the means and the desire to invest heavily in the creation of new processes and products. Monopolists have the perpetual possibility of pursuing the same path.

Technical progress often involves a change in the relationship between factors of production, especially the labour–capital ratio. Many innovations are labour-saving because of a scarcity of particular types of labour or a change in relative factor prices, wages and interest, of labour and capital. In the nineteenth century this was known as 'the machinery question'. Ricardo concluded that workers would suffer from the relatively increased use of capital. He argued that the wage fund would shrink, thus reducing the demand for labour. However, technical progress can be neutral so that economic growth is not at the expense of labour.

Technical change in an economy can be effected by buying under licence the technology of other countries, as has happened in successful Asian manufacturing countries. The USA and the UK have generated much of their own technology through investing in university and industrial research laboratories.

See also: **productivity**

Further reading: Berg 1980; Sylos-Labini 1969

TERMS OF TRADE

The ratio of export prices to import **prices** expressed as a percentage.

Qualifications to this basic ratio have created a variety of terms of trade measures. The simplest, the net barter, or commodity, terms of trade, crudely divides the index of export prices by that for import prices. Gross barter terms of trade show the ratios of quantities of exports to imports. Income terms of trade constitute the ratio of the value of exports to the price of imports. Also there are factorial terms of trade: single factorial if the export price index is multiplied by a productivity index and double if in addition the productivity of the foreign exporting industries is also taken into account. The welfare effects of trade can be considered by using this factorial approach.

It is the lament of poor countries that the terms of trade are against them, evoking the policy response of protection to alter the ratios: by imposing a tariff the demand for imports is reduced and the protected country benefits.

Further reading: Travis 1964

TIME IN ECONOMICS

The elaboration of economic models and policies to incorporate the constant flux in economic conditions.

In **classical economics** long periods of time were analysed as part of a project on **economic growth**. Smith, Ricardo and Marx looked at the relationship between wages, **rent** and **profit** as time passed. There was a fear that economies could be heading to the stationary state of zero economic growth. JS Mill, writing in his *Principles* on the future of the working classes, was exceptional among his contemporaries for questioning the benefits of continuous economic growth if there were a suitable distribution of income.

Early economics concentrated on looking at the interaction of economic variables at a point in time. The Cambridge economist Marshall popularised static models which made use of *ceteris paribus* assumptions, so that the world stood still to study economic problems a bit at a time as a way of coping with change. In the early stages of analysing an economic problem Marshall recommended the mechanical approach of physics, using the concept of **equilibrium** and *ceteris paribus* assumptions. In the later stages a biological and evolutionary approach was suggested (without full explanation). He divided time into different periods: the market day, the short term, the long term and the secular long run. In the market day supply would be completely inelastic. Supply would be slightly elastic in the short period as a consequence of using existing factors of production more intensively, such as happens when workers do overtime and machines are used continuously under a shift system. In the long period supply becomes quite elastic, as new buildings can be erected, machines purchased and workers trained and hired. In the secular long period, population and technology change make the conditions of supply unpredictable.

Time can also be considered with regard to demand. Habit and custom can limit the extent to which consumers change their preferences. Fashion will only cause temporary aberrations from persistent consumption patterns. Marshall recognised, in his *Principles*, book III, chapter IV, that it takes time for consumers to accept substitutes and new products. Also there is a mutual interaction between supply and demand. Unless suppliers produce something new there is a lack of opportunity to change consumption. In a world of little technical progress consumption patterns will be stable.

Gradually dynamic analysis came into economics. Robertson and the Swedish economists of the 1930s such as Lindahl made use of period analysis to trace by time period the effects of an income change such as net investment.

Devices to include time explicitly include using diagrams with shifting curves referring to different dates and the use of different dates for variables in an equation, thus, for example, making current aggregate consumption a function of the previous year's income. Also the technique of discounting allows incomes occurring at future dates to be comparable by being measured at their present values. In econometrics a central technique is the analysis of time series, those lists of dates and contemporaneous values of variables.

Keynes is famous for producing an economics of the short term. In *A Tract on Monetary Reform* (1923: ch. 3), he wrote

> The long run is a misleading guide to current affairs. In the long run we are all dead. Economists set themselves too easy, too useless a task if in tempestuous seasons they can only tell us that when the storm is past the ocean is flat again.

In the *General Theory of Employment, Interest and Money* (1936) Keynes analysed the time preferences of individuals both in determining their propensities to consume and their liquidity preferences. Decisions about future consumption include whether to spend in future out of current income or from **savings**. Interest is granted for parting with liquidity for a time.

An examination of the trade or business **cycle** has always included a division of time into phases of upswings, a peak, downturn, recession and recovery. JS Mill and Marx recognised this. JM Keynes regarded the time element in the cycle as the time period before recovery occurs. The length of a slump he related both to the durability of capital and to the positive or negative rate of growth of population. In his monetary theory he asserted that money enables us to link the present to the future.

If time is discrete it can be described in economic models as a succession of points in time, or time periods, t, $t + 1$, $t + 2$, $t + 3$. This is Newtonian time: movement along a line, hence being described as a spatial view of time. Contrasted with this is dynamic or real time, which sees time as a flow. Time is not in separate periods because in the present we are also remembering the past and anticipating the future. It is a process with unpredictable change.

Ignorance of the future has given rise to much discussion of **expectations**. The future can be the inevitable consequences of present stable conditions, or a spontaneous occurrence entirely unintended.

The optimal inter-temporal allocation of resources was considered by Ramsey in his 1928 study of savings. Creators of the overlapping generations model also raise inter-temporal issues. Samuelson went beyond the familiar economic transaction of all the agents in relation at the same time, and considered trades between generations, using the example of persons retiring at sixty-five years relative to their successors. There is no assumption of the world having a definite beginning or ending. This approach has been elaborated to extend to several generations and many economic agents. It is important to theories of capital and social security policies.

Conditions arising from time can vary within days as well as between them. The pattern of demand varies between peak and off-peak in transport and energy systems daily. This gives rise to the problem of peak-load pricing, with different proposals to relate the price structure to differences in marginal costs. Prices can get stuck in time and hence are sticky prices, or change often with time so are flexible prices.

In **investment** decisions there is always the temptation to choose short-term gains rather than wait for a more distant and possibly larger return. Economic policy making is often criticised for being too short-term, notoriously in the case of demand management. However, there is a case for policy having a large long-term view. JS Mill argued that governments can have a more distant time horizon than private investors, so the time factor will lead to infrastructure investment being in the hands of governments. It is the essence of a **laissez-faire** stance to argue that it is natural forces in the absence of government intervention which gradually in an evolutionary way bring about economic change. In the struggle to renew a national economy there is evidence of the Darwinian theme of the survival of the fittest.

In economic policy making the short term is distinguished from the medium term of three to five years; the long term usually receives less attention but the consequences of climate change have forced governments to look at a more distant horizon.

See also: **equilibrium**; **expectations**

Further reading: O'Driscoll and Rizzo 1985; Samuelson 1958

TRADE THEORY

Explanations of why and where countries trade.

Much of mercantilist thought was concerned with nations becoming strong through trade, often protected by tariffs. The earlier writers believed that trade was a zero-sum game so a gain could only be made at the expense of another nation. They advocated a nation pursuing a permanent balance of trade surplus and prohibited some types of import. By the time of Mun in the seventeenth century it was understood that a deficit in one bilateral trading relation could be matched by a surplus elsewhere. Also trade concerned services such as shipping as well as goods.

Adam Smith used an 'absolute advantage' theory of trade. He saw international trade as a means of extending the **division of labour** principle from the narrow confines of a single country to the world as trade could provide a 'vent for surplus', an outlet for the extra output of more productive workers. Trade was worthwhile as one country had an absolute advantage in costs over another. Torrens and Ricardo made famous the theory of comparative **cost**, or advantage, using as an example a two country model of England and Portugal producing two goods, cloth and wine, to show that even if Portugal could produce everything more cheaply, trade could still be beneficial if the internal cost ratios were different from country to country so that each country would benefit from specialising in the good in which it was more efficient. This theory assumed production under constant costs and immobility of capital. JS Mill refined Ricardian theory by introducing the law of reciprocal demand to indicate the terms at which trade would be conducted and hence the sharing of the gains from trade.

The more sophisticated Heckscher–Ohlin model came to dominate trade theory from the 1930s. Instead of considering only labour, capital was introduced into the model. Assuming that there is perfect competition, no transport costs, perfect mobility of factors of production within but not between countries and production under conditions of constant returns to scale, the theory predicted that a country rich in capital would have a comparative advantage in capital intensive goods, and similarly a labour plentiful country would do better with labour intensive goods. Empirical research for the USA using 1947 data produced the surprising result that the capital rich America was exporting predominantly labour intensive goods: this came to be known as the 'Leontief paradox' after Leontief, who created input–output tables enabling him to test the theory.

International trade theory has broadened to incorporate many aspects of market analysis and **industrial organisation**. As many trade flows occur within multinational or transnational firms, to understand modern trade these firms have to be analysed. Because economists have increasingly moved away from assumptions of perfect competition in their models, international trade under monopolistic and oligopolistic competition subject to increasing returns has been taken into account.

Vernon presented a product cycle theory of trade. In it he asserted that a newly invented product will be exported to increase the scale of production and reduce unit costs. Initially there will be monopoly profits because of the uniqueness of the new product. As the product matures it will be met by imitated substitutes so that in time the original country is importing the product. The volume of the product traded depends on the phase of the product cycle. Initially exports will be low, then there will be a progressive movement to mass production for large markets, then in its old age its sales will be overtaken by rivals.

Strategic trade theory argues that a country can improve its share of trade by a mixture of tariffs and export subsidies, possibly under imperfect competition, to realise increasing returns.

Krugman has recommended a new trade theory, hinted at by earlier writers such as Grubel and Kravis, which replaces the comparative cost introduced by Ricardo and Torrens. He has argued for the inclusion of the assumptions of economies of scale, product differentiation and imperfect competition into a trade theory. The goods which are traded will already have a large domestic market. Increasing returns gained from large production will make it easier to sell abroad at a competitive price and have more competitive prices.

See also: **development economics**; **mercantilism**; **multinational corporation**; **price-specie flow mechanism**

Further reading: Brander and Spencer 1984; Krugman 1980; Mun 1928; Vernon 1966

TRADE (LABOR) UNION

A group of workers paying subscriptions to create an organisation to negotiate wages and other conditions of work on their behalf through **collective bargaining**. Originally in Britain 'a trade union' could either be a group of workers or of employers; in the USA, a labor union.

Entry to union membership is either voluntary, or compulsory under a 'closed shop'. The latter form, now fast vanishing, can be pre-entry with union membership a condition of applying for a job, or post-entry requiring all workers to be union members within a specified time of being employed. The incidence of unionisation, or 'union density', the proportion of a given **labour** force belonging to a union, varies greatly from industry to industry and occupation to occupation. Coal mining, transport and manufacturing were traditionally heavily unionised, so that when structural changes in modern economies made the services sector more important unions found their total membership declining. **Public sector** unions, organising teachers, health care workers and administrators, have taken over private sector unions in size. Traditionally, male workers were more unionised than female, and full-time workers were more likely to join than part-time ones. Unionisation levels are affected by the marginal cost to a union of recruiting a new member; thus there is less unionisation in industries with mainly small firms scattered over a wide area.

Unions can be of benefit to employers. Orderly **collective bargaining** can be less expensive than individual bargaining, which repeats the negotiation of the same issues with worker after worker. Also there can be greater worker satisfaction and productivity if a labour force feels it is getting its just reward. If workers are represented, then it is easier to canvass workers' views.

The perennial question concerning the effects and success of this institution is 'how much do wages rise through the existence of unions?' This union wage effect is difficult to measure if there is not a similar group of workers as a comparator. The union wage premium does vary cyclically. The employment effect is different, as it has long been argued that unions exist to defend their existing members and care little about the unemployment effects of wages being pushed too high. Hence the use of 'insider-outsider' models: these emphasise the selfish nature of union members who are happy to gain wages above the competitive level, despite the impact on outsiders who are unemployed.

Critics of unions argue that they are too concerned with protecting job rights so are opposed to technical change, especially those which attempt to increase productivity through reducing labour-output ratios. 'Featherbedding' is the practice of having an excessive amount of labour employed. The desire of modern economies to have labour market flexibility does challenge the traditional rights of trade union members to retain the same jobs and same range of tasks.

Further reading: Brown 1983

TRAGEDY OF THE COMMONS

The threat to the common good by the group of users of a resource. The 'commons' can be agricultural land or any common resource such as a public park, a lake, or even a city.

This is an application of the problem of common ownership versus private ownership debated as long ago as Plato and Aristotle. With common land, it is to the benefit of the users collectively if there is conservation through attempting to optimise the grazing and other agricultural activities on the land. However, individuals with access can personally benefit by destructive behaviour for their own benefit.

The extent of the tragedy depends on the predominant use made of the land. If a resource is renewable, such as woodland, then there can be cycles in the state of a common resource. In the first phase the population of users increases to the point of destroying the resource. This causes that population to diminish. With less use over time the resource will recover and when it has, the cycle will recommence. A parallel case of oscillations is noted by Malthus in his *Essay on Population*.

In general, this tragedy can be diminished by a mutual agreement of the users to restrain their use. By experimentation there can be a gradual increase in the use of the common resource to establish the optimum point of exploitation.

See also: **altruism**; **exhaustible resources**; **property rights**

Further reading: Hardin 1968

TRANSFER INCOME

A personal income derived not from productive activity but paid under a welfare system or through a generous donation; an inter-government grant.

In **classical economics** services were regarded as non-productive, so the incomes accruing in that sector were not part of the national income but transfers. Despite the decline of the distinction between productive and non-productive income the distinction remains. The creation of the welfare state has introduced new types of transfer income. The provision of pensions for the elderly, the state financing of education, and the offering of benefits to the unemployed and the sick have all increased the volume of transfer incomes in many countries. Also the temporary or permanent migration of persons from poor to rich countries has caused flows of remittances and other gifts within families. Large **firms** and other organisations have many transfer incomes within them which do not create an addition to their total income.

In **national income** accounting it is crucial to separate transfer incomes from factor incomes, as national income is the sum of the latter. To include transfer incomes would exaggerate the size of the national income and make total incomes more than total production.

Internationally, transfer incomes have become important through bilateral and multilateral **aid** and schemes to redeem **debt**. They raise the question of dependency if the help continues for years.

Further reading: Mitchell 1991

TRANSFER PRICING

The internally administered prices used by firms for transactions within themselves but not in external markets.

These are pervasive in **multinational corporations** as the reason for the existence of such firms is to internalise what previously would have been exchanges between separate firms. It is essential for accounting purposes to fix prices on flows of goods and services between the parts of a large firm, but it is difficult to get the pricing right. They will not always represent market values: sub-components might never be traded externally at all. In countries with a substantial amount of government ownership of industry, transfer pricing is also extensively practised.

There is a temptation to choose prices to maximise post-tax corporate income. Transfer prices could be set so that there is little profit in high tax countries and most where tax rates are low. As high tax countries often have generous welfare schemes, any loss of tax revenue is resented. Increasingly, **taxation** authorities sought to make transfer prices be more accurate reflections of the cost of production. By national tax authorities insisting on firms using a transparent formula to fix their transfer prices, it is possible to prevent the setting of prices which do not cover costs and produce profits.

Further reading: Eccles 1985; Feinschreiber 2004

UNEMPLOYMENT

The non-employment of a factor of production, especially **labour**.

Unemployed persons are part of the labour force. Their attachment is the result of being engaged in job-search activity. Being unemployed can also be regarded as a statistical phenomenon, a consequence of the scheme for measuring unemployment. There are both the registered unemployed who are counted because of eligibility for welfare benefits, and the unemployed identified through household surveys, usually producing a higher number of unemployed. Both methods of measurement are imperfect. Those on registers of the unemployed might not be engaged in a genuine search for work but only be concerned to receive financial benefit. Similarly the unemployed noted in surveys might have only a vague attachment to the labour force.

There is also underemployment (also called hidden or disguised unemployment). Persons in this category are employed in low productivity jobs with little output. Principal examples of these are agricultural workers in a less developed economy, workers guaranteed a job under state **capitalism**, and workers protected by trade union regulations which retain rigid job definitions. A method of identifying underemployment is through comparing the labour-output ratio of a particular firm or industry with a benchmark to see if labour is being excessively used.

Unemployment can be viewed as stocks or flows. The labour market is in a constant state of flux. Workers are taking up jobs, or seeking employment as a consequence of leaving full-time employment, international migration or returning from a period of economic inactivity. They leave to retire, endure an unemployment spell before working again, emigrate abroad or stop working because of receiving other sources of income, including welfare benefits. As a consequence of this movement, at any point of time there will be a stock of people without employment but seeking it, i.e. unemployed.

Unemployment is a disequilibrium phenomenon because the supply of labour is greater than the demand for it. An extreme case of disequilibrium is the existence simultaneously of job vacancies, an unsatisfied demand for labour, and unemployment. This can be viewed at the level of a **national economy**, or a region, or an industry or occupation. The disequilibrium can occur because it takes time for markets to clear: if this is the sole reason for unemployment it is termed frictional unemployment and can be identified by its short duration. Full employment is not zero unemployment but largely at the frictional unemployment level because of the inevitability of slow clearing. The disequilibrium may persist longer because of a permanent decline in demand for a type of labour, often because of a major technological shift, as when there is a switch to a different type of transport, or a decline in natural resources – for example, when a coal mine is exhausted. This is structural unemployment, and can persist for an indefinite period but usually is curtailed by a government's policy response. Keynes identified unemployment at the aggregate macroeconomic level as a disequilibrium, or low equilibrium phenomenon. He called this involuntary unemployment; also known as demand-deficient unemployment. The three types of unemployment, frictional, structural and demand-deficient are classified according to cause – the poor functioning of the labour market, the inappropriate skills and abilities of the unemployed or the overall state of demand of the economy. The rate of employment, or (100 − unemployment rate) is used as a proxy for the state of demand in an economy.

Unemployment causes the unemployed a loss of income, status and **happiness**, and the economy loses output. There are thus strong, even absurd, proposals to reduce it. The mercantilists, wishing to build strong states, deplored the waste caused by unemployment. Although classical economists might be thought to be cavalier about unemployment because **Say's law** would naturally bring about full employment, some, including Malthus, were concerned about the post-war depression from 1815 caused by the return of soldiers and sailors to the civilian labour market and the decline in manufacturing. British and Swedish economists of the 1930s were determined to devise policies to cure unemployment. In times of high unemployment public works schemes are recommended. Petty, a mercantilist, went as far as suggesting the removal of Stonehenge from Salisbury Plain to the Tower of London in order to create jobs. Keynes suggested the Treasury employ workers to fill bottles with banknotes, bury them and dig them up again. In practice more sensible schemes can be undertaken, especially road building and other transport schemes. As a high proportion, often at least half, of the stock of the unemployed is unskilled, such public works projects are appropriate. However, expenditure on public works is often criticised. In the 1920s and 1930s in the UK there was the 'Treasury view', later known as 'crowding-out' because the increased taxation and higher interest rates caused by paying for the extra public sector employment, would be matched by lower activity and employment in the private sector so there would be no net gain in employment.

A closer examination of the labour market, and of the unemployed, leads to specific employment policies. Frictional unemployment is blamed on the poor functioning of the labour market. As there can be a poor publication of job vacancy data, from the late nineteenth century UK labour exchanges, or job centres, provided at public expense advertisements of vacancies. For employers seeking workers with scarce skills the search can be long and expensive. Workers reluctant to move home or retrain can take a long time to regain employment. Some frictional unemployment can occur because workers choose to have an unemployment spell to rest or travel.

Responses to structural unemployment follow well trodden roads. Vocational education and specific training programmes are recommended, and regional policies advocated to revive blighted areas. There can be some resentment from existing workers and their **trade unions** if a training programme expands the labour supply and depresses the wages of a particular occupation: for this reason training is often only publicly provided in a narrow range of chronically labour-short occupations.

General macroeconomic policies, chiefly monetary and fiscal, are exercised to stimulate demand in an economy. If the low demand is recurrent because of economic fluctuations it causes cyclical unemployment. Different approaches to stabilise an economy at a particular employment level include using monetary policy to achieve price stability, or following a rule on the expansion of the money supply under monetarism, or making frequent changes in taxes and interest rates under deliberate demand management. Friedman and Phelps argue that there is no demand-deficient unemployment and that there is a natural rate of unemployment, combining frictional and structural unemployment.

The concept of hysteresis, originally concerned with the properties of ferric metals, has been used to account for the failure of unemployment to return to an equilibrium rate. High unemployment persists because higher demand leads to higher wages for existing workers, not more work for the unemployed. At a time of expanding demand, if there are also labour market reforms making labour more efficient, output will grow faster than employment, allowing unemployment to persist.

See also: **labour**

Further reading: Casson 1981; Friedman 1968; Phelps 1968; Sinclair 1987; Weiss 2001

UTILITY

The benefit received from **consumption**. This can be an objective benefit in the sense of usefulness, or a subjective satisfaction. By the end of the eighteenth century the subjective was replacing an objective view.

Because it was asserted that goods could have intrinsic **value** they were of use. The properties of the objects themselves gave rise to their usefulness. This meaning has lingered on in expressions such as 'utility furniture', which was functional rather than decorative.

Hutcheson, Smith's teacher, in discussing price theory in his *Short Introduction to Moral Philosophy* (1747: 209) referred to 'some fitness in the things to yield some use or pleasure in life; without this, they can have no value', using utility in an objective way and relating it to value. In his *An Introduction to the Principles of Morals and Legislation* (1789) Bentham set out the principle of utility as a standard to approve or disapprove of every action. He too had the idea of utility as something objective, a property of any object which produces benefits, pleasures and happiness or prevents the opposite. The happiness of the community cannot be divorced from that of an individual. Thus government measures are based on utility if they promote the net happiness of a community.

Gradually utility came to be regarded as a subjective matter, of giving satisfaction irrespective of the nature of the good itself. Turgot referred to 'esteem value' and the influence of utilitarianism began to infiltrate economics. The notion of marginal utility was used by many early nineteenth century economists, including Nassau Senior of Oxford, noting the tendency for the marginal utility from consuming successive units of the same good to decline. In the 'marginalist revolution' of the 1870s, utility theories became central to theories of value and exchange. Jevons translated value in use into total utility, esteem into final degree (i.e. marginal) and purchasing power into the ratio of exchange. Contrasted with utility is disutility, which even Smith in *The Wealth of Nations* recognised as a phenomenon, as labour does entail 'toil and trouble'; Jevons also used disutility in his theory of labour.

The measurement of utility has long been sought, as this would make possible interpersonal comparisons of the consequences of there being different amounts of goods or wealth or income per person. Bentham, in his pain and pleasure felicific calculus, argued that the value of pleasure and pain depends on seven circumstances: intensity, duration, certainty or uncertainty, propinquity or remoteness, fecundity (the chance of being followed by similar feelings), purity (unlikely to be followed by opposite feelings), and the extent (how many persons are affected). Jevons used only the first four of these in looking at the dimensions of utility. Direct measures of utility are difficult, although bodily behaviour hints at it through sounds emitted and facial expressions. An indirect measure is the behaviour resulting from receiving pain or pleasure expressed in purchasing goods or undertaking tasks. Jevons, following Senior, regarded utility as the relation between things and pain or pleasure and made the distinction between total and marginal utilities.

The distinction between cardinal and ordinal utility is that cardinalists assert that satisfaction can be measured in numbers of utils, whereas ordinalists argue that we can only rank our satisfactions as first, second and so forth. Samuelson popularised the idea of revealed preference in the form of examining consumer responses to changes in incomes and prices. Once the preferences were known, it was possible to plot combinations of two goods on indifference curves. Later, expected utility became a key concept in microeconomics: it is concerned with summing probable utilities.

Edgeworth and Pareto introduced the device of the indifference curve to represent different combinations of two goods which would yield the same amount of utility. The slope of the curve measures the marginal rate of substitution between the two commodities. Instead of speaking of diminishing marginal utility, in this diagram the principle illustrated is the diminishing rate of substitution.

The idea of expected utility is extensively used in modern economics. Building on the idea of ordinal utility and ranking of preferences, uncertain payoffs are ranked according to the expected utility of their outcomes. This is based on the von Neuman-Morgenstern utility function, which shows an individual ranking payoffs according to expected utilities.

See also: **happiness**; **price**

Further reading: Majumdar 1961; Samuelson 1938

VALUE

The fundamental worth or **price** of a good or service.

The discussion of the origin and nature of value can be traced to Ancient Greece. Aristotle used the durable distinction between value in use and value in exchange (market price) which continued to be a tool in the hands of Smith, Ricardo and Marx. Increasingly mainstream Western economics became interested only in the price theory aspect of the value debate.

Smith noted that a good could have value in exchange but little value in use. He employed the aged 'water and diamonds paradox', pointing out that water is useful but commands a low price, whereas diamonds are high in price but have little use. Neoclassical economists were to deal with this paradox by mentioning that diamonds have a higher marginal utility, the basis for a price. In a sense the classical economists had no need to debate this issue as there was an awareness, as shown in the later published *Lectures on Jurisprudence* of Smith that diamonds command a higher price because of their relative scarcity.

The establishment of an exchange economy makes necessary the valuation of what is marketed. Earlier writers of the Middle Ages, including Aquinas and Duns Scotus, debated the nature of a just price ('justum pretium'). It corresponded to a common estimation, which included a measure of market determination. It had to be in accord with a hierarchical society. Later, in order to check whether there is unfairness in the prices set there has often been a desire for an intrinsic value as a standard, although this has long been considered a futile quest. The principal candidate for intrinsic value is the basic **cost** of production. Petty attempted a land and labour theory of value in his statement 'Labour is the father of material-wealth, the earth is its mother', but it was left to Richard Cantillon to show that a value could be alternatively expressed in units of land or labour by linking the value of labour to the amount of land needed to sustain a labourer's family. Smith argued that land, labour and capital all have natural prices and the sum of them will equal the natural prices of goods. The natural value will be the 'central price' around which market prices will fluctuate as demand changes. Supply considerations will determine natural prices; changes in demand will cause market prices to diverge from natural prices. Smith considered three senses of labour – labour disutility (the toil and trouble of production), the labour commanded (the labour we obtain from others through exchange), and labour quantity – to produce three separable labour theories. Both Ricardo and Marx reduced capital to labour and removed rent as a cost of production, thus making labour the only cost.

Ricardo regarded utility as a necessary condition for value in exchange, but argued that only in a few cases, such as rare statues and pictures, would scarcity be the sole determinant of value; for other commodities their value is regulated by the quantity of labour. He assumed that skill and intensity of labour had no effect, and differing lengths of time to bring goods to market could only affect relative values by 6 per cent or 7 per cent, hence Stigler referred to Ricardo's theory as the '93% labour theory of value'.

Marx built on Ricardian theory. In the first volume of *Capital* he stated that use value depends on the physical properties of the commodity concerned which are realised in **consumption**, but exchange value is relative and varies from time to time and place to place. He argued that in exchange the common factor in the items exchanged is labour. To avoid the idea that workers lazy and lacking in skill would produce more valuable goods because they took more time to produce, he introduced the notion of 'socially necessary labour time' based on normal production and average degree of skill and intensity of labour. Ignoring differences in human ability, he argued that skill is the product of training so complex labour can be reduced to simple labour.

As economics moved from classical to neoclassical forms there was a violent rejection of labour theories. Jevons argued that when **labour** is spent in production it is lost and gone forever and no longer has an influence on current price. What counted was the subjective utility, the balance of pleasure over pain, of the exchanging parties. Marshall, however, consciously attempted to combine in his theory of exchange value the Ricardo/JS Mill view with Jevons', creating his own 'scissors diagrams' to represent graphically demand and supply schedules in his theory of price.

Value can be regarded as the consequence of the activity of valuing. This volitional theory of value was employed by Commons in his *Institutional Economics*. He looked at the opinions of judges of the US Supreme Court to obtain an idea of reasonable value. This meant that the theory of value would be constructed out of the habits and customs of social life. This permits a transition from an individualistic approach to value to a social theory of value. Thus value is a consequence of social activity, not of pleasure and pain.

Special cases of value abound. Value-added is the difference between the monetary amount received for output and the monetary amount paid for inputs at each stage of production. The gross domestic product is the sum of the value-added for each industry of that national economy. Contingent values are not produced by the workings of a market but by other forms of estimation; for example, the use of a survey to learn how much landowners appreciate a beautiful view.

See also: **price**; **utility**

Further reading: Brookshire *et al.* 1976; Commons 1990; Marx 1976; Ricardo 1821; Smith 1976; Stigler 1966

WEALTH

What is owned; the stock of assets existing at a point in time; **happiness** and well-being.

As households, firms and governments have distinct legal personalities, they can own property. Wealth must always be distinguished from income, despite income when saved over time becoming a wealth accumulation. In the case of a firm its balance sheet shows its assets and liabilities at a point in time; its profit-and-loss account shows net income over a time period.

Wealth means abundance, the opposite to scarcity. Ruskin coined the term 'illth' as the opposite of wealth. How much one needs to be wealthy will be heavily conditioned by time, place and culture. What is central to the idea is that there are no material constraints on the action of a person. Usually this is possible only for a few people in a population, unless it is a small country with disproportionate resources such as large oil reserves.

Measuring wealth is complex because of the changing physical condition of goods, the hiding of assets to avoid **taxation**, the intangibility of some of them (for example, goodwill), different market valuations and controversy over what should be included. Given such problems it is difficult to have wealth as a tax base, so capital taxes are more expensive to collect than income or sales taxes, and sometimes not worth the trouble. Household members give the fullest indication of wealth when they die. Firms, however, through their balance sheets, have to record their assets and liabilities on a particular day. Governments have an even greater task of measurement, as many of their assets have not received a market evaluation.

The acquisition of wealth comes in different ways. It can be inherited, produced spontaneously by nature, the result of cooperation of labour and other factors of production, stolen, or the consequence of changes in market opinions. Wealth creation usually means a conscious attempt to increase the rate of investment because of taking the long view. Governments with a policy of **economic growth** will encourage the growth of physical and **human capital**.

The earlier mercantilists saw the accumulation of wealth as the goal of a state, but the classical economists, especially Adam Smith, had the different welfare concept of increasing income in the form of annual produce as an aim. At lower levels of income, wealth will be mainly regarded as physical goods, as such are needed to meet the physical needs of food, housing and clothing. When income reaches a higher level, various psychological yearnings can receive attention, thus wealth will include being entertained, and finding peace and happiness.

Well-being is a slippery concept: like utility, much of it is valued subjectively. There are generally agreed prerequisites for well-being, including living in a place not affected by war or crime, being fit and healthy, and having friends. Difficulties arise with non-material sources of satisfaction.

Wealth taxation is imposed either to attempt a greater measure of equality or to have an extra source of taxation. It is always controversial, as it affects the structure of power in a society and leads to difficult problems of asset valuation. The most common type of this taxation is at the time of death when an inventory has to be made and the resources to pay the tax exist. Taxation of the wealth of the living can be punitive if it means the abandonment of a home or business to pay it.

See also: **capital theory**; **economic welfare**; **happiness**; **national income**; **poverty**; **scarcity**; **utility**

Further reading: Brenner *et al.* 1988; Cannan 1948

WELFARE ECONOMICS

A study of the determinants of individual or social welfare.

Individual welfare is personal satisfaction, and is measured by some form of utility. The allocative efficiency of individual welfare is considered, with its consequences for **income distribution**. Increasingly welfare economics has been concerned with the notion of maximising or minimising social welfare, the meaning of optimum conditions, and whether they are products of perfect competition, and how welfare can be achieved under different types of economic system and policy.

An early treatise on welfare economics in the neoclassical tradition, Pigou's *The Economics of Welfare* (1920), regarded economic welfare as a component of total welfare, that part of social welfare which could be measured in monetary terms. In an early exercise in **national income** accounting he considered the nature of total output, which he called 'the national dividend'. He contrasted the marginal private and marginal social products of the use of resources and considered how they could be equalised. A divergence between the two products occurs as the owners of land and capital receive what is the due of workers. Some transfers from the rich to the poor were recommended and a minimum income for the existing population. Much of the welfare problem he identified was associated with the operation of the **labour** market. He assumed there was a law of diminishing marginal **utility** in operation, and that those who suffered from a scheme of redistribution had to be compensated. Marginal methods have also been used to set out the conditions for an optimum output which would require resources be shifted within a national economy until marginal physical products were equalised.

Pareto optimality states that there will be an improvement in economic welfare if everyone is better off without anyone being worse off. For this state of welfare to occur, it is necessary that all consumers have the same marginal rate of substitution in consumption; all producers have the same marginal rate of transformation in production; for all production processes marginal cost equals marginal revenue; and there is equality between the marginal rates of substitution in consumption and the marginal rates of transformation in production.

The 'New Welfare Economics', starting in 1939 in *Economic Journal* debates, was concerned with compensation tests. Harrod raised the case of England benefiting from free trade corn after the abolition of the Corn Laws in 1846 despite landlords losing out. Kaldor suggested that in such cases the government should subsidise the losers. Hicks argued that there could be optimality providing the marginal rates of substitution between consumers and producers was the same. Analysis was aided by the introduction of community indifference curves to show relative preferences at different levels of utility. Under the Kaldor-Hicks test, social welfare will be increased if there is an opportunity for the better off to compensate the worse off. Hicks also considered a compensation for firms under imperfect competition by redistributing producer's surplus to the loser.

The philosophical foundations of welfare economics have had many investigators. Little was concerned with the problem of ascertaining whether there is an increase in welfare if tastes are changing, and how to avoid welfare judgements when stating there is an increase in welfare. His contemporaries appeared to ignore income distribution.

Social welfare can be regarded as the aggregate of individual welfares, or of some collective entity. A 'Benthamite welfare function' consist of the sum of individual utilites, reflecting his principle of the 'greatest happiness for the greatest number'. A long-running debate contrasts cardinal with ordinal utility. The cardinal variety states that numbers of 'utils' can be measured for each act of **consumption**; ordinal utility, less ambitiously, asserts that preferences can be ordered or ranked.

Applications of welfare economics include the **cost–benefit analysis** of public investments, the study of social cost in **environmental economics**, and the application of social welfare functions to policy research.

See also: **consumer's surplus**; **public choice**; **social choice theory**

Further reading: Graaff 1957; Hicks 1939; Kaldor 1934; Little 1957; Nath 1969; Pigou 1932

Bibliography

Abramovitz, M (1968) 'The passing of the Kuznets cycle', *Economica*, 35: 349–67.

Addison, JT and Siebert, WS (1979) *The market for labor: an analytical treatment*. Santa Monica CA: Goodyear.

Ahmad, S (1990) 'Adam Smith's four invisible hands', *History of Political Economy*, 22: 137–43.

Akerlof, GA (1970) 'Market for lemons', *Quarterly Journal of Economics*, 84: 488–500.

Alchian, AA (1950) 'Uncertainty, evolution and economic theory', *Journal of Political Economy*, 58: 211–21.

Alchian, A and Demsetz, H (1973) 'The property rights paradigm', *Journal of Economic History*, 33: 16–27.

Aldridge, AE (2005) *The market*. Cambridge: Polity Press.

Alesina, A, Roubini, N and Cohen, G (1997) *Political cycles and the macroeconomy*. Cambridge MA: MIT Press.

Amable, B (2003) *The diversity of modern capitalism*. Oxford: Oxford University Press.

Andreoni, J (1989) 'Giving with impure altruism: applications to charity and Ricardian equivalence', *Journal of Political Economy*, 97(6): 1447–58.

Antonelli, C (2003) *The economics of innovation, new technologies and structural change*. London and New York: Routledge.

Aoki, M (1984) *The cooperative game theory of the firm*. Oxford: Clarendon Press.

Armstrong, M (1994) *Regulatory reform: economic analysis and British experience*. Cambridge MA and London: MIT Press.

Arrow, KJ (1950) 'A difficulty in the concept of social welfare', *Journal of Political Economy*, 58: 328–46.

—— (1962) 'The economic implications of learning by doing', *Review of Economic Studies*, 29: 155–73.

—— (1966, 2nd edn) *Social Choice and Individual Values*. New York: Wiley.

Arrow, K, Chenery, H, Minhas, B and Solow, R: (1961) 'Capital labor substitution and economic efficiency', *Review of Economics and Statistics*, 43(3): 225–50.

Azariadis, C (1975) 'Implicit contracts and underemployment equilibria', *Journal of Political Economy*, 83: 1183–1202.

Atkinson, AB (1975) *The economics of inequality*. Oxford: Clarendon Press.

Backhouse, RE (1980) 'Fix-price versus flex-price models of macroeconomic equilibrium with rationing', *Oxford Economic Papers*, new series, 32(2): 210–23.

—— (1994) *New directions in economic methodology*. London and New York: Routledge.

Bailey, S (1967 [1825]) *A critical dissertation on the nature, measure and causes of value chiefly in reference to the writings of Mr Ricardo and his followers*. London: Frank Cass.

Banerjee, AV, Bénabon, R and Mookherjee, D (2006) *Understanding Poverty*. Oxford: Clarendon Press.

Barro, RJ (1989) 'The Ricardian approach to budget deficits', *Journal of Economic Perspectives*, 3: 37–54.

Bartlett, B and Roth, TP (1984) *The supply side revolution*. Manhattan Institute for Policy Research. London and Basingstoke: Macmillan.

Barzel, Y (1997, 2nd edn) *Economic analysis of property rights*. Cambridge: Cambridge University Press.

Bastiat, F (1964 [1850]) *Economic harmonies*. Princeton NJ: D van Nostrand.

Baumol, W and Bowen, W (1966) *Performing arts: the economic dilemma*. New York: Twentieth Century Fund.

Beal, EF (1976, 5th edn) *The practice of collective bargaining*. Homewood IL: RD Irwin.

Becker, GS (1964) *Human capital. a theoretical and empirical analysis with special reference to education*. New York: Columbia University Press.

—— (1971) *The economics of discrimination*. Chicago IL: University of Chicago Press.

—— (1974) 'A theory of social interactions', *Journal of Political Economy*, 82: 1063–93.

—— (1981) *A treatise on the family*. Cambridge MA: Harvard University Press.

Beckerman, W (1980, 3rd edn) *An introduction to national income analysis*. London: Weidenfeld and Nicolson.

Benton, M (1994) *Discrimination*. Buckingham: Open University Press.

Berg, M (1980) *The machinery question and the making of political economy 1815–48*. Cambridge: Cambridge University Press.

Bergson, A (1938) 'A reformulation of certain aspects of welfare economics', *Quarterly Journal of Economics*, 52: 310–34.

—— (1980) *The economics of Soviet planning*. Westport CT: Greenwood Press.

Berlin, I (2002, 2nd edn) *Liberty*. Oxford: Oxford University Press.

Bhagwati, J (2004) *In defence of globalization*. New York and Oxford: Oxford University Press.

Binmore, KG (1992) *Fun and games: a text on game theory*. Lexington MA: DC Heath.

Blair, JM (1972) *Economic concentration: structure, behaviour and public policy*. New York: Harcourt Brace Jovanovich.

Blaug, M (1975) 'The empirical status of human capital theory', *Journal of Economic Literature*, 14: 827–55.

—— (1992, 2nd edn) *The methodology of economics, or how economists explain*. Cambridge: Cambridge University Press.

Blaug, M, Eltis, W, O'Brien, D, Patinkin, D and Skidelsky, R (1995) *The quantity theory of money from Locke to Keynes and Friedman*. Aldershot: Edward Elgar.

Bofinger, P (2001) *Monetary policy: goals, institutions, strategies and instruments*. Oxford: Oxford University Press.

Bolton, P and Dewatripont M (2005) *Contract theory*. Cambridge MA: MIT Press.

Boulding, KE (1973) *The economics of love and fear: a preface to a grants economy*. Belmont CA: Belmont Publishing.

—— (1978) *Ecodynamics: a new theory of societal evolution*. Beverly Hills CA: Sage.

Brander, JA and Spencer, BJ (1984) 'Tariff protection and imperfect competition', in Henryk Kierzkowski, ed., *Monopolistic Competition and International Trade*, Oxford: Oxford University Press.

Brenner, YS, Reijnders, JPG and Spithoven, AHGM (eds) (1988) *The theory of income and wealth distribution*. Brighton: Wheatsheaf.

Bronfenbrenner, M (1973) 'Equality and equity', *Annals of the American Academy of Political and Social Science*, 409: 9–23.

Brookshire, D, Ives, B and Schulze, W (1976) 'The valuation of aesthetic preferences', *Journal of Environmental Economics and Management*, 3: 325–46.

Broome, J (1983) *The microeconomics of capitalism*. London: Academic Press.

Brown, HP (1983) *The origins of trade union power*. Oxford: Clarendon Press.

Bruni, L (2004) 'The "technology of happiness" and the tradition of economic science', *Journal of the History of Economic Thought*, 26: 19–23.

Buchanan, JM (1965) 'An economic theory of clubs', *Economica*, new series, 32: 1–14.

—— (1972) 'The Samaritan's dilemma', reprinted in JM Buchanan, *Freedom in Constitutional Contract*, College Station TX: A&M University Press, 1977, 169–85.

—— (1975a) 'The Samaritan's dilemma', in ES Phelps, ed., *Altruism, morality and economic theory*. New York: Russell Sage Foundation.

—— (1975b, 4th edn) *The public finances: an introductory textbook*. Homewood IL: RD Irwin.

—— (1977) *Freedom in constitutional contract*, College Station TX: A&M University Press, 169–85.

Buchanan, JM and Tullock, G (1962) *The calculus of consent: the logical foundations of constitutional democracy*. Ann Arbor MI: University of Michigan Press.

Burns, AF and Mitchell, WC (1946) *Measuring business cycles*. New York: National Bureau of Economic Research.

Cagan, P (1956) 'Monetary dynamics of inflation' in M Friedman, ed., *Studies in the quantity theory of money*. Chicago IL: University of Chicago Press, pp. 25–117.

Cahni, P (2004) *Labor economics*. Cambridge MA and London: MIT Press.

Cairnes, JE (1875, 2nd edn) *The character and logical method of political economy*. London: Macmillan.

Caldwell, B (1982) *Beyond positivism: economic methodology in the twentieth century*. London: George Allen & Unwin.

Caldwell, B (ed.) (1990) *Carl Menger and his legacy in economics*. Durham NC and London: Duke University Press.

Caldwell, JC (1972) 'Toward a restatement of demographic transition theory', *Population and Development Review*, 2: 579–616.

Camerer, C, Loewenstein, G and Prelec, D (2005) 'Neuroeconomics: how neuroscience can inform economics', *Journal of Economic Literature*, 43: 9–64.

Cameron, B (1968) *Input-output analysis and resource allocation.* Cambridge: Cambridge University Press.

Cannan, E (1948, 3rd edn) *Wealth: a brief explanation of the causes of economic welfare.* London: Staples Press.

Cantillon, R (2001 [1752]) *Essay on the nature of commerce in general.* New York: Transaction Publishers.

Casson, M (1981) *Unemployment: a disequilibrium approach.* Oxford: Martin Robertson.

—— (1982) *The entrepreneur: an economic theory.* Oxford: Martin Robertson.

Castro, B and Weingarten, K (1970) 'Toward experimental economics', *Journal of Political Economy,* 78: 598–607.

Caves, R (1996, 2nd edn) *Multinational enterprise and economic analysis.* Cambridge: Cambridge University Press.

Charvet, J (1981) *A critique of freedom and equality.* Cambridge: Cambridge University Press.

Christaller, W (1966) *The central places of Southern Germany.* Englewood Cliffs NJ: Prentice-Hall.

Clark, JM (1917) 'Business acceleration and the law of demand', *Journal of Political Economy,* 25(3): 217–35.

Clegg, HA (1976, 3rd edn) *The system of industrial relations in Great Britain.* Oxford: Blackwell.

Clower, R (1967) 'A reconsideration of the microeconomic foundations of monetary theory', *Western Economic Journal,* 6: 1–8.

Coase, RH (1937) 'The nature of the firm', *Economica,* new series, 4: 386–495.

—— (1960) 'The problem of social cost', *Journal of Law and Economics,* 3: 1–14.

—— (1988) *The firm, the market and the law.* Chicago IL and London: University of Chicago Press.

Coddington, A (1976) 'Keynesian economics: the search for first principles', *Journal of Economic Literature,* 14: 1258–73.

Cohen, AJ and Harcourt, GC (2003) 'Retrospectives: whatever happened in the Cambridge capital theory controversies?', *Journal of Economic Perspectives,* 17: 199–214.

Cohen, B (1997) *The edge of chaos: financial booms, bubbles, crashes and chaos.* Chichester: Wiley.

Cohen, KJ (1975, 2nd edn) *Theory of the firm: resource allocation in a market economy.* Englewood Cliffs NJ: Prentice-Hall.

Collard, D (1975) 'Edgeworth's propositions on altruism', *Economic Journal,* 85: 355–60.

—— (1978) *Altruism and economy: a study in non-selfish economics.* Oxford: Martin Robertson.

Commons, JR (1990 [1934]) *Institutional economics: its place in political economy.* New York: Transaction Publishers.

Corina, JG (1966) *Incomes policy: problems and prospects.* London: Institute of Personnel Management.

Cornes, R and Sandler, T (1986) *The theory of externalities, public goods and club goods.* Cambridge: Cambridge University Press.

Cowling, K (1982) *Monopoly capitalism*. London: Macmillan.

Davidson, P (1982/83) 'Rational expectations: a fallacious foundation for studying crucial decision-making processes', *Journal of Post-Keynesian Economics*, 5: 182–96.

Deane, P (1967, 3rd edn) *British economic growth, 1688–1959: trends and structure*. London: Cambridge University Press.

Denison, EF, assisted by JP Pouillier (1967) *Why growth rates differ*. Washington DC: Brookings Institution Press.

Dewey, D (1965) *Modern capital theory*. New York: Columbia University Press.

Demsetz, H (1967) 'Toward a theory of property rights', *American Economic Review Papers and Proceedings*, 57: 347–59.

Department of Economic and Social Affairs, Statistics Division, United Nations (1999) *Handbook of input-output compilation and analysis*. New York: United Nations.

Domar, E (1957) *Essays in the theory of economic growth*. New York: Oxford University Press.

Dorfman, R (1967) *Prices and markets*. Englewood Cliffs NJ: Prentice-Hall.

Douglas, PH (1948) 'Are there laws of production?', *American Economic Review*, 38: 1–41.

Downs, A (1957) *An economic theory of democracy*. New York: Harper.

Drazen, A (2000) *Political economy in macroeconomics*. Princeton NJ: Princeton University Press.

Duclose, J-Y, Sahn, DE and Younger, SD (2006) 'Robust multidimensional poverty comparisons', *Economic Journal*, 116: 943–68.

Dupuit, AJE (1844) 'On the measurement of the utility of public works', *Annales des ponts et chaussées*. (trans., 1952, *IEP*).

Easterlin, RA (2001) 'Income and happiness', *Economic Journal*, 111: 965–84.

Eccles, RG (1985) *The transfer pricing problem: a theory for practice*. Lexington MA: DC Heath.

Ehrenberg, RG (1997) *Modern labor economics*. New York: Addison-Wesley.

El-Garnal, MA (2006) *Islamic finance: law, economics and practice*. Cambridge: Cambridge University Press.

Eltis, W (1984) *The classical theory of economic growth*. London: Macmillan.

Evans, GW and Honkapohja, S (2001) *Learning and expectations in macroeconomics*. Princeton NJ: Princeton University Press.

Feinschreiber, R (2004) *Transfer pricing methods*. Hoboken NJ: John Wiley.

Felipe, J and Fisher, FM (2003) 'Aggregation in production functions: what applied economists should know', *Metroeconomica*, 58:262.

Fellner, WH (1956) 'Patinkin's integration of monetary and value theory', *American Economic Review*, 46: 947–55.

—— (1960) *Competition among the few: oligopoly and similar market structures*. London and New York: AM Kelley.

Fels, A (1972) *British Prices and Incomes Board*. Cambridge: Cambridge University Press.

Field, J. (2004) *Social capital*. London and New York: Routledge.

Fisher, FM (1972) *The economic theory of price indices: two essays on the effects of taste, quality and technological change*. New York: Academic Press.

—— (1983) *Disequilibrium foundations of equilibrium economics*. Cambridge: Cambridge University Press.

Fleetwood, S (2002) 'Boylan and O'Connor's causal holism: a critical realist evaluation', *Cambridge Journal of Economics*, 26: 27–45.

Fontaine, P (2000) 'Making use of the past: theorists and historians on the economics of altruism', *The European Journal of the History of Economic Thought*, 7(3): 407–22.

Fontaine, P and Leonard, R (2005) *The experiment in the history of economics*. London: Routledge.

Forubotn, EG and Pejovich, S (1972) 'Property rights and economic theory: a survey of recent literature', *Journal of Economic Literature*, 10(4): 1137–62.

Frank, AG (1978) *Dependent accumulation and development*. London: Macmillan.

Freeman, C (1997) *The economics of industrial innovation*. London: Pinter.

Frey, BS and Stutzer, A (2002) 'What can economists learn from happiness research?' *Journal of Economic Literature*, 40: 402–35.

Friedman, M (1953) *Essays in positive economics*. Chicago IL and London: University of Chicago Press.

—— (1968) 'The role of monetary policy', *American Economic Review*, 58: 1–17.

Friedman, M and Friedman, R (1980) *Free to choose*. London: Harcourt Brace Jovanovich.

Friedman, M and Schwartz, A (1963) *A monetary history of the United States*. Princeton NJ: Princeton University Press.

Gayle, DJ and Goodrich, JN (eds) (1991) *Privataisation and deregulation in global perspective*. London: Pinter.

Gemmell, N (ed.) (1987) *Surveys in development economics*. Oxford: Blackwell.

George, DAR (1993) *Economic democracy: the political economy of self-management and participation*. Basingstoke: Macmillan.

George, KD, Joll, C and Lynk, EL (1992, 4th edn) *Industrial organisation: competition, growth and structural change*. London: Routledge.

Giersch, H (ed.) (1994) *Economic aspects of international migration*. Berlin and London: Springer-Verlag.

Glimcher, P (2003) *Decisions, uncertainty, and the brain: the science of neuroeconomics*. Cambridge MA: MIT Press.

Gloria-Palermo, S (1999) *The evolution of Austrian economics: from Menger to Lachman*. London: Routledge.

Gold, B (1981) 'Changing perspectives on size, scale and returns: an interpretative survey', *Journal of Economic Literature*, 19 (March): 5–33.

Graaff, J de V (1957) *Theoretical welfare economics*. Cambridge: Cambridge University Press.

Grampp, WD (1948) 'Adam Smith and the economic man', *Journal of Political Economy*, 56: 315–36.

—— (1952) 'The liberal elements in English mercantilism', *Quarterly Journal of Economics*, 66: 465–501.

Grapard, U (1995) 'Robinson Crusoe: the quintessential economic man?', *Feminist Economics*, 1: 33–52.

Gray, HP (1985) *Free trade or protection? A pragmatic analysis*. London: Macmillan.

Green, P (1981) *The pursuit of inequality*. Oxford: Martin Robertson.

Griffin, JM (1986, 2nd edn) *Energy economics and policy.* Orlando FL and London: Academic Press.

Gruchy, AG (1973) *Contemporary economic thought; the contribution of neo-institutional economics.* London: Macmillan.

Gudeman, S (2001) *The anthropology of economy: community, market and culture.* Oxford: Blackwell.

Haberler, G (1968, 5th edn) *Prosperity and depression.* London: George Allen & Unwin.

Hahn, FH and Matthews, RCO (1964) 'The theory of economic growth: a survey', *Economic Journal,* 74: 779–902.

Hamberg, D (1971) *Models of economic growth.* New York: Harper & Row.

Hardin, G. (1968) 'The tragedy of the commons', *Science,* 162: 1243–48.

Harrod, RF (1948) *Towards a dynamic economics: recent developments of economic theory and their application to policy.* London: Macmillan.

Hart, O (2001) 'Financial contracting', *Journal of Economic Literature,* 39(4): 1079–1101.

Hart, O and Moore, J (1988) 'Incomplete contracts and renegotiation', *Econometrica,* 56: 755–85.

Hausman, DM and McPherson, MS (1993) 'Taking ethics seriously: economics and contemporary moral philosophy', *Journal of Economic Literature,* 31: 671–731.

Hay, P (2002) *A companion to environmental thought.* Edinburgh: Edinburgh University Press.

Hayami, Y and Godo, Y (2005, 3rd edn) *Development economics: from the poverty to the wealth of nations.* Oxford: Oxford University Press.

Hayek, FA (1937) 'Economics and knowledge', *Economica,* new series, 4: 33–56.

—— (1976) *The denationalization of money.* London: Institute of Economic Affairs.

Head, JG (1974) *Public goods and public welfare.* Durham NC: Duke University Press.

Heal, GM (1973) *The theory of economic planning.* Amsterdam: North Holland.

Heathfield, DF (1971) *Production functions.* London: Macmillan.

Heckscher, E (1935) *Mercantilism.* 2 vols, London: George Allen & Unwin.

Heffernan, SA (1996) *Modern banking in theory and practice.* Chichester: Wiley.

Henry, JF (1990) *The making of neoclassical economics.* Boston MA and London: Unwin Hyman.

Hibbs, D (1977) 'Political parties and macroeconomic policy', *American Political Science Review,* 71: 1467–87.

Hicks, JR (1937) 'Mr Keynes and the "classics": a suggested interpretation', *Econometrica,* 5: 147–59.

—— (1939) 'The foundations of welfare economics', *Economic Journal,* 49: 696–712.

—— (1950) *A contribution to the theory of the trade cycle.* Oxford: Clarendon Press.

—— (1965) *Capital and growth.* Oxford: Clarendon Press.

Hicks, JR and Weber, W (1973) *Carl Menger and the Austrian School of economics.* Oxford: Clarendon Press.

Hillier, B (1997) *The economics of asymmetric information*. Basingstoke: Macmillan; New York: St Martin's Press.

Hirsch, F (1976) *The social limits to growth*. London: Routledge & Kegan Paul.

Hirshleifer, J (1980, 2nd edn) *Price theory and applications*. Englewood Cliffs NJ and London: Prentice-Hall.

History of Political Economy (2004) *passim*, vol. 36, supplement.

Hodgson, GM (1993) *Economics and evolution: bringing life back into economics (economics, cognition and society)*. Cambridge: Polity Press.

Hollander, S (1987) *Classical economics*. Oxford: Blackwell.

Honoré, AM (1961) 'Ownership', in Guest, AG: *Oxford essays in jurisprudence*. London: Oxford University Press, ch. 5, pp. 107–47.

Hoover, EM (1948) *The location of economic activity*. New York: McGraw Hill.

Hotelling, H (1931) 'The economics of exhaustible resources', *Journal of Political Economy*, 39(2): 137–75.

Howard, MC (1992) *A history of Marxian economics*. Basingstoke: Macmillan Education.

Howe, RE and Roemer, JE (1981) 'Rawlsian justice as the core of a game', *American Economic Review*, 71: 880–95.

Hughes, GA (1987) 'Fiscal federalism in the UK', *Oxford Review of Economic Policy*, 3: 1–23.

Hume, D (1975 [1777]) *Enquiries concerning human understanding and concerning the principles of morals*. LA Selby-Bigge and PH Nidditch, eds, 3rd edn, Oxford: Clarendon Press.

Humer, S (1993) *Managing the multinational: confronting the global-local dilemma*. New York and London: Prentice-Hall.

Hutchison, TW (1938) *The significance and basic postulates of economic theory*. London: Macmillan.

Hutt, WH (1975) *The theory of collective bargaining 1930–1975*. London: Institute of Economic Affairs.

Hyman, R (1975) *Industrial relations: a Marxist introduction*. London: Macmillan.

Jackman, R, Mulvey, C and Trevithick, J (1981, 2nd edn) *The economics of inflation and performance*. Oxford: Martin Robertson.

Jain, AK (2001) 'Corruption', *Journal of Economic Surveys*, 15: 71–122.

Janssen, LH (1961) *Free trade, protection and customs unions*. London: HE Stenfert Kroese.

Jochnick, C and Preston, FA (eds) (2006) *Sovereign debt at the crossroads: challenges and proposals for resolving the Third World debt crisis*. Oxford: Oxford University Press.

Jomo, KS (2005) *Pioneers of development economics: great economists on development*, London: Zed Books.

Jones, AM (ed.) (2006) *Elgar companion to health economics*. Cheltenham: Edward Elgar.

Jones, RJB (1995) *Globalisation and interdependence in the international political economy: rhetoric and reality*. London: Pinter.

Jonung, L (ed.) (1991) *The Stockholm School of Economics revisited*. Cambridge: Cambridge University Press.

Jorgensen, DW (1995) *Productivity*. 2 vols, Cambridge MA and London: MIT Press.

Junankar, PN (1982) *Marx's economics*. Deddington: Philip Allan.

Kahn, RF (1931) 'The relation of home investment to unemployment', *Economic Journal*, 41: 173–98.

Kaldor, N (1934) 'A classificatory note on the determinateness of equilibrium', *Review of Economic Studies*, 1: 122–36.

Kaldor, N and Mirrlees, JA (1962) 'A new model of economic growth', *Review of Economic Studies*, 24: 174–92.

Kates, S (ed.) (2003) *Two hundred years of Say's law*. Cheltenham: Edward Elgar.

Keynes, JM (1937) 'The general theory of employment', *Quarterly Journal of Economics*, 51(2): 209–23.

Keynes, JN (1891) *The scope and method of political economy*. London: Macmillan.

Kiker, BF (1974) 'Nicholson on human capital', *Scottish Journal of Political Economy*, 21 (June).

King, R, Plosser, C and Rebelo, S (1988a) 'Production, growth and business cycles: I. The basic neoclassical framework', *Journal of Monetary Economics*, March/May, 195–232.

——(1988b) 'Production, growth and business cycles: II. New directions', *Journal of Monetary Economics*, March/May, 309–41.

Kirzner, IM (1973) *Competition and entrepreneurship*. Chicago IL and London: University of Chicago Press.

Kitchin, J (1923) 'Cycles and trends in economic factors', *Review of Economics and Statistics*, 5: 10–16.

Kiyotaki, N and Moore, J (2002) 'Evil is the root of all money', *American Economic Review*, 92: 62–66.

Klein, LR (1952) *The Keynesian revolution*. London: Macmillan.

—— (1970) *An essay on the theory of economic prediction*. Chicago IL: Markham Publishing Co.

Knight, FH (1921)*Risk, uncertainty and profit*. Boston MA and New York: Houghton Mifflin.

Kondratieff, ND (1935) 'The long waves in economic life', *Review of Economics and Statistics*, 17: 105–15.

Kooreman, P and Wunderink, S (1997) *The economics of household behaviour*. Basingstoke: Palgrave Macmillan.

Krautkraemer, JA (1998) 'Non-renewable resource scarcity', *Journal of Economic Literature*, 36: 2065–2107.

Kregel, JA (1976) *Theory of capital*. London: Macmillan.

Kreps, DM (1990) *Game theory and economic modelling*. Oxford: Clarendon Press.

Krishna, V (2002) *Auction theory*. San Diego CA: Academic Press.

Krueger, AO (1974) 'The political economy of the rent-seeking society', *American Economic Review*, 64: 291–303.

Krugman, P (1980) 'Scale economies, product differentiation, and the pattern of trade', *American Economic Review*, 70: 950–59.

Kuhn, TS (1996, 3rd edn) *The structure of scientific revolutions*. Chicago IL and London: University of Chicago Press.

Kukathas, C (1990) *Rawls: A Theory of Justice and its critics*. Cambridge: Polity Press.

Kuznets, SS (1966) *Modern economic growth: rate, structure and spread*. New Haven CT: Yale University Press.

Kydland, FE and Prescott, EC (1990) 'Business cycles: real facts and a monetary myth', *Federal Reserve Bank of Minneapolis Quarterly Review*, 14: 3–18.

Laidler, D (1999) *Fabricating the Keynesian revolution: studies of the inter-war literature, money, the cycle and unemployment*. Cambridge: Cambridge University Press.

Laidler, D, Tobin, J, Matthews, RCO and Meade, JE (1981) 'Conference papers on monetarism – an appraisal', *Economic Journal*, 91: 1–57.

Lakatos, I (1972) *Proofs and refutations: the logic of mathematical discovery*. J Worrall and E Zahar, eds, Cambridge: Cambridge University Press.

Lal, D (1983) *The poverty of 'development economics'*. London: Institute of Economic Affairs.

Lancaster, K (1971) *Consumer demand: a new approach*. New York: Columbia University Press.

Lane, J-E (1993) *The public sector: concepts, models and approaches*. London: Sage.

Latsis, SJ (1972) 'Situational determinism in economics', *British Journal for the Philosophy of Science*, 23: 207–45.

Leibenstein, H (1966) 'Allocative efficiency vs. X-efficiency', *American Economic Review*, 56: 392–415.

Leijonhufvud, A (1968) *On Keynesian economics and the economics of Keynes*. New York: Oxford University Press.

Leontief, WW (1953) 'Domestic production and foreign trade: the American capital position re-examined', *Economia Internazionale*, 7: 3–32.

—— (1956) 'Factor proportions and the structure of American trade: further theoretical and empirical analysis', *Review of Economics and Statistics*, 38: 386–407.

LeRoy, SF and Singell, LD (1987) 'Knight on risk and uncertainty', *Journal of Political Economy*, 95(2): 394–406.

Lewis, WA (1954) 'Economic development with unlimited supplies of labour', *Manchester School*, 22: 139–91.

—— (1979) 'Dual economy revisited', *Manchester School*, 47: 211–29.

Lindahl, E (1939) *Studies in the theory of money and capital*, London: George Allen & Unwin.

Lister, R (2004) *Poverty*. Cambridge: Polity Press.

Lindbeck, A (1971) *The political economy of the left: an outsider's view*. New York: Harper & Row.

Lipman, BL (1995) 'Information processing and bounded rationality: a survey', *Canadian Journal of Economics*, 28: 42–67.

Little, IMD (1957, 2nd edn) *A critique of welfare economics*. Oxford: Clarendon Press.

—— (2002) *Ethics, economics and politics: principles of public policy*. Oxford: Oxford University Press.

Littlechild, SC (2000) *Privatisation, competition and regulation*. London: Institute of Economic Affairs for the Wincott Foundation.

Loasby, B (1991) *Equilibrium and economics: an explanation of connecting principles in economics*. Manchester: Manchester University Press.

Locke, J (1988 [1698]) *Two treatises of government*. P Laslett, ed., Cambridge: Cambridge University Press.

Loehr, W and Sandler, T (eds) 1978) *Public goods and public policy.* Beverly Hills CA: Sage.

Long, J and Plosser, C (1983) 'Real business cycles', *Journal of Political Economy,* 91: 39–69.

Lucas, RE (1972) 'Expectations and the neutrality of money', *Journal of Economic Theory,* 4: 103–24.

—— (1973) 'Some international evidence on output-inflation tradeoffs', *American Economic Review,* 63: 326–34.

—— (1980) 'Methods and problems in business cycle theory', *Journal of Money, Credit, and Banking,* 12: 696–715.

Lupton, D (1999) *Risk.* London: Routledge.

Machlup, F (1963) *Essays on economic semantics.* Englewood Cliffs NJ: Prentice-Hall.

—— (1977) *A history of thought on economic integration.* London: Macmillan.

Macho-Stadler, J and Pérez-Castrillo, JD (1997) *An introduction to the economics of information, incentives and contracts.* Oxford: Oxford University Press.

Majumdar, T (1961) *The measurement of utility.* London: Macmillan.

Mäler, K-G (1974) *Environmental economics: a theoretical inquiry.* Baltimore MD: Johns Hopkins University Press.

Marshall, A (1920, 8th edn) *Principles of economics.* London: Macmillan.

Marx, K (1976 [1867]) *Capital: a critique of political economy.* B Fowkes, trans., Harmondsworth: Penguin Books.

McCallum, BT (1989) 'New classical macroeconomics: a sympathetic account', *Scandinavian Journal of Economics,* 91: 223–52.

McCloskey, DN (1985) *The rhetoric of economics.* Brighton: Wheatsheaf.

McKenzie, GW (1983) *Measuring economic welfare: new methods.* Cambridge: Cambridge University Press.

Madrid Conference on Optimum Currency Areas (1973) *The economics of common currencies.* HG Johnson and AK Swoboda, eds, London: George Allen & Unwin.

Magnusson, L (ed.) (1995) *Mercantilism.* 2 vols, London: George Allen & Unwin.

Meade, JE (1951) *The theory of international economic policy, volume one: the balance of payments.* London: Oxford University Press.

—— (1952) 'External economies and diseconomies in a competitive situation', *Economic Journal,* 62: 54–67.

—— (1970) *The theory of indicative planning: lectures given in the University of Manchester.* Manchester: Manchester University Press.

Meek, RL (1962) *The economics of physiocracy: essays and translations.* London: George Allen & Unwin.

Meier, GM (1984) *Pioneers in development,* New York and Oxford: Oxford University Press for the World Bank.

—— (2005) *Biography of a subject: an evolution of development economics.* Oxford: Oxford University Press.

Meltzer, AH (1991) *Political economy.* New York and Oxford: Oxford University Press.

Merrett, AJ (1968) *Incentive payment systems for managers*. London: Gower.

Mill, JS (1844) *Essays on unsettled questions of political economy*. London: JW Parker.

Minford, P (1991) *The supply side revolution in Britain*. Aldershot: Edward Elgar.

Minford, P and Peel, D (1982) 'The political theory of the business cycle', *European Economic Review*, 10: 253–70.

Mishan, EJ (1972) *Elements of cost-benefit analysis*. London: George Allen & Unwin.

Mitchell, D (1991) *Income transfers in ten welfare states*. Aldershot: Avebury.

Modigliani, F (1944) 'Liquidity preference and the theory of interest and money', *Econometrica*, 12: 45–88.

Mueller, DC (2003) *Public choice III*. Cambridge: Cambridge University Press.

Mun, T (1928 [1664]) *England's Treasure by Forraign Trade*. Oxford: Blackwell.

Muth, JF (1961) 'Rational expectations and the theory of price movements', *Econometrica*, 29: 315–35.

Myrdal, G (1939) *Monetary equilibrium*. Translated from the German, London: W Hodge & Company.

Näslund, B and Sellstedt, B (1978) *Neo-Ricardian theory: with applications to some current economic problems*. Lecture notes in economics and mathematical systems, vol. 156. Berlin and New York: Springer-Verlag.

Nath, SK (1969) *A reappraisal of welfare economics*. London: Routledge & Kegan Paul.

Needham, D (1978) *The economics of industrial structure, conduct and performance*. New York: St Martin's Press.

Nelson, R and Winter, S (1982) *An evolutionary theory of economic change*. Cambridge MA and London: Belknap Press of Harvard University Press.

Nerlove, M (1958) 'Adaptive expectations and cobweb phenomena', *Quarterly Journal of Economics*, 72: 227–40.

Neumann, J von and Morgenstern, O (1947, 2nd edn) *Theory of games and economic behavior*. Princeton NJ: Princeton University Press.

Neves, V (2004) 'Situational analysis beyond single-exit modelling', *Cambridge Journal of Economics*, 28: 921–36.

Ng, U (1978) 'Economic growth and social welfare: the need for a complete study of happiness', *Kyklos*, 314: 575–87.

Nordhaus, WD (1975) 'The political business cycle', *Review of Economic Studies*, 42: 169–90.

Oakley, A (1994) *Classical economic man: human agency and methodology in the political economy of Adam Smith and JS Mill*. Cheltenham: Edward Elgar.

Oakley, A. (1999) 'Economics and the origin of Popper's situational analysis', *History of Economics Review*, 30.

Oates, WE (1991) *Studies in fiscal federalism*. Aldershot: Edward Elgar.

O'Brien, DP (2004) *The classical economists revisited*. Princeton NJ: Princeton University Press.

O'Driscoll, GP and Rizzo, MJ with a contribution from Garrison, RW (1985) *The economics of time and ignorance*. Oxford: Blackwell.

Ohlin, B (1937) 'Some notes on the Stockholm theory of saving and investment', *Economic Journal*, 47: 53–69.

Okun, AM (1974) *Equality and efficiency: the big trade-off.* Washington DC: Brookings Institution Press.

O'Neill, B (1987) 'Non-metric test of the mini-max theory of two-person zero-sum games', *Proceedings of the National Academy of Sciences, USA*, 84: 2106–9.

Osborne, MJ (2004) *Introduction to game theory.* New York and Oxford: Oxford University Press.

Oswald, AJ (1997) 'Happiness and economic performance', *Economic Journal*, 107: 1815–31.

Panzar, LC and Willig, RD (1981) 'Economies of scope'. *American Economic Review Papers and Proceedings*, 71 (May): 268–72.

Papandreou, AA (1994) *Externality and institutions.* Oxford: Clarendon Press.

Parker, D (1991) *Profit and enterprise: the political economy of profit.* New York and London: Harvester Wheatsheaf.

Patinkin, D (1956) *Money, interest and prices: an integration of monetary and value theory.* Evanston IL: Row, Peterson.

Peacock, A (1969) 'Welfare economics and public subsidies to the arts', *Manchester School of Economics and Social Studies*, 4: 323–35.

—— (1992) *Public choice analysis in historical perspective.* Cambridge: Cambridge University Press.

—— (1997) *The political economy of economic freedom.* Cheltenham: Edward Elgar.

—— (2000) 'Public financing of the arts in England', *Fiscal Studies*, 21: 171–205.

Peacock, A and Shaw, GK (1971) *The economic theory of fiscal policy.* London: George Allen & Unwin.

Pen, J (1971) *Income distribution.* London: Allen Lane, the Penguin Press.

Pesaran, MH (1987) *The limits of rational expectations.* New York and Oxford: Blackwell.

Phelps, ES (1968) 'Money wage dynamics and labor market equilibrium', *Journal of Political Economy*, 76: 678–711.

Pigou, AC (1932, 4th edn) *The economics of welfare.* London: Macmillan.

Polanyi, K (1944) *The great transformation: the political and economic origins of our time.* New York: Farrar and Reinhart.

Popper, K (1959) *The logic of scientific discovery.* London: Routledge.

Posner, Richard A (1975) 'The social costs of monopoly and regulation', *Journal of Political Economy*, 83: 807–27.

Quincey, Thomas de (1897 [1844]) *The logic of political economy*, in *Political economy and politics*, volume IX of his *Collected Writings*, ed. David Masson. Reprinted 1970. New York: Augustus M Kelley.

Ramsey, FP (1928) 'A mathematical theory of saving', *Economic Journal*, 38: 543–59.

—— (1931 *The foundations of mathematics and other logical essays.* RB Braithwaite, ed., London: Kegan, Paul, Trench and Trubner; New York: Harcourt Brace.

Rawls, J (1999) *A theory of justice.* Oxford: Oxford University Press.

Ricardo, D (1821, 3rd edn) *On the principles of political economy, and taxation.* London: John Murray.

Resnick, SA (1975) 'State of development economics', *American Economic Review Papers and Proceedings*, 65: 317–22.

Robbins, L (1932) *An essay on the nature and significance of economic science.* London: Macmillan.

Robertson, DH (1915) *A study of industrial fluctuation: an inquiry into character and causes of the so-called cyclical movements of trade.* London: PS King and Son.

Robinson, EAG (1953, 2nd edn) *The structure of competitive industry.* Cambridge: Cambridge University Press.

Robinson, J (1952) *The rate of interest and other essays.* London: Macmillan.

—— (1962) *Economic philosophy.* London: CA Watts.

Rosen, HS (2005, 7th edn) *Public finance.* Boston MA and London: McGraw-Hill.

Rosenzweig, MR (1997) *Handbook of population and family economics.* Amsterdam and Oxford: Elsevier.

Ross, S (1976) 'The arbitrage theory of capital asset pricing', *Journal of Economic Theory*, 13: 341–60.

Rostow, WW (1960) *The stages of economic growth.* Cambridge: Cambridge University Press.

Rothschild, E (2001) *Economic sentiments: Adam Smith, Condorcet and the Enlightenment.* Cambridge MA and London: Harvard University Press.

Rubinstein, A (2000) *Economics and language.* Cambridge: Cambridge University Press.

Ruskin, J (1867, 2nd edn) *The political economy of art.* London: Smith, Elder.

Salanié, B (2000) *The microeconomics of market failures.* Cambridge MA and London: MIT Press.

—— (2003) *The economics of taxation.* Cambridge MA and London: MIT Press.

Samuelson, PA (1938) 'A note on the pure theory of consumers' behavior', *Economica*, new series, 5: 61–71.

—— (1948) *Foundations of economic analysis.* Cambridge MA: Harvard University Press.

—— (1954) 'The pure theory of public expenditure', *Review of Economics and Statistics*, 34(4): 387–89.

—— (1958) 'An exact consumption-loan model of interest with or without the social contrivance of money', *Journal of Political Economy*, 66: 467–82.

Sandler, T and Tschirhart, JT (1980) 'The economic theory of clubs: an evaluative survey', *Journal of Economic Literature*, 18: 1481–1521.

Savage, LJ (1954) *The foundations of statistics.* New York: Wiley.

Schleifer, A and Vishny, RW (1993) 'Corruption', *Quarterly Journal of Economics*, 108: 599–617.

Schmidt, C (ed.) (1996) *Uncertainty in economic thought.* Cheltenham: Edward Elgar.

Schneider, G (2002) *The shadow economy: an international survey.* Cambridge: Cambridge University Press.

Schultz, TW (1971) *Investment in human capital: the role of education and research.* New York: Free Press.

—— (1972) *Human resources.* New York: National Bureau of Economic Research.

BIBLIOGRAPHY

Schumpeter, JA (1934) *The theory of economic development: an inquiry into profits, capital, credit, interest and the business cycle.* Cambridge MA: Harvard University Press; London: H Milford.

—— (1954, 4th edn) *Capitalism, socialism and democracy.* London: George Allen & Unwin.

Scitovsky, T (1972) 'What's wrong with the arts is what's wrong with society', *American Economic Review,* 62(1/2): 62–69.

—— (1976) *The joyless economy: an inquiry into human satisfaction and consumer dissatisfaction.* London: Oxford University Press.

Selgin, GA (1988) *The theory of free banking: money supply under a competitive note issue.* Cato Institute, Totowa NJ: Rowman & Littlefield.

Seligman, ERA (1895) *Essays in taxation.* New York and London: Macmillan.

Sen, A (1977) 'Social choice theory: a re-examination', *Econometrica,* 45: 53–89.

—— (1989) *On ethics and economics.* Oxford: Blackwell.

—— (1999) 'The possibility of social choice', *American Economic Review,* 89: 349–78.

Senior, NW (1827) *An introductory lecture on political economy: delivered before the University of Oxford, on the 6th of December, 1826.* London: J Mawman.

Shackle, GLS (1949) *Expectation in economics.* Cambridge: Cambridge University Press.

—— (1968, 2nd edn) *Expectations, investment and income.* Oxford: Clarendon Press.

—— (1973) *Epistemics and economics: a critique of economic doctrines.* Cambridge: Cambridge University Press.

Sharpe, WF (1964) 'Capital asset prices: a theory of market equilibrium under conditions of risk', *Journal of Finance,* 19: 425–42.

Sherman, H (1972) *Radical political economy: capitalism and socialism from a Marxist-humanist perspective.* New York: Basic Books.

Shubik, M with Levitan, R (1980) *Market structure and behaviour.* Cambridge MA: Harvard University Press.

Simon, HA (1955) 'A behavioural model of rational choice', *Quarterly Journal of Economics,* 69: 99–118.

—— (1993) 'Altruism and economics', *American Economic Review Papers and Proceedings,* 83(2): 156–61.

Sinclair, PJN (1987) *Unemployment: economic theory and evidence.* Oxford: Blackwell.

Singer, HW (1984) *The ethics of aid.* Brighton: Institute of Development Studies.

Smith, A (1976a [1759]) *The theory of moral sentiments.* Oxford: Oxford University Press.

—— (1976b [1776]) *An inquiry into the nature and causes of the wealth of nations.* Oxford: Oxford University Press.

Smith, VL (1989) 'Theory, experiment and economics', *Journal of Economic Perspectives,* 3: 151–69.

Sorkin, AL (1975) *Health economics: an introduction.* Lexington MA: Lexington Books.

Soto, H de (2000) *Mystery of capital: why capitalism triumphs in the West and fails everywhere else.* London: Bantam.

Stein, L (1982) *Monetarism, Keynesian and new classical economics*. New York: New York University Press.

Stern, RM (1973) *The balance of payments: theory and economic policy*. London: Macmillan.

Steuart, J (1998 [1767]) *An inquiry into the principles of political oeconomy*. AS Skinner, ed., with N Kobayashi and H Mizuta, London: Pickering & Chatto.

Stigler, GJ (1962) 'Information in the labour market', *Journal of Political Economy*, 70 (October supplement): 94–105.

—— (1966, 3rd edn) *The theory of price*. New York: Macmillan.

—— (1971) 'The theory of economic regulation', *Bell Journal of Economics*, 2: 3–21.

Stiglitz, JE (1990) *Whither socialism?* Cambridge MA and London: MIT Press.

Stiglitz, JE, Ocampo, JA, Spiegel, S, Ffrench-Davis, R and Nayyar, D (2006) *Stability with growth: macroeconomics, liberalisation and development*. Oxford: Oxford University Press.

Streeten, P (1961) *Economic integration: aspects and problems*. Leyden, the Netherlands: AW Sythoff.

Svensson, J (2005) 'Eight questions about corruption', *Journal of Economic Perspectives*, 19: 19–42.

Sylos-Labini, P (1969) *Oligopoly and technical progress*. Cambridge MA: Harvard University Press.

Tawney, RH (1926) *Religion and the rise of capitalism: a historical study*. London: John Murray.

—— (1964, 5th edn) *Equality*. London: Unwin Books.

Taylor, MP (1995) 'The economics of exchange rates', *Journal of Economic Literature*, 33: 13–47.

Thompson, D, Kay, JA and Mayer, C (eds) (1986) *Privatisation: the UK experience*. Oxford: Clarendon Press.

Throsby, D (1994) 'The production and consumption of the arts', *Journal of Economic Literature*, 32(1): 1–29.

Thweatt, WO (1988) *Classical political economy: a survey of recent literature*. Norwell MA, Dordrecht and Lancaster: Kluwer Academic.

Tiebout, C (1956) 'A pure theory of local government expenditures', *Journal of Political Economy*, 64: 416–24.

Tietenberg, TH (1994) *Environmental economics policy*. New York: Harper-Collins.

Tilman, R (2001) *Ideology and utopia in the social philosophy of the libertarian economists*. Westport CT and London: Greenwood Press.

Townsend, P (1979) *Poverty in the United Kingdom: a survey of household resources and standards of living*. Harmondsworth: Penguin.

Travis, WP (1964) *The theory of trade and protection*. Cambridge MA: Harvard University Press.

Tsuru, S (1993) *Institutional economics revisited*. Cambridge: Cambridge University Press.

Tullock, G (1967a) 'The welfare costs of tariffs, monopolies and theft', *Western Economic Journal*, 5: 224–32.

—— (1967b) 'The general irrelevance of the general impossibility theorem', *Quarterly Journal of Economics*, 81: 256–70.

Vanek, J (1972) *The economics of workers' management: a Yugoslav case study.* London: George Allen & Unwin.

Vanhoove, N (1987, 2nd edn) *Regional policy: a European approach.* Aldershot: Gower.

Veblen, T (1900) 'The preconceptions of economic science. Part III', *Quarterly Journal of Economics*, 14: 240–69.

Vernon, R (1966) 'International investment and international trade in the product cycle', *Quarterly Journal of Economics*, 80: 190–207.

Vickrey, W (1961) 'Counter speculation, auctions and competitive sealed tenders', *Journal of Finance*, 15: 8–37.

Viner, J (1937) *Studies in the theory of international trade.* New York and London: Harper & Brothers.

Vousden, N (1990) *The economics of trade protection.* Cambridge: Cambridge University Press.

Vroe, M de (1999) 'Equilibrium and disequilibrium in economic theory: a comparison of the classical, Marshallian and Walras-Hicksian Conceptions', *Economics and Philosophy*, 15: 161–85.

Wallace, N (2001) 'Lawrence R Klein Lecture 2000: Whither monetary economics?', *International Economic Review*, 42: 847–69.

Walton, P (1972) *From alienation to surplus value.* London: Steed and Ward.

Webb, S (1921) *The consumers' cooperative movement.* London: Longman, Green.

Weber, A (1929) *The theory of the location of industries.* Chicago IL: University of Chicago Press.

Weibull, JW (1995) *Evolutionary game theory.* Cambridge MA and London: MIT Press.

Weintraub, ER (1974) *General equilibrium theory.* London: Macmillan.

Weiss, P (2001) *Unemployment in open economies: a search theoretic analysis.* New York: Springer.

Whately, R (1847, 3rd edn) *Introductory lectures on political economy delivered at Oxford in Easter term 1831.* London: B Fellowes.

White, LH (1995, 2nd edn) *Free banking in Britain: theory, experience and debate, 1800–1845.* Cambridge: Cambridge University Press.

—— (1999) *The theory of monetary institutions.* Malden MA and Oxford: Blackwell.

Whitley, J (1994) *A course in macroeconomic modelling and forecasting.* New York and London: Harvester Wheatsheaf.

Wiles, PJD (1961, 2nd edn) *Price, cost and output.* Oxford: Blackwell.

—— (1977) *Economic institutions compared.* Oxford: Blackwell.

Williamson, OE (1985) *The economic institutions of capitalism: firms, markets, relational contracting.* New York: Free Press; London: Collier Macmillan.

—— (2000) 'The new institutional economics: taking stock, looking ahead', *Journal of Economic Literature*, 38: 595–613.

Wrigglesworth, J (1985) *Libertarian conflicts in social choice.* Cambridge: Cambridge University Press.

Young, AA (1928) 'Increasing returns and economic progress', *Economic Journal*, 38: 527–42.

Names Index

Lösch, August 1906–45: 195
Lucas, Robert E b. 1937: 152–53, 177

Machlup, Fritz 1902–83: 10
Malthus, Thomas Robert 1766–1834: 19–21, 37, 46, 53, 57, 59, 62, 122, 165, 180, 186–88, 211, 214
Mankiw, Nicholas Gregory b. 1958: 127
Marshall, Alfred 1842–1924: 22, 29–30, 39, 41, 53, 62, 68, 71, 78, 81, 83, 90, 96, 103 126, 149, 158, 185, 195, 205, 219
Marx, Karl 1818–83: 16, 17, 19–20, 38, 46, 50, 82–83, 135–37, 166, 184, 193–94, 205–6, 217–19
McCloskey, Deirdre N [Donald] b.1942: 65
Meade, James E 1907–95: 80, 90, 127, 157
Meek, Ronald L 1917–78: 137
Menger, Carl 1840–1921: 9, 18, 133–34, 149
Merton, Robert C b.1944: 183
Mill, James 1773–1836: 186
Mill, John Stuart 1806–73: 19, 21, 46, 51, 58, 62, 71, 81, 157, 159, 183, 187, 189, 192, 205–7, 208, 219
Mirabeau, Victor de Riqueti, Marquis de 1749–91: 154
Mirrlees, James A b.1936: 60
Mises, Ludwig von 1881–1973: 10, 131, 174, 194
Mitchell, Wesley C 1874–1948: 45
Modigliani, Franco 1918–2003: 150
Montchrétien, Antoine de c.1575–1621: 157
Moore, John H Hardman b.1954: 144
More, Thomas 1478–1535: 193
Morgenstern, Oscar 1902–76: 10, 98, 217
Mun, Thomas 1571–1641: 71, 138, 208
Mundell, Robert G b.1930: 43
Muth, John b.1930: 87, 177
Myint, Hla b.1920: 49–50
Myrdal, Gunnar 1898–1987: 49–50, 84, 87, 96, 197

Nash, John F b.1928: 80, 99, 152
Nelson, Richard R b.1930: 83
Neuman, John von 1903–57: 10, 98, 217
Newton, Isaac 1642–1727: 64
Nicholson, Joseph Shield 1850–1927: 109
Nordhaus William D b. 1941: 156
Nozick, Robert 1938–2002: 202

Ohlin, Bertil G 1899–1979: 63, 149, 197, 208
Okun, Arthur M 1928–80: 77
Owen, Robert 1771–1858: 34, 130, 192–93

Pareto, Vilfredo 1848–1923: 67, 217, 222
Pasinetti, Luigi L b.1930: 19, 151
Patinkin, Don 1922–95: 126
Peacock, Alan Turner b.1922: 41
Pesaran, M Hashem b. 1946: 88
Petty, William 1623–87: 19, 49, 109, 138, 148, 185, 214, 218
Phelps, Edmund S b. 1933: 215
Phillips, AWilliam H 1914–75: 116, 152
Pigou, Arthur Cecil 1877–1959: 24, 89–90, 174, 221
Plato c.427–347 BC: 98, 192–93, 211
Polanyi, Karl 1886–1964: 56
Ponzi, Carlo 1882–1949: 15
Popper, Karl 1902–93: 64, 66 175
Prebisch, Raul 1901–85: 49
Prescott, Edward C b. 1940: 177

Quesnay, Francois 1694–1774: 120, 132, 148, 154–55
Quincey, Thomas de 1785–1859:118, 166

Ramsey, Frank P 1903–30: 60, 183, 186
Rawls, John 1921–2002: 176–77
Reid, Thomas 1710–96: 193
Resnick, Stephen A b. 1938: 50
Ricardo, David 1772–1823: 19–21, 38, 64, 74, 132–33, 136–37, 148, 150, 165–66, 180, 187, 202, 205, 207–9, 217–19

Subject Index

Note: page numbers in **bold** indicate the entry for a subject.

single factorial terms of trade 204
social capital **190**
social choice theory **190–92**
social contract 131
social cost 5, 23–24, 37–38, 73, 90,
    167–68, 182
social optimum 70
social welfare function 110, 149, 153,
    176, 191, 222
socialism **192–94**
socialist calculation 10, 194
socially necessary labour time 136
soft currency 42–43
sovereign debt 47, 153
Soviet type economy 26, 147, 186,
    194, 199
spatial economics **194–96**
spatial monopoly 195
spatial oligopoly 196
special drawing right 42
specific training 110
speculation 14–15
speculative demand for money 96,
    143–44
spontaneous economy 131
spontaneous order 4, 10, 17, 67, 105,
    119, 121, 124, 131
stabilisation policy **196**
stages theory 49, 55, 59, 83, 135
stagflation 117
standard commodity 151
state capitalism 16–17, 194, 213
static model 205
sticky price 127, 207
stochastic model 65, 133
Stockholm School **197**
strategic trade theory 209
strikes 115–16
structural adjustment **197–98**
structural disequilibrium 53
structural forecasting 133
structural unemployment 198, 214–15
structure of an economy **198–99**
structure-conduct-performance 114
subjective utility 215–16
substitution effect 160–61
sunspot equilibrium 80
supplementary cost 37
supply elasticity 71, 205
supply side economics **199**

surplus value **200**
sustainable development 50

tableau économique 120, 132, 154
take-off 59
tariff 44, 168–69, 204, 208–9
tatonnement 8
taxation **201–3**
tax competition 203
Tax Freedom Day 202
tax haven 203
tax incidence 202
technical efficiency 69
technical progress **203–4**
term structure of interest rates 122
terms of trade **204**
thrift 185
Tiebout hypothesis 195
time in economics **205–7**
time series 48, 132–33, 141, 206
total utility 216
trade creation 44–45
trade cycle *see* cycles
trade diversion 45
trade theory **207–9**
trade union **209–10**
tragedy of the commons **211–12**
training 110
transaction cost 8, 24–25, 43, 190,
    194
transactions demand for money 143
transfer income **211–12**
transfer pricing **212**
transformation problem 136
transitory consumption 31
transitory income 31
transmission mechanism 141
Treasury view 214
tropism 56
trust 34, 39, 119, 129, 142, 144, 179,
    190

uncertainty *see* risk and uncertainty
underdevelopment 49–50
underground economy 147
unemployment **212–15**
union density 210
union wage effect 210
unionisation 210
unit banking 13